# PATENTS
## From a Different Perspective

# JOHN P. SUTTON

# PROLOGUE

The United States Court of Appeals for the Federal Circuit is usually viewed as the Congressional solution to the problem of inconsistent patent decisions of the regional United States Courts of Appeal which had jurisdiction over appeals in patent cases from regional United States District Courts. Some regions were perceived as "pro-patent," and others were perceived as "anti-patent." This led to forum-shopping, where patent owners would seek jurisdiction in "pro-patent" regions and those contesting patents would seek jurisdiction in "anti-patent" regions.

The solution to forum-shopping was thought to be in creating a single specialist Court of Appeals having jurisdiction over patent cases on appeal from all United States District Courts. The new appellate court would replace the regional Courts of Appeal that were created in 1890 as intermediate courts of appeal between the district courts and the Supreme Court. Before 1890, there were no intermediate courts of appeal between district courts and the Supreme Court, all of which were courts of general jurisdiction, not specializing in any particular area of law.

The concept of a specialized Court of Appeals was not new in 1982, when the Federal Circuit was created. The first specialized Court of Appeals was the United States Court of Customs Appeals created in 1910. It was an administrative court under the direction of the Treasury Department. In 1890, the year that the regional Courts of Appeal were created as courts of general jurisdiction, Congress also created the specialized Court of Customs Appeals to review decisions of the Board of General Appraisers.

Litigation over the duties imposed by the government was under the jurisdiction of the United States District Court for the district where the port of entry was located. The decisions of the Board of appraiser specialists were first addressed by non-specialist district court judges who were seldom trained in either appraising customs duties or in the classification of customs duties. The district court decisions were reviewed by the specialist Court of Customs Appeals. The sequence of decisions by specialist appraisers, first review by generalist district courts, and then review of district court decisions by the specialist Court of Customs Appeals was cumbersome, but not as cumbersome as the system it replaced. The prior system had decisions of customs appraisers reviewed by trial courts on the record before the Board of General Appraisers; trial court's decisions reviewed by regional Courts of Appeal; and Court of Appeals decisions reviewed by the Supreme Court. When the Court of Customs Appeals was created in 1910, review of decisions of the specialized appellate court could not be reviewed by the Supreme Court. Judge Rich, in *A Brief History of the United States Court of Customs and Patent Appeals* (hereinafter "Brief History"), at page 7, called the creation of the specialized customs court a "major step in bringing about decongestion and uniformity in customs jurisprudence."

In 1914, Congress passed "Public Law No. 180 granting certiorari review by the Supreme Court" (Brief History 48).

On April 1, 1929, Congress renamed the Court of Customs Appeals as the "Court of Customs and Patent Appeals" with added jurisdiction over appeals from district courts in patent cases (Brief History 66). On May 20, 1929, the Supreme Court declared that the new Court of Customs and Patent Appeals was "not a court created under Article III of the Constitution, but was a mere administrative tribunal" (*id.*). *Ex parte Bakelite*, 279 U.S. 438 (1929) "slapped the court down" (*id.*). This language indicates the respect he had for the specialist court he was appointed to, and the contempt that Judge Rich held for the high court that "down-graded" the Court of Customs and Patent Appeals (CCPA).

Later, the Supreme Court held that the CCPA was an Article III court in *Glidden Co. v. Zdanok*, 370 U.S. 530 (1962), after Congress enacted a law stating that the CCPA was an Article III court.

The problem with giving the CCPA jurisdiction over both patent cases and customs cases is that there is only one kind of customs appeal, namely, from decisions on classification of duties and the amount of duties. All customs cases are decided, in the first instance, by the Board of Customs Appraisers (or its successor). There is no grant by the government to exclude importation, similar to the patent right to exclude infringement.

On the other hand, a patent is a right to exclude others from using the patented invention without permission of the patent owner. There are two kinds of patent cases that are appealable to higher courts. First is the decision to grant the patent or not, which is determined by the Patent and Trademark Office (originally Patent Office), much like the decision to appraise and classify customs duties. That decision is reviewed by the CCPA (now the Federal Circuit).

Second is the enforcement of the patent right, which is usually not determined by the PTO, but rather is decided by a district court. The judicial determination is whether the patent owner prevails or the patent challenger prevails. There is no corresponding litigation involving customs law because there is no right to exclude others in customs law.

Unlike the cost of customs duties, which is relatively small, the cost of enforcement of the right to exclude the use of a patent can often exceed a million dollars by each side of a patent infringement case today. This is wholly separate from the value of the right to exclude or the money damages that may be awarded, which can reach hundreds of millions of dollars. The money involved in customs cases is vastly different from the money involved in patent infringement litigation.

The money involved in obtaining a patent is in the same ball park as customs duties. Both are *ex parte* disputes between an actor and the government. The judicial disputes between a patent owner and an accused infringer in an *inter parte* proceeding in district court are enormously different. There is no corresponding proceeding in customs law.

There was a substantial difference between the review of customs cases and patent cases before the Court of Customs and

Patent Appeals ("CCPA"). In customs cases, the sequence was first a decision by the Board of Customs Appraisers; a review by the Circuit Court (now District Court) in the district where the port of entry was located; a review by the regional Circuit Court of Appeals; and possible review by the Supreme Court.

Later, the first level of review to the district court and the second level to the court of appeals were eliminated. Appeals from the Board of Appraisers went directly to the Court of Customs Appeals, a less cumbersome path.

In contrast, in patent appeals there is a divergence between patent infringement issues and patent grant issues. Appeals from the agency determination not to grant a patent used to be appealed to the CCPA, with possible review by the Supreme Court. If the agency determination is to grant the patent, the owner of the patent may sue alleged infringers in the district court having jurisdiction over the defendant. As previously noted, the district court decision used to be reviewed by the regional Court of Appeals, with possible review of that decision by the Supreme Court.

Likewise, one challenging a patent used to be able to sue the patentee in a district court having jurisdiction, with an appeal as of right to the regional Court of Appeals, and possible review by certiorari to the Supreme Court.

When the CCPA was abolished in 1982, the new Federal Circuit reviewed both *ex parte* cases from the PTO and *inter partes* cases from the district courts. Review by regional Courts of Appeal was replaced by review by the Federal Circuit.

The difference in the appellate path, depending upon whether (1) the case is an appeal from an administrative agency or (2) is a judicial determination of a case or controversy does not exist in customs cases. There is only one appellate path in customs cases: a determination of the Board of Appraisers is the only decision that can be appealed. There are no *inter parte* disputes in customs law, so there can be no litigation in judicial courts.

The result is that the specialized patent court now has jurisdiction not only over the administrative decisions of the PTO, but also the judicial decisions in disputes between plaintiffs and defendants in every patent case in every district in the United States. At a stroke, Congress created a specialist patent court, (no longer considering customs cases), but reviewing administrative decisions of the PTO (as its predecessor CCPA had since 1929), but also cases involving disputes regarding patent validity and infringement, a huge volume of cases in which the CCPA had absolutely no previous experience.

District courts and regional Courts of Appeal were governed by the Federal Rules of Civil Procedure and the Federal Rules of Evidence. The CCPA, charged with reviewing administrative decisions by the Court of Customs Appeals and the Board of Appeals and Interferences of the PTO, was not bound by those Federal Rules. The CCPA was guided by the belief that, as the highest authority in patent cases and customs cases, it did not need to defer to anyone.

However, Federal Rule 52(a) requires that "findings of fact, whether based on oral or documentary evidence, shall not be set aside unless clearly erroneous." Neither customs cases nor patent cases before the CCPA were so restricted.

The judges of the Federal Circuit, formerly of the CCPA, no longer had to review customs cases. But they were not trained to review district court decisions that were governed by the Rules of Civil Procedure. Customs decisions on duties or the classification of the imported products were administrative determinations, as were PTO decisions in (the grant of a patent *vel non*). They did not involve a trier of fact in the first instance before the government. The government makes a decision on the mixed issue of fact and law. Fact is decided by the government agency and law is also decided by the agency. There is no separation as contemplated by Rule 52.

A completely different appellate path was in place for *inter partes* patent disputes: the court of first instance is the district court, with appeal to the regional Court of Appeals, and possible appeal to the Supreme Court. This was all changed with the creation of the Federal Circuit, which replaced review by the regional courts of appeal.

Although the Federal Circuit perceives itself as the fountainhead of patent law (chapter 2), now that patent cases are not reviewed by regional Courts of Appeal, it was hoped that conflicts among circuits could be avoided. Now, with all district court patent decisions reviewed by the Federal Circuit, inter-circuit conflicts were thought to be avoided.

In fact, the lack of experience with Federal Rules, especially deference to the trier of fact, has led to many errors in Federal Circuit decisions. These errors are examined in this book.

Ultimately, it is the Supreme Court, a generalist court, which is the final authority on patent law as well as every other kind of law. The specialist patent court, lacking judges trained in the Federal Rules, is less successful in deciding judicial disputes than the generalist regional Courts of Appeal that were familiar with those Rules. Deference is not something that comes easily to the specialist patent court.

When the specialist Federal Circuit was created in 1982, Judge Rich expected that it would "bring[] about decongestion and uniformity" in patent jurisprudence, just as he had said the Court of Customs Appeals had done with customs jurisprudence. His firm belief in specialized courts was grounded in the marriage of technology and law before a single court.

A specialist patent court could combine a grasp of patent law with a grasp of science and technology, subjects that generalist judges are usually not trained to address.

Commentators have almost universally hailed the relatively new patent court as a success in creating new, consistent, uniform jurisprudence that is far superior to what had resulted from the non-specialist Courts of Appeals since they were created in 1890.

I believe it is error to view patent law from the perspective of the Federal Circuit and its predecessor specialized patent court, the CCPA. The patent courts are inferior to the Supreme Court, and patent law must be viewed from the perspective of the Supreme Court, the head of the judicial department of government that has the duty "to say what the law is" (*Marbury v. Madison*, 5 U.S. 137, 178 (1803)).

Even though the Patent Clause of the Constitution gives Congress the power to secure exclusive rights to inventors, it does not give power to Congress to create a specialized court to say what the law is. Resolution of judicial disputes is reserved to the judicial department, and the specialized patent courts are inferior to the Supreme Court for saying what the law is.

Because the Supreme Court rejects the reasoning of the patent courts most of the time (two out of three patent court decisions are reversed or vacated when considered by the Supreme Court), I believe the proper perspective for viewing patent law is from the perspective of the high court, not that of the specialist courts.

The perspective of the patent courts is not even superior to other federal courts of appeal in individual cases. The mere fact that some of the patent court judges had previous experience in patent law is no reason to reject the wisdom in patent cases of the other courts of appeal of equal rank to the patent courts.

Most of the specialized patent court judges from 1929 to 2012 that had previous patent law experience were engaged in patent prosecution, not in litigation of patent infringement disputes. Although the Federal Circuit now has a former district court judge with experience in the trial of patent infringement cases, the patent courts had none during the first eighty years.

I would argue that a regional court of appeals having a panel with at least one judge with experience in trials of patent infringement cases could be better qualified to judge appeals of *inter partes* patent infringement cases than would patent court judges lacking that experience.

Judge Learned Hand, perhaps the most experienced patent judge in the history of the United States, comes to mind. He served as judge of the District Court for the Southern District of New York and on the Court of Appeals for the Second Circuit, both of which heard many patent cases.

His patent law opinions are collected in "*Learned Hand on Patent Law*" (1983). His perspective is described in Hershel Shanks's, "*The Art and Craft of Judging, The Decisions of Judge Learned Hand*" (1968). He subscribed to Alexander Hamilton's view that "the judiciary . . . may truly be said to have neither *force* nor *will*, but merely judgment" (1968, 15). This perspective is entirely contrary to the conventional wisdom of commentators on patent law.

Some commentators claim that Congress created the Federal Circuit and set its "goal to 'foster uniformity in patent law,'" (Abate and Fisher, *Supreme Court Review of the United States Court of Appeals for the Federal Circuit 1982-1992*, Fed. Cir. B.J. 307, 333 (1992)). But that is no reason to believe that the Supreme Court would defer to decisions of the Federal Circuit as experts, as the authors speculated.

Fourteen years later, Judge Gajarsa of the Federal Circuit and one of his law clerks reviewed the Supreme Court decisions on appeal from the Federal Circuit "In The Federal Circuit and the Supreme Court" 821Am. U. L. Rev. 821, 842, Gajarsa and Cogswell (2006))." They concluded that the "Federal Circuit is by far the principal expounder of the patent law." But far from finding Supreme Court deference to Federal Circuit expertise, they concluded, "Quite possibly, the Federal Circuit is poised to become the 'Ninth Circuit' of the twenty-first century" (844). (The Ninth Circuit Court of Appeals is notorious as the regional court of appeals most often reversed by the Supreme Court).

Another of Judge Gajarsa's law clerks, Bruce D. Abramson, wrote a book entitled *The Secret Circuit: The Little-Known Court Where the Rules of the Information Age Unfold (2006)*." He cites the Gajarsa and Cogswell article in support of the proposition that the "Supreme Court reviewed only fifty-two Federal Circuit rulings and reversed only a fraction of them," (2007, 5) citing the Abate paper quoted in the Gajarsa article. That was not what Judge Gajarsa concluded in his article. Quite the opposite: Judge Gajarsa found that the Federal Circuit is reversed nearly as often as the Ninth Circuit in cases that reach the Supreme Court.

Abramson expanded further, and asserted that the Federal Circuit acted "to strengthen a weak patent system whose inability to motivate innovation threatened to perpetuate the economic malaise of the 1970s" (2007, 5). This misunderstands the function of the judicial branch which lacks the powers of the political branches of government to strengthen a weak patent system.

Abramson (2007, 6-7) said the patent court "was created to address the critical question–What sorts of rules would motivate America's technology industries to expand in ways that enhance both domestic employment opportunities and global leadership?"

Again, these are political goals for the political branches to address, not the judicial branch. Later, he suggests that President Reagan envisioned a new economy with new institutions like the Federal Circuit (9). I question that perspective. Courts have no responsibility to create a new economy.

In this book, I explore the thirty-three Supreme Court reviews of patent court decisions (twenty-seven by the Federal Circuit, not fifty-two as Abramson stated). Two-thirds have been overturned. While that is a "fraction," as Abramson wrote, it is not diminutive, as Abramson implied. Two-thirds is a larger fraction than the fraction of reversals of Ninth Circuit decisions by the Court.

Judge Newman of the Federal Circuit, before her appointment to the court, participated in the Domestic Policy Review of Industrial Innovation during the Carter Administration in the late 1970's. She wrote about it in "The Federal Circuit: Judicial Stability or Judicial Activism" 42 Am. U. L. Rev. 683, 688 (1993). Her view was that the Federal Circuit was created for judicial stability, not judicial activism. She condemned "policy-driven activism whereby the application of the law will not be known until the Federal Circuit hears the case." In other words, the Federal Circuit was created to be the final authority on patent law. I do not share that view either. The Supreme Court, as we shall see, is the final authority on patent law and every other kind of law.

The Policy Review concluded that the "patent system's constitutional and statutory incentive to promote technological progress" had been "diminished by the inconsistencies of judge-made law concerning patent rights and remedies" (1993, 684-85). The solution, according to the Policy Review, was to create a national specialist patent court that "would be free of intercircuit differences, and thereby provide a stable body of law upon which reliance could be placed by inventors and investors (685).

It seems to me that "intercircuit differences" is a judicial problem, not a political problem for Congress to address. The judicial branch had already created a solution to the problem of intercircuit differences. It is expressed in Supreme Court Rule 10(a):

Considerations Governing Review on Certiorari

Review on a writ of certiorari is not a matter of right, but of judicial discretion [review by the Federal Circuit is a right]. A petition for a writ of certiorari will be granted only for compelling reasons. The following, although neither controlling nor fully measuring the Court's discretion, indicate the character of the reasons the Court considers:

(a) A United States court of appeals has entered a decision in conflict with the decision of another United States court of appeals on the same important matter.

The judicial branch solution to the problem of "intercircuit differences" is simple, elegant, and makes much more sense than the legislative branch's solution, which involved eliminating jurisdiction over patent issues in all United States regional courts of appeal. The regional courts of appeal continued to have jurisdiction over patent issues raised in Sherman Act anti-trust cases and many other patent-related issues. Congress has not attempted to diminish the judicial branch's jurisdiction over patent/anti-trust disputes.

The executive branch solution proposed in the Policy Review was that jurisdiction over patent issues would be vested in a new court specializing in patent matters. The new court was not required to have judges whose professional lives were devoted to resolution of judicial disputes. In fact, the executive department solution did not even require the specialized court judges to have expertise in patent infringement litigation, as Judge Hand and many other court of appeals judges did. The solution of the executive branch, being a political branch, was its usual method of selecting judges, namely, considering political factors, not judicial qualifications.

I say "usual method of selecting judges" advisedly, after studying the specialized patent courts since 1962 when I was hired to serve on the first patent court, the CCPA. From 1929 (when the CCPA was created) until 1973, most of the judges appointed to the CCPA were former politicians: senators, congressmen, governors, and so forth. Only two, Judge Lindsay Almond and Judge Donald Lane, had previous experience as a trial judge.

Since 1973, there have been patent court judges with previous experience as elected officials, though some had been staffers for elected politicians. None have had previous experience as a trial judge, unlike some appointees to regional courts of appeal. Learning how to judge by wrestling in the trenches of district courts, or reviewing decisions of district courts, as Judge Hand did, is beyond the experience of all of the specialist patent court judges except the new Federal Circuit Judge O'Malley, a former district court judge.

The executive branch solution following the Policy Review was referred to Congress for enactment of this monumental intervention into the judiciary function. It is the judicial branch, not Congress, that has the responsibility "to say what the law is" when one court of appeals enters a decision in conflict with a decision of another court of appeals.

Congress clearly has the power "To constitute tribunals inferior to the Supreme Court" (Art. I, Sect. 8, cl. 9), so there is no Constitutional issue in the executive and legislative solutions to the "intercircuit differences" problem. It is equally clear that the Policy Review by the executive branch never seriously considered the wisdom of discarding almost a century of jurisprudence by United States Courts of Appeal in patent infringement cases by some of the giants of the judicial branch (e. g. Judge Learned Hand).

If the problem of "intercircuit differences" is the result of inadequate use of Rule 10 (where a decision of one circuit conflicts with a decision of another circuit), then a solution short of abolishing ninety-two years of patent cases by experienced regional court judges should have been considered. Instead, the first decision by the Federal Circuit abolished as precedent every patent decision by every court of appeals since 1890 (*South Corp. v. United States,* 690 F. 2d 1388 (Fed Cir. *en banc* 1982)).

The many opinions of Judge Learned Hand were therefore made non-precedential by order of the new patent court, whose judges had never heard or reviewed a district court patent case. Abolition of all patent infringement decisions by all courts of appeal might have been acceptable if the replacement judges had experience in either trying patent infringement cases in district court, or as judges reviewing patent infringement cases on appeal. But the Federal Circuit judges have not had substantial prior experience in trying patent infringement disputes. Throwing out every court of appeals patent decision from 1890 to 1982 because of "intercircuit differences" is draconian, to say the least.

The Supreme Court has never considered the Federal Circuit's decision not to rely upon regional circuit cases as precedential statements of the law. But in the most recent decision of the Court that reviewed a Federal Circuit decision, *Kappos v. Hyatt*, Justices Sotomayor and Breyer joined in a concurring opinion affirming the decision of the Federal Circuit. The opinion cited Judge Hand's opinion for the Second Circuit Dowling v. Jones, 67 F.2d 537, 538 (CA 2, 1933) as supporting affirmance of the Federal Circuit decision. This suggests that two justices of the Supreme Court find a regional court of appeals decision precedential in reviewing a Federal Circuit patent case.

Judge Newman's view in her law review article that "intercircuit differences" were eliminated by the creation of a single specialist patent court is not supported by her writings during many years as judge on the Federal Circuit. She is the author of many dissenting opinions. My view is that her dissents seem wiser than the majority opinions in many of those cases. But the issue is not which is "right" and which is "wrong." Rather, her dissents show that what used to be intercircuit differences have become "*intra* circuit differences." The differences have not gone away; they are now differences between the majority and minority in the same circuit, rather than between circuits.

Judge Newman believed that the "failure of the 'two cultures' of law and science to understand each other" resulted in "the [regional circuit] judiciary reflecting in its patent decisions a variety of perceptions of the place of patents in the nation's economy" (1993, 685-86). From Judge Hand's perspective, whether law and science understand each other is not a judicial problem. Nor is it a judicial problem as to where patents belong in the nation's economy. These are political problems for the political branches to address, not for the judicial branch.

Later, Judge Newman asserted that a Federal Circuit accomplishment was that it "removed many of the artifices and doctrines that had puzzled inventors and confounded jurists" (1993, 687). From my perspective, as shown in this book, it is the Supreme Court that has removed many of the "artifices and doctrines" of the Federal Circuit's interpretation of the law in its 33 reviews of patent court decisions. Precedents of the Supreme Court and of the regional courts of appeal are ignored because the patent courts assumed that a specialist courts need not defer to the precedents of generalist courts. That assumption is simply wrong. Specialists cannot ignore decisions of generalist courts simply because they are specialists.

These "artifices and doctrines" are many, but a preview of two examples is illustrative. First, the Federal Circuit's practice of setting aside facts found by a district court without finding them to be "clearly erroneous" was overturned in the very first Court review of a Federal Circuit decision: *Dennison v. Panduit*, 475 U.S. 809 (1986).

Second, the Federal Circuit's removal of "obvious to try" from the obviousness inquiry in interpreting Section 103 under its "own law" was struck down in *KSR v. Teleflex*, 550 U.S. 398 (2007). These two cases will be more thoroughly discussed below, but they are cited here to illustrate how the Supreme Court "removed many of the artifices and doctrines" that had been created by the Federal Circuit.

Still others writing about the new patent court applauded the omniscience of the specialist Federal Circuit. Professor Rochelle Cooper Dreyfuss, in *The Federal Circuit; A Case Study in Specialized Courts* (1989), sought to "determine whether the law in the CAFC's hands is more responsive to the philosophy of the Patent Act, to national competition policies, and to the needs of researchers and technology users" (1989, 5). Learned Hand, in contrast, believed the issue is whether the court has "judgment," not *force* or *will.*

From my perspective, stated in *Patent Trials after CAFC,*10 APLA Q. J. 309, 318-19 (1982), the law is not in the hands of the Federal Circuit. It is one of many intermediate appellate courts in the federal judiciary, all of which are inferior to the Supreme Court. It is not a task for the Federal Circuit to make the law "more responsive to the philosophy of the Patent Act," or "to national competition policies," or "to the needs of" users as Dreyfuss states. These are all tasks for the political branches, executive and legislative, not the judicial branch. The Federal Circuit's hands are tied by the various texts of Federal Rules and by decisions of a higher judicial authority.

The procedural rules are intended "to secure the just, speedy, and inexpensive determination of every action" (Federal Rule of Civil Procedure 1). If a "philosophy" is needed, it must be shaped by the legislature. Justice is blind, and has no philosophy. Justice weighs the evidence dispassionately, and has no preconceived ideas.

Dreyfuss found it a "benefit" that the Federal Circuit was able to synthesize "patent law principles that escaped the regional circuits" (1989, 8). (That blanket condemnation included all of the thoughtful work of Judge Hand on the Second Circuit which showed judgment, not force or will).

Dreyfuss "looked at the degree to which the court has attempted to advance what it regards as national policy" (1989, 14). Again, policy is for political departments, not the judicial department.

Her view was that Federal Rule 52(a)(6) (which contains the judicial branch's prohibition of an appellate court setting aside findings below unless "clearly erroneous"), "operates perversely as regards the CAFC" (1989, 47). The patent court, in her view, should be able to overturn findings by a district court based upon expert testimony if the appellate judges "think that the finding is wrong, but not clearly erroneous" (48). The "CAFC must find some method for reversing decisions that it believes are unresponsive to its teachings" (50). I do not share those views. The inferior court lacks the power to modify the Rules of the judicial branch to make them responsive to the lower court's "teachings."

While there are many other commentators with a different perspective than mine, I will end with just one more, a believer in the omniscience of the Federal Circuit. Kimberly A. Moore, now a judge on the Federal Circuit, wrote an article before her appointment: "*Are District Court Judges Equipped to Resolve Patent Cases?*," 15 Harvard J. of L. and Tech. 1 (2001). Her view was that trial judges are not so equipped, because she assumes that the Federal Circuit is correct when it disagrees with a district court's interpretation of a claim. Because the appellate court disagrees with the district court interpretation in many of the cases she studied in her article, she assumes that the district court's interpretation is wrong and therefore district court judges are not equipped to resolve patent cases. This analysis reflects a misunderstanding of the judicial system. There are two parts to resolving disputes, whether patent cases or any other kind of dispute. First, facts must be found in the trial court. Second, the trial court must apply the law to the facts. When a district court sits without a jury, the judge performs both of these duties, finding facts and applying the law. Finding facts, whether by a jury or by a judge, requires weighing the evidence admitted at trial. Whether the fact-finder is "equipped" to resolve or determine facts depends upon the supporting evidence, not on the "equipment" of the fact-finder, such as education, prior experience, or intellect. If there is no evidence to support a finding, it makes no difference how well the trier of fact is "equipped" by knowledge of technology, law, or any other expertise.

This book shows that the Supreme Court disagrees with the decision of either the CCPA or the Federal Circuit in two-thirds of the cases it has reviewed. Only one-third of the cases are affirmed, and even in some of those cases the patent court is criticized for faulty reasoning. Using Moore's reasoning, then, the Federal Circuit is not equipped to resolve patent cases because of that ratio of reversals to affirmances.

The Moore article nowhere mentions or applies Federal Rule of Civil Procedure 52(a)(6), which prohibits an appellate court from setting aside findings of a district court unless they are clearly erroneous. As the advisory note to the 1985 amendment to Rule 52(a) puts it, deference must be given to "the trial court's findings." "To permit courts of appeal to share more actively in the fact finding function [especially findings based on non-demeanor testimony] would tend to undermine the legitimacy of district courts in the eyes of litigants, multiply appeals by encouraging appellate retrial of some factual issues, and needlessly reallocate judicial authority." The "trial court, not the appellate tribunal, should be the finder of facts."

This clear mandate from the judicial branch falls on deaf ears with both Dreyfuss and Moore, who seek "appellate retrial of some factual issues, and [not to] needlessly reallocate judicial authority" to lower courts. The perspective of both Dreyfuss and Moore is clearly wrong. These authors assume that Rule 52(a) does not apply to the Federal Circuit. This assumption, in turn, assumes that there are no facts in claims, and there is no need for deference to district court findings of fact.

Claims define the invention. How could a definition of an invention not contain facts? What Dreyfuss and Moore advocate is that the Federal Circuit may substitute its view of what a claim means for that of the fact-finder. This disregards Rule 52(a), and is improper.

From my perspective (10 APLA Q. J. 309), the Federal Circuit must "be more deferential to findings of fact by lower tribunals. . . . CAFC will have to apply the same standards of review in all cases. . . . CAFC will likely evolve to be more like other Circuit Courts where 'the parties are entitled to a consideration in the first instance of all the facts touching the obviousness issue, by a fact-finder who sees and hears the witnesses' (Markey, C.J. sitting by designation in *E.I. DuPont de Nemours v. Berkeley & Co., Inc.*, 620 F. 2d 1247 (Eighth Cir. 1980))" (318-319).

Judge Markey's statement in 1980 when he sat with the Eighth Circuit was not followed in the opinion he wrote on behalf of the Federal Circuit in *Panduit Corp. v. Dennison Mfg. Co.*, 774 F. 2d 1082 (Fed. Cir.1985). In the *Panduit* case, he set aside findings of the district court without citing Rule 52(a) or showing clear error. The Supreme Court vacated the decision and remanded the case to the Federal Circuit to consider Rule 52(a).

Moore's article did not acknowledge the Rule 52(a)(6) prohibition against appellate courts modifying trial court findings of facts. Instead, she cited *Cybor Corp. v. FAS Technologies, Inc.*, 138 F. 3d 1448 (Fed. Cir. 1998) and *Markman v. Westview Instruments, Inc.*, 52 F. 3d 967 (Fed Cir. 1995), that hold that there are no facts in claims. The mere statement of this proposition is laughable, (or "absurd" as Abramson's book states), yet that is the perspective of the Federal Circuit. I believe that a patent claim, which defines an invention, necessarily has facts.

Moore's assertion (2001, 20) is that *Cybor* and *Markman* made claim construction "purely a question of law devoid of fact findings." The truth is that experts can only testify as to facts, not law. The Supreme Court, in reviewing the Federal Circuit decision in *Markman*, cited Walker, *Patent Laws*, for the proposition that construction of claim terms, "aided by expert testimony, are questions for the court" (517 U.S., 387). If expert testimony is the basis, it must be factual, that can "aid" the court.

Likewise, *Markman* (517 U.S. 388) cited William C. Robinson's, *The Law of Patents for Useful Inventions* (1890): in cases in which claim terms "are unknown to the judge, the testimony of witnesses may be received on these subjects." The testimony of experts must relate to facts, not law. The Federal Circuit fails to understand that claim construction is a "mongrel" practice mixing fact and law, with "construing a term of art following receipt of evidence" being in the fact part. The mongrel practice cannot be "devoid of fact findings," as Moore contended.

Finally, the Moore article (2001, 7) states that district courts cannot receive testimony or other evidence "to vary the plain meaning of a claim term." But "if the Federal Circuit disagrees with the district court's claim construction, it may adopt the construction of the appealing party . . . or it could proffer its own claim construction never before considered by either party" (*id.*, 13).

This peculiar interpretation is unquestionably contrary to Rule 52(a). If the district court finding of claim construction is "clearly erroneous," it may be set aside. But no law permits simply substituting a reviewing court's view of facts for that of the trier of fact. If there is no evidence in the record supporting an alternative view of the facts, the case must be remanded. A court of appeals cannot be a fact-finder. Facts must be found by "a fact-finder who sees and hears the witnesses," not a court of appeals, under Rule 52.

Admission of evidence is a matter of trial court discretion, not appellate whim. "Cases arise where it is very much a matter of discretion with the court whether to receive or exclude evidence; but the appellate court will not reverse in such a case, unless the ruling is manifestly erroneous" *Spring v. Edgar*, 99 U.S. 645 (1879). Setting aside findings of the trial court that are "clearly erroneous" in the 1879 *Spring* case is the same standard as in Rule 52(a): "manifestly erroneous." The Federal Circuit cannot "proffer its own claim construction" without any supporting factual evidence having been admitted in evidence in the district court.

The conventional wisdom of those commentators cited above reveals a perspective contrary to mine. I hear a different drummer. I see patent law from a different perspective.

The Federal Circuit's "own law" is found wanting time after time in Supreme Court reviews, as this book illustrates. The fine garments Dreyfuss and Moore have made for their Emperor, the Federal Circuit, are imaginary. It is time for a little boy to cry "But the Emperor has nothing on at all" (Anderson, *The Emperor Has No Clothes*, (1837)).

# CHAPTER 1

# INTRODUCTION

This book is about the two specialist patent courts, the United States Court of Customs and Patent Appeals (CCPA) and the United States Court of Appeals for the Federal Circuit (Federal Circuit).

In 1890, Congress created intermediate appellate courts between the federal courts of first instance, now called district courts, and the Supreme Court. All levels of federal courts: district courts, courts of appeal and Supreme Court; were staffed by generalist judges rather than specialists in particular areas of the law. Presidents often appointed trial specialists to the federal courts, but the jurisdiction of the federal courts was general, not specialized.

Congress created administrative agencies staffed by specialists in various areas of the law. One of the earliest federal agencies was the US Patent Office, which has experts not only in patent law, but also in specific areas of technology in which patent applications are filed. Later, dozens of federal agencies were created to deal with special areas of the law. Experts in these areas (e.g. customs law, criminal law, and anti-trust law) would decide issues before the agency in the first instance, and the agencies usually had internal appellate boards to review those decisions.

The judges of the appellate boards, then as now, were not Article III judges, that is, part of the judicial branch of government. Rather, they were Article I judges, created by Congress as part of the legislative branch. The primary difference between the two types of judges is that Article III judges have lifetime tenure.

Review of decisions by administrative agencies was usually allowed by legislation, but the location of reviewing tribunals in the judicial hierarchy varied. Sometimes, further review of agency decisions was by district courts, whose decisions were reviewed by courts of appeal. Other times, a review of administrative agency decisions was permitted by appeal directly to regional courts of appeal.

In patent cases, a review of the agency's decisions originally went to the District Court of the District of Columbia, an Article III court, with further review by the Court of Appeals for the District of Columbia, another Article III court. In 1929, a specialized administrative court for patent cases was created and combined with the existing Court of Customs Appeals. It had jurisdiction over appeals from the patent agency as well as from the customs agency, and the name of the combined court was the Court of Customs and Patent Appeals (CCPA).

The only link in a judicial decision between customs law and patent law that I have ever found is the case of *Hartranft v. Weigmann*, 121 U.S. 609, 615 (1887). It was a customs case, not a patent case. Weigmann bought polished ornamental shells in London and imported them into the United States. A jury decided that the duty Weigmann would pay was $55.29 for "manufactures of shells." The trial court held out the possibility that some or all of the shells might be natural products and not manufactures, in which case no duty was to be paid.

The circuit court decided, and the Supreme Court affirmed, that grinding or etching the outer layer of shells to improve their ornamental qualities did not make the shells "manufactures." As the Supreme Court put it, "They were still shells. They had not been manufactured into a new and different article having a distinctive name, character, or use from that of a shell."

The Supreme Court has repeatedly cited *Hartranft* for the proposition that products of nature are not patentable subject matter, although no patent was involved in that case. The free list of the customs statute had a category "shells of every description, not manufactured." The patent statute has always provided that a patent could be granted for a "manufacture." Today, 35 U.S.C. §101 provides that "any new and useful . . . manufacture" is entitled to a patent. The word "manufacture" is common to both the customs statute and the patent statute, one providing that the government is entitled to no duty for a shell "not manufactured" and the other providing that a manufactured product may be patented if new and useful. The Supreme Court connected the two in deciding cases raising the issue of whether the subject matter of a patent application is patentable (chapter 5).

The Supreme Court has reviewed thirty-three of the decisions of the two patent courts. Six of the cases came from the CCPA and twenty-seven from the Federal Circuit. The first four of the six CCPA decisions were overturned, either vacated or reversed. Only 33% of the CCPA cases reviewed by the Supreme Court were affirmed. Seventeen of the first twenty-one Federal Circuit decisions were overturned, but the record has improved in recent years. As this is written at the end of the Supreme Court's 2011 term in 2012, the total is 22 of the patent court decisions were overturned, and 11 were affirmed by the Supreme Court, or exactly 67% of the decisions were overturned, and 33% were affirmed; not a very good record. It was worse in 2008, when 6 of 27 cases, or 22%, were affirmed, or almost four out of five reversed. To state the problem of review then, more than two-thirds of the decisions of the patent courts were overturned when reviewed by the Supreme Court.

Why such a poor record? That is the question pursued in this book. There are many reasons, and I try to explain them. Most commentators view the two patent courts as the Congressional vehicle for making consistent patent law decisions that are at the junction of law and technology. The specialized patent courts are deemed by those commentators to be the fountainhead of patent law.

My belief is that the patent courts do not have the power to make their "own law." Rather, as intermediate appellate courts in the hierarchy of Article III of the Constitution, the patent courts are inferior to the Supreme Court, which is the final authority on the judicial law of the land. The patent courts are therefore not the fountainhead of judicial patent law. They must follow the decisions of the Supreme Court. This different perspective gave rise to the title of this book.

I have followed all thirty-three of the Supreme Court reviews of patent court decisions since 1966. The very first one was a petition for writ of certiorari of a case decided by the CCPA when I was a law clerk there in 1964.

I have sorted the cases referred to in this book according to the sources of the applicable rules: constitutional provisions, statutes, precedents, the Federal Rules of Civil Procedure, Rules of Appellate Procedure, and Rules of Evidence. I have occasionally referred to cases within my own experience to illustrate points.

I hope to provide a different perspective on the workings of the two patent courts to show why their record is worse than the record in patent cases compiled by the regional courts of appeal from 1890 to 1982. Specialist patent courts are not necessarily better at deciding patent cases than generalist courts.

Briefly, the remainder of the book is arranged this way:

Chapter 2 seeks to explain how the patent courts came to believe they are the final authority on patent law, and how each of the two specialist courts attempted to develop its own law.

Chapter 3 is a scorecard of the 33 Supreme Court decisions since 1966 that reviewed decisions of the two patent courts. Eleven of the cases were affirmed, even though in many of those the reasoning of the patent court was in part rejected. Twenty-two patent court decisions were either vacated or reversed. Further musings on what this means are contained in chapter 3.

Chapter 4 analyzes Supreme Court reviews of patent court decisions involving constitutional rights. Due process of law is the subject of cases interpreting the Fifth and Fourteenth Amendments. The Seventh Amendment right to jury trial is covered in another case. The last case in chapter 4 involves the immunity of states under the Eleventh Amendment.

Chapter 5 begins the analysis of patent cases involving acts of Congress, starting with 35 U.S.C. §101. There are more Supreme Court decisions involving patentable subject matter under Section 101 than any other topic.

Chapter 6 covers the one case involving 35 U.S.C. §102(b).

Chapter 7 discusses 35 U.S.C. §103, which is by far the most litigated section of the patent code, but only tangentially involved in Supreme Court reviews of patent court decisions. *Graham v. John Deere Co.*, the first Court interpretation of Section 103 was not an appeal from a patent court decision, so it is not one of the 33 patent court cases studied here. It was a review of three appeals from regional courts of appeal, but it was such an important development in patent law that it is included in this chapter.

Chapter 8 relates to the Bayh-Dole Act, 35 U.S.C. §200-212, an attempt by Congress to sort out the rights of participants in government funded research.

Chapter 9 relates to 35 U.S.C. §271(b), induced infringement of a patent.

Chapter 10 relates to 35 U.S.C. §271(e), regarding drug and medical device patents regulated by the Food and Drug Administration.

Chapter 11 relates to §271(f), combinations of components made outside the United States, and the two Supreme Court decisions dealing with the issue.

Chapter 12 addresses the remedy for infringement of a patent under 35 U.S.C. §281.

Chapter 13 deals with the recent case concerning the presumption of validity under 35 U.S.C. §282.

Chapter 14 deals with the one case that reviewed an injunction under 35 U.S.C. §283.

Chapter 15 moves from the patent code to the Administrative Procedure Act as related to patent cases. Specifically, 5 U.S.C. §706 deals with court review of agency decisions. The very last of the 33 Court decisions, *Kappos v. Hyatt*, also relates to the Administrative Procedure Act.

Chapter 16 departs from statutory provisions and begins study of the Federal Rules of Civil Procedure, beginning with Rule 50(a). Because the *Markman* decision made reference to the receipt of evidence from experts in construing patent claims, Rules of Evidence 702-706 are included in this chapter rather than in a separate chapter. *Markman* is discussed in the prologue as well.

Further discussion of this important case in a separate chapter on Evidence Rules seemed unnecessary.

Chapter 17 addresses cases interpreting Rule 52(a), although the Rule is referred to repeatedly in earlier chapters.

Chapter 18 relates to Rule 56(c), summary judgment.

Chapter 19 leaves the Federal Rules and enters Supreme Court precedents on the Doctrine of Equivalents.

Chapter 20 discusses Court reviews of Federal Circuit decisions on the well-pleaded complaint.

Chapter 21 is a summation of some of the problems addressed here and focuses upon possible corrections to some of those problems.

# CHAPTER 2

# OMNISCIENT PATENT COURTS

A major reason why the patent courts' decisions have not fared well at the Supreme Court is because the patent courts assumed they are the omniscient fountainhead of patent law. Congress created a specialized patent court because it concluded that specialists in patent law would be better able to resolve appeals in patent cases than the generalist judges in regional courts of appeal. The perception of omniscience is derived in part by the fact that the very first patent court judge was Giles S, Rich, who had, before his appointment, been qualified to practice before the Patent Office. Rich was co-author of the Patent Act of 1952, an accomplishment that may have led, when he was a judge, to the court's perception of omniscience. Before 1956, when Rich was appointed to the CCPA, there had never been a former specialist in patent law appointed to the court.

Charles Alan Wright, lead author of *Federal Practice and Procedure*, the definitive treatise on the Federal Rules of Civil Procedure, wrote a law review article about deference when he was a young man. *The Doubtful Omniscience of Appellate Courts* (1957) took its title from the dissent in *Orvis v. Higgins*, 180 F. 2d 537, 542 n. 57 (2nd Cir. 1950):

"This is a typical instance for the application of Fed. R. Civ. P. 52(a). Though trial judges may at times be mistaken as to facts, appellate judges are not always omniscient" (Wright 1957, 779). The majority in *Orvis* held that for facts not proved by oral testimony, Rule 52(a) does not require deference to the credibility determination of the trial court. The appellate court is capable of reviewing findings based on non-demeanor testimony without deference, according to the majority.

Wright argued that not deferring to the facts as found by the district court "impairs the confidence of litigants and the public in the decisions of the trial courts, and it multiplies the number of appeals" (*id.*)

The battle between the Wright view and the Moore view (not the same Moore that wrote an article in 2001) in his treatise *Federal Practice* (1982) was resolved by the ADVISORY COMMITTEE NOTES for the 1985 Amendment to Rule 52(a). Wright's law review article was cited in the Note, along with his treatise *Federal Practice and Procedure* (1971) in adopting Wright's view. The Note concluded that to "permit courts of appeal to share more actively in the fact-finding function would tend to undermine the legitimacy of the district courts in the eyes of litigants, multiply appeals by encouraging appellate retrial of some factual issues, and needlessly reallocate judicial authority."

This was the final resolution of the issue of an appellate court's obligation to defer to district court findings of fact. But that final resolution has never seeped into the practice of the Federal Circuit. The patent court continues to believe in its omniscience and follows its "own law," without following the mandate of Federal Rule 52(a). That Rule, approved by the Supreme Court, must be followed by every court of appeals. The Federal Circuit avoids that mandate by holding that patent claims (that define the invention) contain no facts, as noted in the *Cybor* discussion in the prologue above.

The only possible reason for this preposterous idea that a patent claim is devoid of facts is to be able to ignore the requirement of Rule 52(a) that an appellate court must defer to the district court's findings of facts. "Findings of facts, whether based on oral or documentary evidence, shall not be set aside unless clearly erroneous." If an inventor testifies as to what his invention is, as a matter of fact, and the district court, sitting with or without a jury, believes the testimony to be true and makes findings of fact, those facts may not be set aside unless clearly erroneous.

Instead of following the high standard of Rule 52(a), the Federal Circuit has created its "own law," that the appellate court can substitute its view of the meaning of claim terms for that of the trier of fact because patent claims are "devoid of facts," and therefore may be interpreted any way that the appellate court chooses. No deference need be paid to the trier of fact, so the reasoning goes.

Following *Cybor*, the Federal Circuit believes that claim interpretation is decided *de novo* on appeal as a matter of law without deference to the trial court interpretation. In other words, the Federal Circuit chooses to "undermine the legitimacy of the district courts," "encourage[e] appellate retrial of some factual issues," and "needlessly reallocate judicial authority" in direct violation of the mandate of the 1985 advisory committee notes.

The patent court judges apparently do not abide by the 1985 notes because they lack substantial experience in patent infringement cases. The first patent court only had jurisdiction over decisions of administrative agencies, and never reviewed decisions of district court judges. Only a single one of the judges of the two patent courts has ever served as a district court judge before appointment to the patent court, unlike other federal courts of appeal judges. Judge O'Malley, a former district court judge, has just recently been appointed to the Federal Circuit.

The other judges of the patent courts have failed to defer to jury findings of fact, district court findings, precedents by sister courts of appeal, precedents of the Supreme Court, federal rules, and congressional enactments (as opposed to comments by individual legislators or witness testimony to Congress). These shortcomings shall be explored. But first I shall try to trace the development of the omniscient, specialist courts and the reasons for the hubris and arrogance.

Judge Giles Rich was easily the most influential force in patent law in the second half of the Twentieth Century. Like his father before him, he prosecuted patent applications before the Patent

Office for decades. "Prosecution" in the criminal law sense means a government lawyer pursuing criminals to punish crime. In the patent law sense, "prosecution" means opposing the government in pursuit of patents on behalf of inventors and owners of inventions. "Patent prosecution" is drafting persuasive patent applications defining the invention in order to convince the patent examiner to grant the patent on the invention to the inventor or to the inventor's assignee. The patent examiner represents the public interest in determining that all requirements of the patent laws have been met.

The inventor's representative is "pro-patent" in the sense that he or she seeks the government grant to the inventor. To the extent that the patent examiner opposes the grant if the patent application fails to satisfy all statutory requirements (since 1952, these have been new, useful, nonobvious, and properly described), the government is "anti-patent" in protecting the public interest.

Having spent his professional life prosecuting patent applications before his appointment to the bench, Judge Rich was decidedly "pro-patent." He also had the unique experience of participating in the drafting the first overhaul of patent law by Congress since 1836, the 1952 Patent Act.

Two people, Giles Rich, representing the pro-patent representatives of inventors, and Pasquale ("Pat") Federico, representing the Patent Office, were the primary drafters of the 1952 patent law. The two became friends primarily through their mutual respect for the other's knowledge and intellect. There was no "pro-patent" or "anti-patent" animosity between them, just a shared interest in clarifying patent law that had become unclear since 1836.

When Judge Rich was appointed to the CCPA in 1956, he brought his experience of opposing patent examiners for nearly thirty years as well as his intimate working experience with Federico, a former patent examiner and Patent Office Solicitor. He also brought a thorough knowledge of the new patent act of 1952. He had worked with congressional committees in pursuing the new act, but Judge Rich had not been a politician and had never held elected office.

The only autobiography of Judge Rich that I have found is two and a half pages in his book *A Brief History of the United States Court of Customs and Patent Appeals* (1980, 131–33). He was born in 1904 in Rochester, New York. His father, also named Giles Rich, was a patent lawyer in Rochester and moved the family to New York City in 1919, where he continued to practice patent law.

Judge Rich went to Harvard from 1922 to 1926, and he received a degree in "history, economics and government." Many patent lawyers have degrees in science or engineering, but Judge Rich did not. He received a law degree from Columbia University in 1929, became a member of the New York bar, and went to work at his father's law firm "almost simultaneously with the great stock market crash of that year" (1980, 131).

Judge Rich wrote that he had lectured undergraduates at Columbia University on patent law from 1942 until 1956. Undergraduates, unlike even beginning law students, have no training in how the judicial process works, so it was unlikely that the rules of evidence and civil procedure used to decide judicial disputes played any significant role in his lectures. The fundamentals of patent law are not related to the judicial process.

In the book, Judge Rich wrote a brief biography of each of the twenty-five judges who had served on the Court of Customs Appeals and the Court of Customs and Patent Appeals in the preceding seventy years. For his own biography, he stated that in "the early 1940's . . . Rich wrote a monograph on 'The Relation between Patent Practices and the Antimonopoly Laws,'" which was published in five issues in the Journal of the Patent Office Society (1980, 180). Because anti-monopoly laws may be considered "anti-patent" by those who believe that patents are monopolies, it was clear which side Rich was on.

"He was at the same time active in the work of the New York Patent Law Association, and when it undertook, after the virtual destruction of the doctrine of contributory infringement by the Supreme Court in the *Mercoid* cases in 1944, to introduce and foster legislation to correct the anti-monopoly situation, Rich became deeply involved with it. As NYPLA Vice President in 1948 and 1949 it was his responsibility to explain this legislation to Congressional committees. As a result of bills which the NYPLA wrote and had introduced, and other bills in the patent law field, the House Patents

Subcommittee . . . decided to revise and codify the patent statutes. . . . [Rich and Federico were] a two-man drafting committee . . . preparing the bills which became, eventually, the Patent Act of 1952." This work led to his appointment to the CCPA in 1956.

This modest account of how Rich, on behalf of NYPLA, drafted bills "in the patent law field" that became, with the help of Pat Federico as his partner in a "two-man drafting committee," the greatest reformulation of patent law since 1836. It is no wonder that Judge Rich rightly regarded himself as the drafter of the 1952 act and thus the most knowledgeable expert on patent law in the country. Hubris, though unbecoming, is understandable given his accomplishments.

Unfortunately, the ability to draft bills in the patent field is not helpful in deciding judicial disputes. Courts are not the fountainhead of law; legislators are. Courts must follow rules laid down by the Judicial Conference and, ultimately, the Supreme Court. These rules require deference to Supreme Court precedents, to facts found by the trier of facts, and to trial courts' decisions on admissibility of evidence and the application of law in the trial court.

Being knowledgeable in patent law does not mean knowledge of civil procedure and admissibility of evidence in district courts and in regional courts of appeal..

Judge Rich reshaped the CCPA and later the Federal Circuit in his own image of omniscience. His expertise did not need to defer to any other body; not a jury, not a tribunal below it, not any court of appeals of equal rank, and not even the Supreme Court. The Federal Circuit has even gone so far as to develop its "own law," to be followed as it wishes, regardless of differences from law applied in other courts.

Judge Rich believed that the Supreme Court was anti-patent because of its anti-monopoly decisions like the *Mercoid* cases, as well as the fact that it lacked knowledge of the patent law that he knew so well. The disdain that Judge Rich had for the Supreme Court was reflected in the remark in his autobiography (1980) about "the virtual destruction of the doctrine of contributory infringement."

Rich attempted, in drafting the 1952 patent act, to have Congress alter the *Mercoid* holding, but the1952 act was not directed expressly toward overruling *Mercoid*. The Supreme Court continues to follow *Mercoid* (see *Quanta* in chapter 4).

The author of the *Mercoid* opinion was Justice Douglas, whose arguably anti-patent views were formed during his government service in antitrust law. Rich also opposed what he believed was the anti-patent concurring opinion by Justice Douglas in *Great Atlantic & Pacific Tea Co. v. Supermarket Equipment Corp.*, 340 U.S. 147 (1950). Douglas in *Mercoid* had written that a patent was a privilege granted for a public purpose. In *A & P*, Justice Douglas wrote that a "patent had to serve the ends of science—to push back the frontiers of chemistry, physics, and the like, to make a distinctive contribution to scientific knowledge." Rich sought to alter that anti-patent view through the 1952 patent act, which specified that a patent could be granted for a "nonobvious" invention, even if it did not push back the frontiers. Rich believed nonobviousness was a much lower threshold than that specified by Justice Douglas in *A & P*.

Yet another opinion of Justice Douglas that bothered Rich was his dissent in *Glidden v. Zdanok*, 370 U.S. 530 (1962), which affirmed the decision in *Benny Lurk v. United States*, 296 F. 2d 360 (D.C. Cir. 1961). Benny Lurk was tried for the robbery of $58.31 in the District of Columbia district court. The presiding judge at the trial was Judge Joseph Jackson of the CCPA, sitting by designation. Lurk was convicted and sentenced to four to fourteen years in prison. On appeal, the court appointed Eugene Gressman, a former Supreme Court law clerk, to represent Lurk.

Lurk claimed that Judge Jackson was not qualified to preside over a criminal trial in a district court and to sentence Lurk to years in prison because the CCPA was not an Article III court. That is, Judge Jackson was appointed to serve on the CCPA, and the Supreme Court had ruled in *Ex Parte Bakelite*, 279 U.S. 438 (1929) that the Court of Customs Appeals (which became the CCPA in 1929) was a legislative court under Article I of the Constitution, and was not a judicial court under Article III. To the same effect was *Williams v. United States*, 269 U.S. 553 (1933) holding judges of the CCPA were not Article III judges.

Determining customs duties by the Court of Customs Appeals was deemed an administrative function and not the determination of a case or controversy, as in a criminal trial.

The Court of Appeals in *Benny Lurk* upheld the conviction because Congress had expressly held in 1958 that the judges of the CCPA were Article III judges. The Supreme Court affirmed the *Lurk* decision in *Glidden Co. v, Zdanok*, 368 U.S. 814 (1961). Justice Douglas dissented, asserting that Article I judges do not decide cases or controversies involving jury trials and the range of disputes of property, life and liberty. In short, they are not "real" judges, just administrative judges. This dissent was not anti-patent, but it was against lawyers and judges who only decided administrative matters in the PTO, and not cases in courts. The total effect of these cases, and many more, was an irreconcilable divide between pro-patent and anti-patent views.

What Judge Rich encountered when he arrived 1956, was a court made up of politicians that had no prior experience in patent law. Judge O'Connell had been a newspaper man who turned to politics during the Depression and was appointed to the CCPA in 1944, during President Roosevelt's third term. Judge Johnson, who became chief judge of the CCPA on the same day that Judge Rich was sworn in, had been a prosecuting attorney ("prosecution" in the criminal law sense, not the patent law sense) and a congressman from Indiana during his professional life. Judge Worley had been elected to the Texas legislature in 1935 and to congress in 1940 and served until 1950 when President Truman appointed him to the CCPA. Judge Cole had been a congressman from Maryland for fourteen years before his appointment to the Customs Court and then to the CCPA.

These four politicians, whose on-the-job training came from serving on the CCPA, were Judge Rich's seniors when he arrived. The seniors were not so much "anti-patent" as "*non*-patent" in outlook. As lawyers, they knew that deference was to be paid to facts found by juries and by administrative agency experts. The default mode of decision-making was to affirm the Patent Office decision unless appellant established that the agency had erred.

When I was a law clerk at the CCPA in the early 1960's, then Chief Judge Worley began the hearing of nearly every case by asking appellant's counsel how the Board of Appeals or the Trademark Trial and Appeal Board had erred. Many appellant lawyers were not prepared to address that question and instead immediately began their canned arguments. Failure to answer Judge Worley's opening question began on the wrong foot, and often cost the appellant Judge Worley's vote on the outcome.

Judge Rich, on the other hand, having battled patent examiners who had rejected his patent claims, did not presume that the Patent Office appellate tribunals were correct, as the other four judges did. All of the judges were sworn to uphold the law and all of them faithfully followed that mandate. However, prior life experiences color the decision-making process. Judge Rich's pro-patent experience differed from the non-patent experience of the former politicians.

Although Judge Rich privately objected to the anti-patent rulings by courts more familiar with anti-trust law than patent law, he did not generally espouse his pro-patent views publicly. An exception is his 1974 dissent in *In re Johnston*, 502 F. 2d 765 (CCPA 1974).

Before *Johnston*, the Supreme Court had reversed the decision of the CCPA (authored by Judge Rich) in *Gottschalk v. Benson*, 409 U.S. 63 (1972). *Benson* involved the issue of whether computer programs were patentable subject matter under §101. Judge Rich, on behalf of the CCPA, held that a new program for an old general purpose digital computer was patentable subject matter, but the Court reversed, holding that the Benson invention was not patentable subject matter.

*Johnston* came before the CCPA two years after the Court decided *Benson*. The only difference between *Benson* and *Johnston* was that *Benson* involved claims to a process, and *Johnston* involved claims to a machine. The majority of the CCPA held that *Benson* was limited to software defined as a process, and claims to a machine were therefore patentable subject matter. Judge Rich dissented on the ground that there is no "essential difference in substance between these apparatus claims . . . [and] the steps of the data processing method as being carried out by any conventional data processing machine," as stated by the board. In Judge Rich's view, "Every competent patent draftsman knows how to" cast claims as either a method or an apparatus. He believed that the *Benson* message is "loud and clear" regarding patentable subject matter, regardless of form as a method or an apparatus.

The Court's statements in *Benson* showed that it did *not* hold that a "patent for any program servicing a computer" was precluded, and that its decision did *not* "freeze process patents to old technologies, leaving no room for new, onrushing technology." Judge Rich said that these were "comforting words to which inventors of software and owners of software inventions look for solace," but he found "it more significant to contemplate the identities of the troops lined up for battle in Benson and observe which side obtained victory."

The government was on one side "against patenting programs or software, supported by the collective forces of major hardware (i.e. computer) manufacturers and their representative associations who, for economic reasons, did not want patents granted on programs for their machines. On the other side was [sic] Benson et al and their assignee and assorted lawyers and legal groups who were in favor of patent protection for programs or software. The anti-patenting forces won the victory."

The war analogy between the pro-patent forces of inventors and patent lawyers and the anti-patent forces of the government and others opposed to patenting software has never been more starkly portrayed. Judge Rich revealed which camp he was in, but the pro-patent forces lost the war because the Court said that Congress, not the courts, had to decide whether software was patentable. He expressly stated that he does "not agree with the Supreme Court's decision," but "it is the duty of a judge of a lower court to try to follow in spirit decisions of the Supreme Court—that is their 'thrust.'" Though several CCPA decisions had held that software could be patented, *Benson* had superseded those decisions and Judge Rich believed that the issue had been settled by the Court.

He admitted defeat by "the anti-patenting forces." Later Supreme Court decisions, while citing *Benson* with approval, showed that the issue of whether computer-assisted inventions were patentable subject matter was *not* settled in *Benson*. The war was not over, and the pro-patent forces lived to fight another day.

The Supreme Court took up the *Johnston* case, but it did not decide whether *Benson* controlled the outcome. Rather than consider the §101 issue of patentable subject matter, the Court decided the case based on obviousness, an alternative issue raised by the appeal. The CCPA was reversed, but not because the program was not patentable subject matter. Rather, the Court found the invention obvious, which was the view expressed by Chief Judge Markey in his dissent in the CCPA. *Benson* was not cited by the Supreme Court in *Johnston*. The Court did not determine in *Johnston* that "[t]he anti-patenting forces won the victory," as Judge Rich had concluded in his dissent below.

The next case considered by the Supreme Court on certiorari from the CCPA was *Parker v. Flook*, 437 U.S. 584 (1978). The second sentence of the Court's opinion read: "The only novel feature of the method is a mathematical formula." Novelty was not the issue raised in the CCPA; patentable subject matter was the issue. However, "mathematical formula" raises the issue of §101, and the Court held that *Benson* controlled and required the reversal of the CCPA finding of patentable subject matter. The Court was careful to limit its reversal to the *Benson* holding that a "law of nature cannot be the subject of a patent." *Flook* was not "a judgment that patent protection of certain novel and useful computer programs will not promote the progress of science and the useful arts, or that such protection is undesirable as a matter of policy." *Flook* thus left open the question whether computer programs could be patented, the issue Judge Rich believed *Benson* had closed.

All four of the first cases from the CCPA to reach the Supreme Court were reversed on petitions filed by the Commissioner of Patents. *Brenner v. Manson*, 388 U.S. 519 (1966), the first case decided by the CCPA to be reviewed by the Supreme Court, did not involve computer software. Rather, it involved a steroid, dihydrotestosterone, which ultimately led to the birth control pill introduced by Syntex. The steroid was described and claimed in a patent issued to an inventor named Ringold, suggesting that it was suitable for one seeking an "antiestrogenic effect" in a drug.

Manson, a scientist working for Syntex, believed that he had invented the same steroid before Ringold did. He filed a patent application for the steroid in order to provoke an interference proceeding in the PTO in order to determine which inventor was prior in time.

The patent application filed by Manson stated that the steroid was a "known product" that was described in the Ringold patent. Manson did not specify what the steroid was useful for, but instead just said that it was a known product, presumably to avoid revealing that the owner of the Manson invention was a potential competitor of the owner of the Ringold invention.

The patent examiner did not set up the desired interference because the Manson application did not indicate what the steroid was good for, but instead just that it was a "known product." In order to set up an interference proceeding, the examiner must determine that the inventions in the applications of both parties to the interference are patentable. Because Manson failed to disclose that the steroid was "useful" under §101, the examiner rejected the Manson patent application. The Board of Appeals affirmed, because Manson failed to disclose a "utility for the compound produced by the process at the time he invented the process" (333 F. 2d 236).

The CCPA reversed, holding that it was enough to show that a "process which operated as disclosed to produce a known product is useful within the meaning of Section 101" (id.). The author of the CCPA opinion was Judge Arthur Smith, a former patent attorney who had spent thirty-three years representing inventors before the Patent Office. He was definitely in the pro-patent camp, and believed that "nonobviousness" was sufficient to warrant the grant of a patent. A process that is useful for making a product that was already patented was good enough for Judge Smith.

I was a law clerk at the CCPA when *Manson* was decided. There had been very few cases in which a patent application was rejected as not being "useful." The standard was quite low. I was not surprised that the CCPA reversed the board decision. Because the Supreme Court had never granted certiorari to review a CCPA decision in the thirty-five years before the CCPA decision in *Manson*, it never occurred to me that the Court would be interested in the *Manson* case. To my surprise, it was the first CCPA case ever to reach the Supreme Court.

The Supreme Court reversed the CCPA decision. It said that the "basic *quid pro quo* contemplated by the Constitution and the Congress for granting the patent monopoly is one the benefit derived by the public from an invention with *substantial utility.*" (534).

This sentence illustrates the differences in analytical approach between the Supreme Court and the patent courts. "*Quid pro quo*" teaches that a bargain is reached between the inventor and the public. In return for bringing forth new knowledge for the benefit of society, the inventor receives an exclusionary right to his product for a limited time. The Court said the right to exclude was the "patent monopoly" given to the inventor as part of the bargain. (The "anti-monopoly" concept of *Mercoid* still exists).

The CCPA believed the patent was not a bargain, but rather a right belonging to the creator. It was not a limited monopoly, secured by the benefit to society from the new knowledge. Instead, the patent was a reward for a nonobvious contribution.

The Supreme Court analysis is surely correct. Because Manson disclosed no use for the steroid; he failed to uphold his end of the bargain to come forward with useful knowledge. Just because the steroid was "known," was no reason to grant a monopoly on the birth control pill which was revolutionary in importance.

Not that Ringold fully deserved a patent monopoly on the birth control pill. Having an "antiestrogenic effect" from use of the steroid (minimizing the effect of a sex hormone), is hardly an instruction that unwanted pregnancies can be prevented by its use, which would have enormous benefit to society. At the end of the day, Syntex achieved enormous commercial success from the birth control pill, while it is unknown what the Ringold patent contributed.

If Syntex had obtained a patent on the Manson invention in 1966, when the Supreme Court held that simply being "known" did not warrant a seventeen year monopoly, the birth control revolution would have had a different outcome in the years between 1966 and 1983, when the Manson patent would have expired.

The founding fathers of our nation could not have foreseen, when the patent monopoly was conceived, the enormous economic effect that patents might have. For example, the owner of the Lipitor patent benefitted to the tune of as much as twelve billion dollars annually from the sale of the patented product. It is hard to imagine that the benefit to society from having the knowledge disclosed in that patent was worth the bargain of giving the patent owner the right to exclude others from using the invention for the life of the patent. Perhaps income tax is sufficient to even the bargain, but twelve billion dollars a year is a lot of *quid* for the *quo*.

The good news is that *Manson* ended the draught of oversight by the Supreme Court of the specialized patent court.

Returning to the other §101 cases following *Manson*, the Supreme Court in *Benson*, and *Flook* reversed the CCPA's holding that the subject matter of the invention in each case was not within §101. This issue, §101 was raised in *Johnston*, but the Court decided that case on the alternative ground of §103. With every case emanating from the pro-patent CCPA reviewed by the Supreme Court up to 1978 having been reversed, it appeared to Judge Rich in his dissent in *Johnston* that the "anti-patenting forces won the victory" in the Supreme Court.

Still, there was a glimmer of hope that the Supreme Court was not entirely anti-patent because the Court had said in both *Benson* and *Flook* that the reversal in each case was not a precedent that no patent can be issued on computer programs or mathematical formulae. Judge Rich perceived, from his experience with Congress in the enactment of the 1952 patent law, that Congress was pro-patent, and the Court would follow what Congress enacted if it understood Congress's intent.

Judge Rich sought to educate the Supreme Court on the pro-patent wisdom of Congress in the next cases, rather than continuing to criticize what he perceived as anti-patent cases, like *Benson*. Shortly after *Flook* was decided, Acting Commissioner Parker, the successful petitioner in *Flook*, filed two more petitions in the Supreme Court seeking review of the CCPA decisions in *In re Bergy* and *In re Chakrabarty*.

The fifth case to be presented to the Supreme Court by the Commissioner of Patents was *Parker v. Bergy*, which asked for a review of the CCPA decision in *In re Bergy*, 596 F. 2d 952 (CCPA, 1979), which reversed the Patent Office's holding that the subject matter of a living plant was not patentable. The *Flook* reversal of the CCPA decision had just been handed down, and the Supreme Court immediately granted certiorari to consider the impact of *Flook* on the *Bergy* decision. This might suggest that the Court was resolutely anti-patent, as Judge Rich had concluded in his dissent in *Johnston*. Still, the issue was not closed, as the Court is reluctant to make broad rules, preferring to leave open the possibility of filling the interstices between cases in later decisions.

Acting Commissioner Parker filed a petition for review of yet another §101 decision of the CCPA in *In re Chakrabarty*, decided shortly after the CCPA had reversed the board in *Bergy*. The Court granted the petitions in both *Bergy* and *Chakrabarty* and remanded both cases to the CCPA with instructions to consider the impact of *Flook*.

For his part, Judge Rich realized that the CCPA was given the opportunity, in the remand of both *Bergy* and *Chakrabarty*, to explain precisely what the 1952 patent act had accomplished, a subject Judge Rich knew better than anyone, Pat Federico having passed away. Judge Rich often said that the 1952 patent act was intended to alter by act of Congress the unrealistic (anti-patent) views of the Court. His contempt for Supreme Court patent decisions was shown in 1975, when he wrote that he had "a favorite axiom: 'The higher you go, the less they know.'" (Rich, *How Systematic is the Patent System*, 57 J. Pat. Off. Society 96 (1975)). That is, the Supreme Court knows less about patent law than the specialist patent court generally and Judge Rich specifically as drafter of the 1952 Patent Act.

Rather than complaining that *Benson* had closed the door on patents for computer programs (as he did in his *Flook* dissent), Judge Rich articulated his insights into the 1952 Patent Act that had not been presented to the Supreme Court before the remand of *Bergy* and *Chakrabarty*.

In the combined *Bergy* and *Chakrabarty* decision on remand, Judge Rich revealed that Congress had enlarged the scope of patentable subject matter to include plant inventions, not just "chemistry, physics, and the like," as Justice Douglas had suggested.

Judge Rich pointed out in *Bergy* that Congress, in enacting §101, intended "in general terms to broadly encompass unforeseeable future developments, as, broadly, we suggest, as section 2 of the Sherman Act, 15 USC 2" (596 F. 2d 952, 974). He cited P. J. Federico (his co-author of the 1952 act) for the proposition that the broad language of §101 delineated a "general industrial boundary" (footnote 11).

The Supreme Court never considered §101 of the patent act between 1929 and1965 when it first addressed the issue of patentable subject matter (*Brenner v. Manson*). The Court had, in contrast, decided many cases interpreting the Sherman Act during those years, concluding that the simple statutory language of the act is to be viewed broadly.

Picking up on the "general industrial boundary" language of Federico, Judge Rich then said (974-75): "What we deal with in each appeal is an industrial product used in an industrial process in a useful or technological art;" microorganisms in both *Bergy* and *Chakrabarty*.

Judge Rich went on to explain that the purpose of the Plant Patent Act of 1930 was to extend the patent system to agriculture and horticulture. In 1790, when the first patent act was passed, manufacturing was "the production of any and all things made by the hand of man. . . . In the md-1800's, however, it became apparent that scientific principles could be applied to agriculture and horticulture" (981). The 1930 plant patent act was "an effort to apply the patent system where it had not been applied before in order to fuel the fire under plant breeding and to protect the experimenters in that as yet nonindustrial field" (*id.*). "Congress had in mind the stimulation of a *field of endeavor* that, unlike chemistry, for example, had not yet flowered into an industry. . . . What is crystal clear is the intent of Congress to extend the patent system to a *nonindustrial area,* ignoring completely the fact that plants were alive" (982, Rich's italics).

Because products of nature cannot be patented, the 1930 act did not include sexually produced plants such as "trees of the forest and plants of the earth," and was limited to an asexually produced plant that is "a discovery resulting from cultivation [that] is unique, isolated, and is not repeated by nature, nor can it be reproduced by nature unaided by man" (983). There is no apparent difference between "the part played by the plant originator in the development of new plants and the part played by the chemist in the development of new compositions of matter."

Rich refuted the argument that living things cannot be patented by pointing out the many patents granted for yeasts, bacteria, mushrooms, viruses, and the fact that the PTO had allowed a *Chakrabarty* claim to a carrier and the bacteria he invented.

At page 987, the Rich opinion quoted the House and Senate reports in passing the 1952 act: "a machine, or a manufacture . . . may include *anything under the sun that is made by man*" (Rich's italics). Footnote 25 suggests that this quote is "an expression of Congressional will."

However, because the identical language appears in both the House version and in the Senate version, it likely is not an expression of a Congressman or a Senator. If the sausage of legislation was made in the same way in 1952 as it is made today, the quotation could well have been prepared by Giles Rich, a drafter of the legislation. Rich wrote "Congressional Intent or Who Wrote the 1952 Act," (Rich 1963). I submit, without knowing, that Judge Rich emphasized, in the *Bergy* opinion, either his own words or Pat Federico's words regarding *"anything under the sun"* in preparing reports for the House and Senate. These words were a cute expression of Rich's view, but they are not necessarily "an expression of Congressional will," as Rich argued.

*Bergy* may have been Judge Rich's finest opinion. It certainly impressed the Supreme Court, which decided, for the first time in history, to uphold the CCPA decision and reject the PTO petition in *Diamond v. Chakrabarty,* 447 U.S. 303 (1980). The Court did not overrule any of the preceding decisions that reversed the CCPA on the issue of patentable subject matter, but *Chakrabarty* was decidedly more pro-patent than any of the earlier Court decisions favoring the PTO.

The *Chakrabarty* opinion begins by indicating its narrow scope, whether a man-made microorganism is "a 'manufacture' or 'composition of matter' within the meaning of the statute" (35 U.S.C. §101). "This case does not involve the other 'conditions and requirements' of the patent laws, such as novelty or nonobviousness" (307). The Court cited with approval *Benson* and *Flook*, in which the CCPA holdings that the subject matter fell within §101 were reversed. It also cited many other precedents in which laws of nature were held not to be patentable subject matter.

However, the Court affirmed the decision of the CCPA that the new bacteria, made by man, unlike any other bacteria could be patented. The bacteria had different properties, a different use in treating oil spills, and a different form from other bacteria. "Accordingly, it is patentable subject matter under §101" (310).

The emphasis in the *Bergy* opinion upon what Congress has done and said in its legislative history, rather than disagreeing with Supreme Court precedents, seems to have paid off. Assuming that the Supreme Court knows less than the CCPA, as in Judge Rich's "favorite axiom" recorded in his 1975 JPOS article, the axiom is counterproductive. Educating the Court as to the intent of Congress is productive.

The next review of a CCPA decision was *Diamond v. Diehr*, 450 U.S. 175 (1981). There, as in nearly all of the other Supreme Court reviews of CCPA decisions, the anti-patent Patent Office held that a computer-assisted system for calculating the cure time for making shaped polymeric products was not patentable subject matter, citing *Benson* and *Flook*. Judge Rich, again speaking for the CCPA as he had in *Bergy* (which was affirmed in *Chakrabarty*), ignored his own dissent in *Johnston* that *Benson* controlled computer program cases. Instead, he relied upon *Chakrabarty* for the proposition that Congress had expanded the scope of §101 to include anything under the sun that is made by man, including a new curing process that more accurately controlled temperature.

The Rich opinion in *Diehr* made no reference to the anti-patent forces having won the war, and there was no suggestion of a conflict between software producers and hardware producers. A new dawn had come from *Chakrabarty*.

The Supreme Court bought the argument and affirmed the CCPA decision. Again, the Court did not overrule *Benson* or *Flook*; it simply reached the same result as *Chakrabarty*. Commentators can speculate about whether a change in Court personnel, public opinion, or other facts led the Court to make seemingly irreconcilable decisions without overruling its prior decisions.

In any event, Judge Rich, having authored the only two CCPA opinions that were affirmed by the Supreme Court, continued to seek the expansion of patentable subject matter in later cases to "new field[s] of endeavor" in non-industrial areas, as he wrote in *Bergy*. (Other Supreme Court reviews of Federal Circuit decisions regarding asexually reproduced plants are discussed in chapter 5). If Congress determined that asexually reproduced plants are patentable subject matter, as he explained in *Bergy*, and that microorganisms are patentable subject matter under *Chakrabarty*, it follows that computer programs in non-industrial areas might logically be included in the broad language used by Congress in §101. *Benson*, after all, had left open the prospect of a patent for an appropriate "program for servicing a computer." Judge Rich had overlooked that caveat in *Benson* when he declared in his *Johnston* dissent that the anti-patent forces had won the war over patenting computer software.

Judge Rich apparently realized that at least some computer-assisted processes are patentable subject matter under §101 after *Benson*, and *Diehr* clearly confirmed that.

The CCPA did not learn that it was not infallible before it was eliminated in 1982, even though four of its six cases that were reviewed by the Supreme Court were reversed. The two patent courts have revealed little grasp of the requirement of deference to findings of fact by lower tribunals. While many cases appear in following chapters to illustrate the lack of deference and the assumption of omniscience, a sampling of four decisions that did *not* reach the Supreme Court illustrates the problem of arrogance in place of deference.

## In re Zeidler, 682 F. 2d 961 (CCPA 1982)

In 1982, I was asked to write an article for the then American Patent Law Association Quarterly Journal about changes in the jurisdiction of the new court to include review of district court decisions. The article (10 APLA Q.J. 309 (1982)) predicted that the new patent court would have to comply with the rules applicable to reviewing decisions in judicial disputes in district courts. In *Zeidler*, the CCPA ignored the facts found by the trier of fact. Instead, it substituted its view of the facts for the facts found by patent examiner and the board.

Judge Rich, for the CCPA, said it was appropriate for the CCPA to "substitute its judgment for the judgment of the Examiner, since the examiner was in no better position than the reviewing court to evaluate the testimony of the witness." This view was soundly rejected by the 1985 advisory committee notes to the amendment of Rule 52(a) discussed earlier in this chapter.

The testimony in *Zeidler* was contained in two written declarations. It was not live testimony by a witness testifying under oath and subject to cross-examination in a federal courtroom before a trier of fact, as in district court proceedings. To my knowledge, Judge Rich, the author of the *Zeidler* opinion, had never been a judge or lead counsel in a district court trial with live testimony.

The invention in *Zeidler* was a dye for coloring leather. The patent examiner was presumably one skilled in the art of coloring leather. He was not a trier of fact in a court of law, but he searched the relevant prior art for coloring leather, and found prior art showing dyes similar to applicant's dyes for coloring leather. Instead of setting forth separately stated findings of fact, as district courts must do when finding facts, the examiner merely cited the contents of prior patents and stated the legal conclusion that the differences between the prior art dye formulas and the claimed dye formulas would have been obvious to a person having ordinary skill in the art.

The assignee of the Zeidler patent application submitted two declarations by a staff dye chemist employed by the assignee of the patent application. The declarations were offered to prove the legal conclusion that the invention was not obvious to one skilled in the art. They did not purport to set forth facts that might be submitted in evidence. Instead, the declarations asserted that the differences were not obvious.

Testimony of another employee of the same company that owned the patent application would not be admissible in evidence in a district court patent infringement trial to prove facts regarding the invention.

Evidence Rule 702 is quite clear that the testimony of an expert must be (1) "based upon sufficient facts or data; (2) the testimony is the product of reliable principles and methods, and (3) the witness has applied the principles and methods reliably to the facts of the case." The testimony in the two declarations was biased; contained essentially no facts or data; gave no principles or methods; and was not related to the facts of the case.

Judge Rich, the author of the *Zeidler* opinion, never cited Rule 702, probably because he had never tried a case in a district court as a lawyer or as a judge. Neither the PTO nor the CCPA raised admissibility issue in this or in any other administrative proceeding that I am aware of. Federal Rules of Evidence are never applied in PTO proceedings, although they should be.

The witness was clearly biased, feeding at the same corporate trough as the inventor. The declarations gave no facts or data, no reliable principles and methods relating to the similar dye formulas, and no application of principles to the facts of the case. This "expert" would have been tossed from a district court case and would have been precluded from testifying before a jury.

Instead, the witness was allowed to declare that the "dyes have surprising advantages in the dying of retanned chrome leather." No claims recited the limitation "retanned chrome leather." There was no indication of what the "surprising advantages" were or how the claimed invention resulted in those unnamed advantages.

All of the claims were to compositions of triazo dyes, not a method of dying "retanned chrome leather." The CCPA weighed the evidence and gave greater weight to the conclusory statement of the staff dye chemist for the owner of the patent application than to the PTO conclusion. Judge Rich said that "an expert's evaluation in this field is entitled to more weight than that of a layman." The CCPA reversed the PTO board decision. The testimony was not "an expert's evaluation," was biased, and was inadmissible. A patent examiner is not a "layman." The CCPA erred in reversing the PTO decision.

The Seventh Amendment leaves the weight to be applied to evidence to the trier of fact, not to a reviewing court of appeals that did not receive the evidence in the first instance.

### *In re Sarkli, Ltd.*, 721 F. 2d 353 (Fed. Cir. 1983)

The specialist patent court was not limited to just patent jurisdiction. The Federal Circuit, like the CCPA, believed it was the final authority on trademark matters as well. The *Sarkli* case, decided a year after the Federal Circuit was created, related to the meaning of the French word "repechage."

The examining attorney in the PTO found, as fact, that "REPECHAGE" meant "second chance," and there was an existing registration for "second chance" for skin care products. The legal conclusion reached by the examining attorney was that there was a likelihood of confusion between "REPECHAGE" and "SECOND CHANCE" when used on closely related toiletry products.

The Trademark Trial and Appeal Board deferred to the examining attorney's findings of fact and affirmed the decision to refuse registration of the applicant's mark "REPECHAGE" for skin care products. On appeal to the board, appellant argued that excerpts from French dictionaries showed that the primary meaning of "REPECHAGE" has to do with fishing up or fishing out or rescuing.

The board found, as a matter of fact, that the argument "does not seem to be consistent with the evidence in the record, namely, excerpts from French language dictionaries." The board further found that an American dictionary was more relevant evidence of the primary meaning of "REPECHAGE" to "an appreciable segment of *American* purchasers familiar with the French language" (italics in original).

At oral argument before the board, the appellant contended that the word "is a rare word in French which would not be likely to have any significant impact regarding purchaser confusion in the United States." The board found that "the word is defined in leading American dictionaries," which was sufficient to rebut the appellant's argument.

The board found, as a matter of fact, that a primary meaning in an American dictionary is adequate evidence of meaning to an appreciable segment of American purchasers.

On appeal to the Federal Circuit, Judge Nies, a trademark expert in private practice before her appointment to the bench, wrote that the court agreed with the finding that the goods of the parties were "closely related cosmetic products which would be likely to come from a single source." But the Federal Circuit stated that "the examiner had relied on the following French-English dictionary definition" meaning "Rescuing." Whether the examining attorney had relied upon that definition is not available from the published opinions of the board and the Federal Circuit.

The board opinion undoubtedly did *not* rely upon French-English dictionaries, and insisted that the American dictionary was the best evidence.

The appeal was from the PTO decision by the board, not from the examining attorney. The Federal Circuit was mistaken in representing that the PTO relied on a French-English dictionary instead of an American dictionary in finding the meaning to "an appreciable segment of *American* purchasers."

The Federal Circuit held that "the board erred in holding that the record established the equivalency of the expressions." The court relied upon three French-English dictionaries as evidence that "none of these definitions makes 'second chance' the exact translation of 'repecharge.'" The court conceded that the French language dictionaries that it relied on defined "epreuve de repecharge" means "second chance (offered to those who have failed in a test of any kind.)"

The Federal Circuit said that the dictionary meanings each connote "giving a second chance, but this is not the same as saying that 'repechage' is *equivalent* to 'second chance.'" Considering the "dissimilarity in appearance, sound and all the other factors, before reaching a conclusion on likelihood of confusion as to source," the Federal Circuit concluded that "'repecharge' is not the equivalent of 'second chance' in English, but rather has only a very specialized meaning, in sports parlance, of a trial heat. . . . [likelihood of confusion] has not been shown between SCOND CHANCE and REPECHAGE."

The PTO weighed the evidence. It gave greater weight to an American dictionary for assessing the primary meaning to American purchasers. It concluded that the evidence supported a finding of likelihood of confusion. The board never found as fact that the terms were "exact translations" of each other.

The Federal Circuit did not recite the facts found by the board. It did not show that the findings were "clearly erroneous." The board decision was reversed because the reviewing court construed the facts differently from the trier of fact. No deference was paid by the reviewing court to the facts found below.

Instead, it weighed the evidence submitted by appellant and found it more compelling than the evidence relied upon by the board.

That is not how appellate courts must review decisions of lower tribunals. Weighing evidence is a task for the finder of facts, not the appellate court. Error was found by the Federal Circuit simply because it found other evidence more convincing than the evidence relied upon by the finder of fact.

The "clear error" must be shown in the facts found by the trier of fact. It may not be shown by evidence rejected by the finder of fact as less likely to be true. Even if the appellate court would have reached a different conclusion had it been the finder of facts, it must defer to the findings by the tribunal that receives and weighs the evidence.

An inferior court cannot substitute its view of the facts for that of the trier of fact, but Congress did not create the Federal Circuit as the final authority in patent and trademark cases. Rather, it created a federal court of law, inferior to the Supreme Court, that must follow the federal rules, not its own rules.

### Verdegaal Brothers, Inc. v. Union Oil Company of California, 814 F. 2d 628 (Fed. Cir. 1987)

This case was one of the cases I tried shortly after the Federal Circuit was created. The Verdegaal brothers were two farmers in the Central Valley of California, perhaps the richest farmland in the country. They were not educated, and they learned farming by doing. One of the features of land in the western United States is that the soil is calcareous, derived from calcium carbonate and low in acidity, as compared to soils in the eastern part of the country.

The brothers were not the first to learn that dressing the roots of plants with sulfuric acid lowered the pH of the soil, improved water penetrability, and made the soil more fertile. While still farming, the brothers established a side business of buying tanker trucks, filling them with diluted sulfuric acid, and dressing plants grown by other farmers. The business was successful, but capital intensive in the need for trucks, drivers, and materials.

They came up with the idea of both fertilizing the soil with nitrogen-based fertilizer and sulfuric acid-based soil conditioner. The known fertilizer with the highest percentage of nitrogen was urea. Urea, a fairly simple compound, is not expensive, compared to concentrated sulfuric acid. The combination of urea and sulfuric acid would greatly increase the fertilizer's value to farmers by because it allowed for both soil improvement and plant nutrients at the same time.

The idea was sound, but implementation was difficult. As every high school chemistry student has learned, mixing water and concentrated sulfuric acid can be explosive if not done in the right order. Neither Verdegaal brother had taken high school chemistry, but they both learned of the heat of reaction the hard way.

Union Oil of California (now part of Chevron) refined oil and sold urea, a by-product, to the public through a subsidiary called Union Chemicals. Verdegaal Brothers solved the heat of reaction problem by having a heat sink capable of absorbing the heat from the hydration of concentrated sulfuric acid.

The relationship with Union Oil began cooperatively. Verdegaal Brothers bought urea from Union Chemicals, combined it with concentrated sulfuric acid, and sold the product to Brea Agricultural Services, another Union Oil subsidiary. Brea was much larger than Verdegaal and had more tank trucks, people, chemists, and lawyers than Verdegaal did. The product was successful and generated a lot of money for both Union and Verdegaal.

Union Oil employees were involved in the sale and distribution of the product, and they learned how it was made. Verdegaal Brothers did not have trade secrets contracts with the Union Oil employees who were helping Verdegaal Brothers launch the new product on a large scale. Still, Union Oil respected the ownership rights of the Verdegaal product, at least initially.

Later, the relationship between the Verdegaals and Union Oil soured. I had been retained to obtain a patent for making the Verdegaal product. Union Oil then stopped buying the patented product from the Verdegaals and stopped communicating altogether with the brothers. The brothers learned that Union Oil had set up its own plant to make the product and stopped developing the Verdegaal market in favor of developing its own market for the identical product.

When Brea stopped selling the Verdegaal product, called "US 28," and sold the same urea-sulfuric acid product under its own name, Verdegaal Brothers lost a great deal of business. There was no question that Union Oil had learned how to make US 28 from Verdegaal Brothers and was selling the same product to the same customers.

We sued Union Oil in a district court in California. After skirmishes regarding pleadings that went to the Federal Circuit a first time, the case went to trial before a jury in Fresno, California. Union Oil alleged that the key concept in the patent claims of absorbing the heat of hydration of concentrated sulfuric acid by providing a heat sink was anticipated by a patent grated to Stoller. U.S. patent 4,315,783 was for making a different kind of fertilizer from the Verdegaal fertilizer, but it involved heat of hydration.

Stoller filed a first patent application for a process that did not include a heat sink. However, a continuation-in-part application filed by Stoller did disclose the concept of a heat sink. The second Stoller application was filed *after* the Verdegaal invention was made, and therefore was not "prior art" to the Verdegaal application. This narrow point of patent law should have determined the outcome of the trial.

I had retained Don Chisum, author of the treatise *Chisum on Patents*, as an expert in patent law for the trial. The trial judge, newly appointed to the district court, made it clear that the jury would be instructed on the law by the judge, and not by a paid expert on patent law.

In preparing the case for trial, Chisum brought to my attention the CCPA case of *In re Wertheim*, 646 F. 2d 527 (CCPA 1981). He stated that the Union Oil argument regarding the Stoller patent was mistaken. The controlling statute is 35 U.S.C. §102(e), which at the time of the 1952 act read:

"A person shall be entitled to a patent unless—

(e) the invention was described in a patent granted on an application for patent by another filed in the United States before the invention thereof by the applicant for patent..."

The *Wertheim* opinion was written by Judge Rich. He wrote that Section 102(e) is "a codification of the rule of *Alexander Milburn v. Davis-Bournonville Co.*"

Rich wrote that in *Alexander Milburn*, 270 U.S. 390 (1926) the Supreme Court "held that material disclosed but not claimed in a United States patent may be used as a reference to anticipate a later invention as of the date the reference application was filed, rather than the date the patent finally issued." Sometimes there is a lag of years between the filing date of a patent application and the date the patent is granted.

In *Milburn*, the lag between the two dates was fifteen months. During that period, the Patent Office had granted a patent on an application filed before the patent application that became the patent in suit. The earlier patent "gave a complete and adequate description of the thing patented [later] but . . . did not claim it."

The issue in *Milburn* was whether the earlier patent was prior art as of its grant date or as of its filing date. The Supreme Court held that "the delays of the Patent Office ought not to cut down the effect of what has been done." The earlier patent had described the invention and became public knowledge before the later disclosure of the same invention. The fact that there is a lag between filing and grant does not determine the priority of disclosure. "Letters Patent" means a document disclosing an invention for public benefit. The filing date is all important, not the grant date. The priority of the first disclosure controls.

Judge Rich in *Wertheim* cited the writing of Federico, his drafting teammate, that showed that 35 U.S.C. §102(e) was a codification of the *Milburn* case.

*Wertheim* did not apply the *Milburn* rule because there is an exception to that rule in which the patent said to anticipate is a continuation-in-part (CIP) of a parent patent application that does *not* contain the anticipating disclosure. In *Wertheim*, the anticipating disclosure contained in the granted patent was *not* contained in the original patent application. That was precisely the situation with the Stoller patent, where the description of the "heat sink" concept was not in the original disclosure, but was added in a continuation-in-part application that included the heat sink concept.

Although the invention was disclosed in the CIP application, it was not in the parent application, so the heat sink concept was not a prior disclosure. Professor Chisum was prepared to explain this development of the law to show that the filing date of the first Stoller patent application could not be relied upon because it did not disclose the concept of a heel or heat sink. The example describing the use of a heel in the Stoller patent was not in the parent application. In the words of *Wertheim*, "[w]ithout the presence of a patentable invention, no patent could issue 'but for' the delays of the PTO."

I did not disclose Professor Chisum's analysis in opposing the Union Oil motion to bar his testimony because the analysis tells what the law is. Judge Coyle had made it abundantly clear that only he could instruct the jury on what the law is.

Instead I argued that Professor Chisum had "specialized knowledge [that] will assist the trier of fact to understand the evidence or to determine a fact in issue" under Evidence Rule 702. Judge Coyle, who had ruled against me on the pleading issue earlier, was adamant that Chisum could not instruct the jury on what the law is.

I had to figure out how could I get Professor Chisum to testify that Stoller was not prior art? How could I draft a jury instruction succinct enough to guide the jury through the 1926 *Alexander Milburn* case and the 1981 *Wertheim* case without Professor Chisum's guidance?

Judge Coyle had sliced off two thirds of the counts in my complaint. The patent infringement count was all that was left. If I asked Chisum a single question about *Milburn* or *Wertheim*, I would have my head handed to me. Having the trial judge scold counsel before the jury is often fatal to his party's case. I was determined not to anger Judge Coyle.

My strategy was to gingerly ask Chisum a single question about the Stoller patent. Was it prior art? If I received a negative answer from Chisum, I would not ask the obvious follow up question "Why?" If opposing counsel asked him to explain his answer, the author of the foremost patent law treatise would be more than capable of a clear and cogent answer. I doubted that opposing counsel would ask any follow-up questions because he knew the first rule of cross-examination: do not ask a question if you do not know the answer to the question.

There remained the issue of a jury instruction. Because I had not shared Professor Chisum's full analysis with opposing counsel, I was able to make some innocuous revisions to the instruction drafted by Union Oil's counsel. The result was this agreed-upon jury instruction:

Stoller filed two patent applications—an original application on October 30th, 1978, and a second on February 7th, 1980. Under the patent laws, the claims of the 343 [Verdegaal] patent "patent application was filed," followed by the existing "so it was clear." are invalid if you find that the original application (Exhibit BL) anticipates the process claimed in the 343 patent."

All that I needed to do was to prove that the original Stoller application did not contain the example using a heat sink as that example appeared only in the later issued Stoller patent. The Stoller patent shows on its face that it was granted a month after the Verdegaal patent, so it was clear that the issued Stoller patent was not prior to Verdegaal.

I asked Professor Chisum the usual questions about his education and qualifications. My opponent wisely did not challenge Chisum's expertise. It is often a mistake to attack an expert's qualifications because the jury is usually impressed by the expert's education and qualifications.

I asked about the process of filing a patent application, examination of patent applications, and the granting a patent. I asked about CIP applications and the fact that Stoller had an original and a continuation-in-part application. My single question about prior art was: "And, do you know whether the Stoller patent is prior art to the application of the Verdegaal patent?" There was no objection. Chisum answered "I don't know that it is, no."

It was a negative answer, so I asked no follow-up questions that might have elicited an objection and an admonition. I would have preferred an answer like "I know that it is not prior art," but I settled for the more passive negative answer. Experts seldom are more forceful than they have to be. The best answer would have been: "It is not prior art because it was filed a month after the Verdegaal application was filed."

Union Oil had no witness to contradict Chisum and state that the Stoller patent was indeed prior art. The technical expert that Union Oil called was not asked whether the heat sink concept was in the parent Stoller application, so the only testimony on the issue was Professor Chisum's cautious "no."

Although not forcefully stated, Professor Chisum provided substantial evidence that in his expert opinion the Stoller patent was not prior art.

The jury returned a verdict in favor of Verdegaal and against Union Oil. As with most jury verdicts, it is difficult to know what factors led to the result. Was it because of Professor Chisum's tentative "no"? Was it because a big oil company ripped off the Verdegaal service for farmers in a farming community? Was it because Bill Verdegaal (his brother had died of cancer before trial) talked the talk and walked the walk of the farmers on the jury? One never knows.

Union Oil filed a post-trial motion for judgment as a matter of law, accusing me of misconduct in misleading the jury and accusing Professor Chisum of not knowing what the law is on prior art. Judge Coyle saw the witnesses and heard the testimony and arguments as the jury did and found that there was a reasonable basis for the jury verdict based on the evidence. The Union Oil motion was denied.

Union Oil appealed to the Federal Circuit, making the same arguments against my client, my witnesses, and me. The second *Verdegaal* appeal (reported at 814 F. 2d 628), was heard by a panel of Chief Judge Markey, Judge Davis, and Judge Nies. Judge Nies wrote the opinion for a unanimous panel, none of whom had ever tried a patent case before a jury.

Instead of deferring to the jury findings, as the Seventh Amendment requires, and the district judge who denied the motion for a directed verdict, the omniscient patent court reversed and substituted its view of the record for that of the judge and jury that heard the evidence, made credibility assessments, and determined that the Verdegaal patent was valid and infringed.

Although Professor Chisum apparently convinced the jury that the Stoller was not prior art under Judge Coyle's instruction, Judge Nies wrote that Professor Chisum testified that "*he did not know*" (Nies' emphasis) the law on prior art. When new matter (matter not present in the parent application) is added in a continuation-in-part application that becomes a patent, the filing date of the parent application cannot be carried over to the continuation-in-part.

Judge Nies cited no authorities refuting Professor Chisum's negative answer to the question of whether Stoller was prior art. The Nies opinion quotes my brief stating that *Wertheim* and *Chisum on Patents* §3.07[3] support the conclusion that Stoller was not prior art, just as the jury must have concluded. Judge Nies states unequivocally that Chisum's testimony "leaves no doubt on this point" that Chisum did not know the law.

It is an insult to Professor Chisum to hold, contrary to his testimony and the jury's finding, that the filing date of the parent (which did not disclose a heat sink) determines the priority date. The finder of fact, the jury, concluded that Stoller was not prior art. The Federal Circuit disregarded the facts found by the jury and confirmed by the trial judge, and substituted its view that the foremost expert on U.S. patent law did not know patent law.

The Nies opinion was also insulting to me in stating that my brief was false: "Seldom have we encountered such a blatant distortion of the record." The Federal Circuit did not hear the testimony or receive the evidence, and it should not reverse the verdict by those who tried the facts. Judge Nies believed that the "no" in Professor Chisum's answer was wrong because "Union Oil asserted that . . . Stoller was prior art as of its filing date which was well before the filing date of Verdegaal's application."

Chisum gave his negative answer because the filing date of the application that became the Stoller patent came *after* the date of Verdegaal's application. Union Oil deceived the Federal Circuit by stating that the filing date of the *parent* Stoller application, which made no mention of a heat sink, was the filing date of the Stoller patent. It was not. The Federal Circuit got the facts wrong and unjustly reversed based on the assertions of Union Oil.

A party's "assertions" are not evidence and cannot be a basis for rejecting the *Wertheim* case or the Chisum treatise or Chisum's negative answer. They certainly do not prove that Judge Coyle erred.

Judge Nies also found it "incredible" that I "cavalierly ignored" the jury instruction that I had approved. On the contrary, the jury must have found that "the original [Stoller] application [did not] anticipate [] the process claimed in the 343 patent." The court of appeals had no basis for reversing that finding of fact.

"Anticipation" is a question of fact. Reversing the jury finding of fact, approved by the district judge, is reexamining a fact without support in the rules of the common law and prohibited by the Seventh Amendment.

Judge Nies held that I was "precluded from arguing that the Stoller patent should not be considered prior art." The Federal Circuit lacks jurisdiction to hold that a lawyer cannot make an argument, supported by expert testimony, when the jury and the district court accept that argument.

Finally, the Federal Circuit weighed the evidence and concluded that no jury could have reached the verdict that the jury here reached. The Federal Circuit may not substitute its view of the evidence for that of a jury's. Moreover, the district court must have found that substantial evidence supported the verdict, because he denied the motion for judgment as a matter of law.

The patent court does not understand deference and does not know how to judge facts in patent infringement cases. Again, the lack of experience in patent infringement cases brings out the worst in administrative judges that were suddenly given jurisdiction over judicial decisions in patent infringement cases.

The Supreme Court has explained how a court of appeals must view a jury verdict in *Lavender v. Kurn*, 327 U.S. 645, 653 (1946):

"Whenever facts are in dispute or the evidence is such that fair-minded men may draw different inferences, a measure of speculation and conjecture is required on the part of those whose duty it is to settle the dispute by choosing what seems to them to be the most reasonable inference. Only when there is a complete absence of probative facts to support the conclusion reached does a reversible error appear. But where, as here, there is an evidentiary basis for the jury's verdict, the jury is free to discard or disbelieve whatever facts are inconsistent with its conclusion. And the appellate court's function is exhausted when that evidentiary basis becomes apparent, it being immaterial that the court might draw a contrary inference or feel that another conclusion is more reasonable."

Infringement is a "question of fact, to be submitted to a jury" *Winans v. Denmead*, 15 How. 330, 338 (1854). Whether Professor Chisum knew what he was talking about as a qualified expert is for the jury, not the court of appeals, to evaluate. If the jury chose to believe that Stoller was not prior art based on the Chisum testimony and rejects Union Oil's argument, the appellate court may not disregard that conclusion simply because it "feel[s] that another conclusion is more reasonable."

It was an error for the Federal Circuit to hold that "no reasonable juror" could have reached the verdict it reached and the trial judge agreed with. The Federal Circuit chose to "draw a contrary inference."

*Phonometrics v. Hospitality Franchise Systems, Inc.*
No published or citable order (Fed. Cir. Aug. 14, 2003)

The last example of a mistaken specialist court, unable to properly judge district court rulings on appeal, is one of the many Phonometrics cases I was involved in. Phonometrics had a patent on a telephone system having multiple extensions, such as hotels. I sued dozens of hotel chains for infringing the patent. The issue on appeal of the consolidated cases was whether a court of appeals, specifically the Federal Circuit, has jurisdiction to correct a clerical mistake in a Notice of Appeal.

All of the defendants who were sued for patent infringement filed a joint motion for summary judgment after deposing the inventor. The deposition of the inventor revealed that he had no assets and would be unable to satisfy an award of attorney fees for having filed the complaints without just cause.

Most of the defendants filed a motion against me personally under the seldom used statute 28 U.S.C. §1927, which permits a claim against "any attorney . . . who so multiplies the proceedings in any case unreasonably and vexatiously may be required by the court to satisfy personally the excess costs, expenses, and attorney fees reasonably incurred because of such conduct."

Phonometrics owned a patent for an invention. Twenty-two companies used the invention of the presumptively valid patent, and I sued all of them. The Judicial Panel on Multidistrict Litigation granted my motion to consolidate all cases for pretrial proceedings. That is the exact opposite of "multipl[ying] the proceedings . . . unreasonably and vexatiously." My motion was for the purpose of *avoiding* multiplication of the proceedings.

The only judicial proceeding that followed the filing of the complaint was the deposition of the inventor, an act by the *defendants*, not by me. There was absolutely no act by me that could be characterized as multiplying the proceedings "unreasonably and vexatiously."

Nevertheless, the district judge granted the motion filed by most of the defendants for an award of attorney fees against me personally. However, the defendants had difficulty showing that the attorney fees they charged their clients were "incurred because of [my unreasonable and vexatious] conduct." The fees for attending the one deposition of the inventor taken by defendants could not fairly be incurred by my conduct. The district judge found the motions for attorney fees to be inadequately supported, and gave defendants ten days to show how the fees sought were incurred by reason of my conduct. Not all defendants were willing to pursue an award against me personally. Some of those who were willing dropped out when they were required to support the amount of the fees claimed as caused by my conduct. However, many defendants, smelling blood, rushed forward with dollar amounts claimed. Twelve of the original twenty-two defendants that were sued remained to the end.

The district judge divided the cases into two groups, with a separate order for each of the two groups, one February 5, 2003 and the other February 10, 2003.

I filed a single notice of appeal in the Federal Circuit on March 3, 2003, identifying all of the defendants that filed the revised claims for attorney fees. However, only the date of the first order, relating to most of the original moving parties, was in the notice of appeal. The date of the later order was omitted, a clerical error. Copies of the notice were sent to each one of the parties, whether the orders were dated February 5 or February 10. The notice of appeal was also filed in the district court; it specified all of the parties, and the court to which it was appealed, as required by Federal Rule of Appellate Procedure 3.

The Federal Circuit did not include those defendants whose orders were dated February 10 in the official caption of the appeal, limiting the appeal to the first order. Appellate Rule 3(c)(4) expressly states "An appeal must not be dismissed for informality of form or title of the notice of appeal, or for failure to name a party whose intent to appeal is otherwise clear from the notice."

I filed in the Federal Circuit a Motion to Correct Clerical Mistake under Federal Rule of Civil Procedure 60(a), which permits correction by an appellate court. The omniscient patent court disregarded Rule 60(a), which expressly states that an appellate court has the power to correct a mistake.

Judge Prost, on behalf of the Federal Circuit, held that the mistake of not having the correct date for a few of the named defendants in the notice of appeal "cannot be corrected and was not 'clerical.' The failure to correctly designate what is appealed is a jurisdictional defect."

All parties were named and served. The court has jurisdiction to decide an appeal properly noticed and served. Judge Prost wrote that the "court has jurisdiction to review only the February 5, 2003 awards," because the notice of appeal failed to state that some of the defendants were granted attorney fees five days later. The failure to have the correct date of the award for some appellees deprived the Federal Circuit of *jurisdiction*, the court said, over a patent infringement case that had a motion for summary judgment and an award of attorney fees against a non-party to the case.

I asked for a three-judge panel to review the decision of Judge Prost under Appellate Rule 27(c). Judge Prost, on behalf of a three-judge panel of the Federal Circuit, held that Judge Prost was correct in holding that the Federal Circuit lacked the power to correct the dates for the orders on the joint motion brought by all defendants. A request for *en banc* review by the Federal Circuit was denied. A petition for writ of certiorari in the Supreme Court was also denied.

Appellate Rule 3(a)(1) states "An appeal permitted by law as of right from a district court to a court of appeals may be taken." Phonometrics had a right to appeal the awards given on defendants' motion. The omniscient patent court was plain wrong in holding that it lacked *jurisdiction* over an appeal as of right of the decisions on the joint motion simply because of a clerical mistake related to a few defendants.

The reduced amount awarded by the district court to the defendants, to be paid by me for unreasonable and vexatious multiplying proceedings, totaled about a million dollars. Most of the successful defendants dropped out when the appeal to the Federal Circuit was filed. Spending more money for briefing and arguing the appeal was not a wise expenditure by defendants as my behavior was clearly not vexatious or unreasonable.

The Federal Circuit affirmed the awards under §1927. More defendants dropped out when the petition to the Supreme Court was filed. Only one of the original sixteen defendants persisted in pursuing a "pound of flesh" against opposing counsel. RHI Hotels, Inc. owners of the "Radisson" brand, filed the successful opposition to the motion to correct the clerical error. It was not included in the list of defendants in the Federal Circuit case because its award was dated February 10, and the court held it had no jurisdiction over the February 10 defendants. RHI filed suit against me personally in the Northern District of California and pursued it relentlessly for years. It obtained a six figure judgment against me, and filed liens against all of my real estate properties. So much for civility among members of the bar working their trade. The single award relentlessly pursued by one of the many defendants was ultimately paid.

These cases are illustrative of the patent courts' departure from the mainstream of judicial procedure and common sense. The Federal Circuit is not omniscient and must learn to abide by what Congress states in statutes, not by what witnesses allege in congressional hearings. The courts must follow Supreme Court precedents, and the Federal Rules approved by the Supreme

Court and amended with advisory committee notes. It must learn to distinguish between fact and law and to defer to fact-finders rather than decide facts *de novo* on appeal without deference.

The next to last review by the Supreme Court of a Federal Circuit decision regarding §101 patentable subject matter is *Mayo Labs v. Prometheus Labs.*, 132 S. Ct. 1289 (2012). Prometheus was the exclusive licensee of two patents for determining the appropriate dosage level of certain drugs prescribed for patients with autoimmune diseases. If the dosage is too low, the treatment will be ineffective. If the dosage is too high, the treatment may induce harmful side effects. The issue was whether the relationship between the concentration of drug metabolites in the blood to drug effectiveness is a law of nature. A law of nature is not patentable.

If the processes claimed in the patents have transformed an unpatentable law of nature into patentable applications of those laws, it may be patentable. The Supreme Court unanimously held that the subject matter was not patentable under §101 and reversed the Federal Circuit decision.

"Our conclusion rests upon an examination of the particular claims before us in light of the Court's precedents." All of the cited Court precedents are discussed in this book, whether the Federal Circuit was affirmed or not. An English case (*Neilson v. Harford*, Webster's Patent Cases 295, 371 (1841)) is the only case cited by the Court in *Mayo* that is not one of its own precedents.

It concluded that apart from the laws of nature, the steps recited in the claims were "well-understood, routine, conventional activity previously engaged in by researchers in the field," and not patentable subject matter. While such steps might not be novel under 35 U.S.C. §102, or nonobvious under §103, the Federal Circuit decision was grounded on §101, not the following sections.

Prometheus, the licensee of the patents, sold its tests protected by the patents to the industry, including Mayo. Mayo wanted slightly different concentrations than were in the Prometheus tests, and came up with a slightly different test of its own and stopped buying the Prometheus products. Prometheus believed that the difference was insufficient to avoid liability for patent infringement and sued Mayo. Mayo defended by asserting that the licensed patents did not cover patentable subject matter. The district court granted the Mayo motion for summary judgment on the ground that the patents claimed laws of nature.

The Federal Circuit disagreed, finding that the claims fell within the Federal Circuit's "machine or transformation test" in that either the patient's body or blood was "transformed." The Supreme Court did not expressly overrule the Federal Circuit's "own law" that it calls the "machine or transformation test" in reversing *Mayo*, but one should be wary about alleging that a human body or human blood is "transformed" by a process under that test.

The Supreme Court granted Mayo's first petition for certiorari and immediately remanded the case back to the Federal Circuit to consider the Court's decision in *Bilski*, which characterized the Federal Circuit's "machine or transformation" as <u>not</u> being a definitive test of patentable subject matter under §101, but only an important and useful clue. The Federal Circuit misinterpreted the Supreme Court language in *Bilski* as approving its "machine or transformation test," and led to the "clear and compelling conclusion" that transforming a body or blood did not "encompass laws of nature or preempt natural correlations." That conclusion of the Federal Circuit was soundly reversed by the Supreme Court in *Mayo*, and the "machine of transformation" test is unquestionably diminished, though it may still be a useful clue.

The unanimous Supreme Court decision in *Mayo* should not be interpreted as a defeat for the pro-patent forces by the anti-patent forces, as Judge Rich asserted in his *Johnston* dissent. *Benson* is cited repeatedly in *Mayo*, and the fact that *Mayo* was reversed and *Bilski* was affirmed does not influence their respective teachings.

The Federal Circuit indulges in wishful thinking when the last word of a Court opinion is "affirmed," and fears defeat by the anti-patent forces when the last word is "reversed." *Bilski* and *Mayo* are reconcilable, just as *Benson* and *Diehr* are reconcilable, despite Judge Rich's alarm expressed in his *Johnston* dissent.

Supreme Court decisions are seldom black or white. They must be read carefully for the consistencies with precedents, not for inconsistencies. The Court almost never slams the door shut. It always leaves room for nuance. *Mayo* certainly allows for development of the law under §101.

# Chapter 3

# SCORECARD

**M**y disillusion with the decisions of the patent courts followed my formative years as a law clerk at the CCPA, when I subscribed fully to the omniscience of the CCPA. In part, my concern that the decisions of the patent courts might be wrong was confirmed when patent court decisions were reviewed by the Supreme Court. The first review of a patent court decision by the Supreme Court was in 1966, when the CCPA decision in *Brenner v. Manson* was reversed by the Supreme Court. From then on, when patent court decisions were looked at by the Supreme Court on appeal, they were found to be wrong much of the time.

I have kept a scorecard showing how the patent courts have fared on appeal to the Supreme Court. The high court did not review a single decision of the CCPA from 1929, when it was created to review decisions of the Patent Office, until 1966, when the first case was reviewed by the Supreme Court.

From 1966 until 2012, the decisions of the patent courts have been reviewed by the Supreme Court in thirty-three cases. In only eleven cases have the decisions of patent courts been affirmed. All of the other twenty-two cases resulted in either vacating the patent court decision or reversing it.

Thus, two-thirds of the decisions of the patent courts have been overturned. In the text below, I have arranged all of the cases according to the issues addressed, rather than chronologically. The scorecard indicates Court review of a wide range of patent issues, but by no means all such issues.

For historical accuracy, the thirty-three cases are here listed numerically in chronological order in the first column. The case name is in the second column. The citation is shown in the third column. The outcome of each case is in the fourth column.

| No. | Case name | Citation | Outcome |
|---|---|---|---|
| 1. | *Brenner v. Manson* | 383 U.S. 519 (1966) | Reversed |
| 2. | *Gottschalk v. Benson* | 409 U.S. 63 (1972) | Reversed |
| 3. | *Dann v. Johnston* | 425 U.S. 219 (1976) | Reversed |
| 4. | *Parker v. Flook* | 37 U.S. 584 (1978) | Reversed |
| 5. | *Diamond v. Chakrabarty* | 447 U.S. 303 (1980) | Affirmed |
| 6. | *Diamond v. Diehr* | 450 U.S. 175 (1981) | Affirmed |

The remaining twenty-seven cases are appeals from decisions of the Federal Circuit:

| No. | Case name | Citation | Outcome |
|---|---|---|---|
| 7. | *Dennison Mfg., Co. v. Panduit Corp.* | 475 U.S. 809 (1986) | Vacated |
| 8. | *Christianson v. Colt Industries Op. Corp.* | 486 U.S. 800 (1988) | Vacated |
| 9. | *Eli Lilly & Co. v. Medtronic, Inc.* | 496 U.S. 661 (1990) | Affirmed |
| 10. | *Cardinal Chemical Co. v. Morton Int'l, Inc.* | 508 U.S. 83 (1993) | Vacated |
| 11. | *Asgrow Seed Co. v. Winterboer* | 513 U.S. 179 (1995) | Reversed |
| 12. | *Markman v. Westview Instruments, Inc.* | 517 U.S. 370 (1996) | Affirmed |
| 13. | *Warner-Jenkinson v. Hilton Davis Chem.* | 520 U.S. 17 (1997) | Reversed |
| 14. | *Pfaff v. Wells Electronics, Inc.* | 525 U.S. 55 (1998) | Affirmed |
| 15. | *Dickenson v. Zurko* | 527 U.S. 150 (1999) | Reversed |
| 16. | *Florida Prepaid v. College Savings Bank* | 527 U.S. 627 (1999) | Reversed |
| 17. | *Nelson v. Adams USA, Inc.* | 529 U.S. 460 (2000) | Reversed |

| | | | |
|---|---|---|---|
| 18. | *J. E. M. Ag. Supply. v. Pioneer Hi-Bred* | 534 U.S. 124 (2001) | Affirmed |
| 19. | *Festo Corp. v. Shoketsu Kinzoku Kogyo* | 535 U.S. 722 (2002) | Vacated |
| 20. | *Holmes Group, Inc. v. Vornado Air Circ.* | 535 U.S. 826 (2002) | Vacated |
| 21. | *Merck KGaA v. Integra Lifesciences, Ltd.* | 545 U.S. 193 (2005) | Vacated |
| 22. | *Unitherm Food Sys. v. Swift-Eckrich, Inc.* | 546 U.S. 394 (2006) | Reversed |
| 23. | *eBay, Inc. v. Merc Exchange, LLC* | 547 U.S. 388 (2006) | Vacated |
| 24. | *Medimmune Inc. v. Genentech, Inc.* | 549 U.S. 118 (2007) | Reversed |
| 25. | *KSR Int'l Co. v. Teleflex, Inc.* | 550 U.S. 398 (2007) | Reversed |
| 26. | *Microsoft Corp. v. AT&T Corp* | 550 U.S. 437 (2007) | Reversed |
| 27. | *Quanta Computer, Inc. v. LG Electronics* | 553 U.S. 617 (2008) | Reversed |
| 28. | *Bilski v. Kappos* | 561 U.S. (2010) | Affirmed |
| 29. | *Global-Tech Appliances, Inc. v. SEB, S.A.* | 563 U.S. (2011) | Affirmed |
| 30. | *Board of Trustees (Stanford) v. Roche* | 563 U.S. (2011) | Affirmed |
| 31. | *Microsoft Corp. v. i4i.* | 564 U.S. (2011) | Affirmed |
| 32. | *Mayo Medical v. Prometheus Labs., Inc.* | 565 U.S. (2012) | Reversed |
| 33. | *Kappos v. Hyatt* | 566 U. S. (2012) | Affirmed |

Although eleven of the thirty-thee Supreme Court decisions were affirmances, only two patent court decisions (*Microsoft*, No. 31 and *Kappos*, No. 33) were unanimously affirmed by the Supreme Court (although there were two opinions in each). *Chakrabarty*, the first case that was affirmed, was a 5-4 decision with Justices Brennan, White, Marshall and Powell dissenting.

In *Diehr*, the second affirmance, the majority remanded for further proceedings. At 450 U.S. 191, the majority said "In this case, it may later be determined that the respondents process is not deserving of patent protection because it fails to satisfy the statutory conditions of novelty under §102 or nonobviousness under §103," and the Court left open the possibility of rejection on remand. *Diehr* was also a 5-4 decision, with Stevens, Brennan, Marshall and Blackmun dissenting. Stevens and Blackmun had been in the majority in *Chakrabarty*. Had either of those two voted to reverse in *Chakrabarty*, that case would also have been a reversal of the patent court.

The third affirmance, *Eli Lilly*, was also remanded for further proceedings in the patent court. It was therefore not a complete win for the patent court. Also, Justices Kennedy and White dissented, so the affirmance was not unanimous.

The fourth affirmance, *Markman*, held that the trial judge, not the jury, was in the best position to construe written documents like patents. The Court said that the trial judge may receive evidence, such as expert testimony, in construing claim terms. The Court did not affirm the patent court's "own law" that it has the power to decide *de novo* any issue involving claim terms without deference to the decision of the trial judge who receives the evidence in the first instance.

The fifth affirmance, *Pfaff*, struck down the Federal Circuit test of "totality of the circumstances" in "on sale bar" cases. Such a "rule that makes the timeliness of an application depend of the date when the invention is 'substantially complete' undermines the interest in certainty. Moreover, such a rule finds no support in the text of the statute" (525 U.S. at 65-66).

The sixth instance, *J.E.M. Ag. Supply*, had two dissenters, Breyer and Stevens, who interpreted the apparently inconsistent patent statutes differently from the majority. Though the Court affirmed, it had different reasoning than that of the Federal Circuit.

The seventh affirmance of Supreme Court review of patent court decisions, *Bilski*, struck down the Federal Circuit ban on all business method patents. It also struck down its sole test of §101 that a process must be "tied to a machine or transformation of an article." Although the case was affirmed, the Federal Circuit suffered a sharp rebuke in *Bilski*.

The eighth affirmance, *Global-Tech*, involved a U.S. patent on a deep fryer. Global-Tech had a subsidiary make a copy of the deep fryer and sell it at a lower price than the patented SEB fryer. SEB sued for induced infringement under patent law. Global-Tech claimed that it did not know the product infringed. The district court, the Federal Circuit, and the Supreme Court held that "willful blindness" does not avoid liability for induced infringement. Justice Kennedy dissented.

The ninth affirmance, *Stanford v. Roche*, involved federally funded inventions. Stanford owned patents funded in part by National Institutes of Health. The inventor later assigned rights to Cetus that became Roche. The Federal Circuit and the Supreme Court held that federal funding did not vest title in Stanford, and the inventor could assign the patent rights to Roche. Breyer and Ginsburg dissented.

The tenth affirmance, *Microsoft v. i4i*, involved the presumption of validity, which means that one challenging the validity of a patent must prove it by clear and convincing evidence. The record did not reveal such evidence. Justices Breyer, Scalia, Alito and Thomas concurred in the judgment with opinions.

The last affirmance, *Kappos v. Hyatt* in 2012, involved the alternative appellate route through the District of Columbia instead of directly to the Federal Circuit. The Administrative Procedure Act governs, and permits new evidence in a Section 145 case. The judgment was unanimous, but Sotomayor and Breyer filed a concurring opinion.

At the end of the 2011 Court Term, the scorecard had 11 affirmances and 22 losses for the patent court. That is, two thirds of the patent court decisions were disapproved by the Supreme Court. *Mayo*, the last of the Supreme Court reversals, was unanimous, a first. *Microsoft* and *Hyatt*, two of the last cases discussed in this book, were affirmances with no dissents, but each had concurring opinions. 5-4 splits in the Court seem to be diminishing in recent patent cases.

CHAPTER 4

# CONSTITUTIONAL PROVISIONS

The United States is the only country in the world in which the founding Constitution includes a provision for patent law. Article I, Section 8, clause 8 empowers Congress "To promote the progress of science and the useful arts, by securing for limited times to authors and inventors the exclusive right to their respective writings and discoveries."

This is a "balanced" clause that gave rise to two different systems, copyright and patent. Copyright is connected to "science," "authors" and "writings." Patent is connected to "useful arts," "inventors," and "discoveries." Both systems had been established in England well before 1789, when the Constitution was signed. .

In the century and a half after the establishment of the Jamestown and Plymouth colonies in the early Nineteenth Century, England went through the Reformation and Restoration, which left the nation somewhat different from what existed when the colonies were established. Of importance to the present discussion, the first copyright law, the Statute of Anne, came into force in 1710.

Before that time, members of the Stationers' Guild were the masters of copyrights and authors were mere servants. Publishing was fully controlled by publishers, and authors had no ownership rights to their works. The Statute of Anne broke the rule of masters over servants and secured to authors the exclusive right to their writings for limited times. There can be no doubt that the copyright half of the clause in the Constitution is directly traceable to the Statute of Anne.

The word "science" in the clause seems odd to twenty-first-century ears, which are used to associating copyrights with Mickey Mouse or other entertainment figures. It can be explained by Diderot's Systematic Dictionary of the Sciences, Arts, and Crafts, published between 1751and 1772. It had a profound impact upon the founding fathers, who were trying to establish a new country with a new copyright system.

The patent half of the Constitutional clause is also traceable to the breaking of the grip of masters over the fruits of the labor of servants in England. Letters patents originally were patents of importation in England. The monarch granted monopolies to individuals bringing new technology into the kingdom from elsewhere. The monopolies came to be a way to raise money for the monarch by charging patent-holders, who did not create the protected inventions, instead of taxing the patented products. The patent-holders were masters by reason of the grant of the monopoly, and servants surrendered the fruits of their labor to the masters.

The Statute of Monopolies (1624) abolished patent monopolies granted by the monarch and instead granted inventors the exclusive right to their discoveries for a limited time. That is, the servant did not have to give up his invention to his master because the right was secured to inventors.

The English repudiation of master-servant law in copyrights and patents was not brought to the English colonies in America. The reason that masters controlled servants in the colonies is that masters paid for servants to come to America and therefore had the right to the fruits of the servants' labors, whether the labor was to provide crops from plantations, manufactured goods, or inventions.

There were three primary categories of English emigrants to America: indentured servants, convicts and redemptioners. Abbott Emerson Smith, in *Colonists in Bondage: White Servitude and Convict Labor in America 1607-1776* (1947, 16-17) explained,

"The usual form of indenture was simple. It was a legal contract, by which the servant bound himself well and faithfully to serve the master in such employments as the master might assign, for a given length of time, and usually in a specified plantation. In return, the master undertook to transport the servant to the colony, furnish him with adequate food, drink, clothing, and shelter during his service, and perhaps give him a specified reward when his term was ended."

Smith indicated that in the seventeenth century, "indentured servitude was practically the only method by which a poor person could get to the colonies" (20). In the eighteenth century, German and Swiss "redemptioners" came to the colonies, trading servitude to a master in the colony who paid the ship captain for the portion of the cost of transportation that the redemptioner was unable to pay in advance. The primary difference between indentured servants and redemptioners was that indentured servants came alone to escape debts and problems in the Old world, while whole families came as redemptioners seeking a new life in the New World.

The life of indentured servants was much worse than those of the redemptioners. "A servant could not marry without the consent of his master. He could not vote. He could hold property, but he must not engage in trade, and there were severe penalties in all colonies for freemen who traded with servants, presumably because the latter would steal or embezzle their masters goods and dispose of them to unscrupulous freemen. The servant's special abilities, if any, were exercised for the benefit of the master... the colonists felt that masters had property in the labor of their servants" (Smith 1947, 233-34).

*Webster's Third New Int'l Dictionary* (1968) defines "redemptioner" as "an emigrant from Europe to America in the 18th and 19th centuries obtaining passage by becoming an indentured servant at the disposal of the ship-owner or master for a specified length of time."

The Smith book continued at page 336 that by the American Revolution, "it is safe to say that not less than half, nor more than two-thirds, of all white immigrants to the colonies were indentured servants or redemptioners or convicts."

The majority of American citizens at the time of founding the new nation had either experienced this kind of oppression or were descendants of indentured servants or redemptioners who were treated as though their labor was the property of their masters. It follows that there were strong beliefs that citizens' creations in the form of writings and discoveries should belong to the creators and not to their masters.

Given this background, it is clear that the patent and copyright clause was intended to be a repudiation of master-servant law that had shaped, or at least impacted, half or more of the population of the country. From this perspective, the founding fathers seriously intended that "securing for limited times to authors and inventors" meant securing rights to the creators, not their masters.

Unfortunately, this historical analysis has been lost on Congress, the patent profession, and patent court judges. Congress has never repudiated master-servant law in determining whether patents should be secured to the creators or to their masters.

The conventional wisdom in the United States is that in order "To promote the progress of science and the useful arts," as the Constitution says, one must encourage investment. Certainly patent court judges believe that.

Judge Rich, in his papers and in the opinions he authored, was convinced that patent law existed to stimulate the economy. One example is *In re Bergy*, 596 F. 2d 952, 981 (CCPA 1979) (which was affirmed as *Diamond v. Chakrabarty*, 447 U.S. 303 (1980)):

"At the inception of the American patent system in 1790, the growth of the new country demanded a *stimulus* for the manufacture of all kinds of goods for the benefit of the *public* [not inventors]. This field of manufacturing was generally regarded as "*industry*;" its domain was the production of any and all things made by the hand of man [not man's inventions]. At the time, existing industry was not sufficient to supply even agriculture with its needs, which found itself with limitless land, a shortage of manpower, and a crying need for tools and machines [not just *new and useful* tools and machines]."

Eventually, after Luther Burbank had dramatized the *economic plight* of the amateur horticulturalists, the clamor in Congress for legislative help to plant breeders culminated in the Plant Patent Act of 1930. The statute was, in toto, an effort to apply the patent system where it had not been applied before in order to *fuel the fire* under plant breeding and to protect experimenters in that as yet nonindustrial field. There were legal niceties to overcome the product of nature rejection that had already been applied by the Patent Office to pre-Burbank plants [products of nature were not precluded by §101 in his view, it was just a "legal nicety"] but the intent of Congress in passing the act is beyond doubt" (*id.*, italics added).

Rich continued:

"The purpose of the [Plant Patent] bill is to afford agriculture, so far as is practicable, the same opportunity to participate in the *benefits of the patent system* as has been given industry, and thus assist in placing agriculture on a basis of *economic equality* with industry."

"Congress had in mind the *stimulation* of a *field of endeavor* that, unlike chemistry, for example, had not as yet flowered into an industry. Hence, to 'assist in placing agriculture on a basis of *economic equality* with industry,' it extended the *benefits* of the patent system to these as yet non-industrial plant breeders like Luther Burbank.

"It's a little hard for plant men to understand why Article 1, §8 of the Constitution should not have been earlier construed to include the *promotion of the art of plant breeding*" (983; italics added). The Constitution does not promote the useful arts; it promotes *progress* by securing rights to inventors as "a reward, an inducement, to bring forth new knowledge" (*Graham v. John Deere Co.*, 383 U.S. 1, 9 (1966), italics added).

Judge Newman advanced a similar view of stimulating investment. In "*Introduction: the Federal Circuit: Judicial Stability or Judicial Activism 42 Am. U. L. Rev. 683 (1993)*," (1993, 684-85), she wrote that the "Domestic Policy Review of Industrial Innovation" expressed "forceful concern of the nation's technological leadership [read masters] about the effect on industrial innovation of judge-made patent law." The report expressed the view that the new court, unencumbered by inconsistent regional courts of appeal's "judge-made patent law" would provide a "stable body of law upon which reliance could be placed" by investors. (The masters had no interest in securing rights to inventors (servants) as a "reward, and inducement to bring forth new knowledge." Rather, progress is promoted by rewarding innovators that invest. Follow the money, in the original scheme).

More recently, Chief Judge Michel wrote in "*Leading Citizens*" (2010, 266) Fed. Cir. B. J. 265, 266 (2010) that the "founders well understood the causal connection between patents and national prosperity, economic growth and technological progress." This adheres to the British rewards to masters, not to inventors. On the contrary, the founders carefully expressed in the Constitution the clear intent of "WE, the People of the United States, in order to form a more perfect Union [than the disparate states arising from colonies], establish Justice [to replace the oppression of indentured servitude and Master-Servant law], insure domestic Tranquility [without labor of servants being property of the masters], provide for the common Defense [against Indians and colonizers from England, France and Spain], promote the general Welfare [another jab at master-servant law], and secure the Blessings of Liberty to ourselves and our Posterity [to marry without seeking a master's consent and have posterity], do ordain and establish this CONSTITUTION for the United States of America."

Where in this founding document is there anything about "the *benefits of the patent system* as has been given industry, and thus assist in placing agriculture on a basis of *economic equality* with industry" (Rich); a "stable body of law upon which reliance could be placed" by investors (Newman); or "causal connection between patents and national prosperity [and] economic growth" (Michel)?

Why would Franklin and Jefferson, both inventors, putting together a Union of former colonies, oppressed for well over a century, long before the industrial revolution, give a damn about the investors that gave us involuntary servitude, redemption and slavery? I disagree with Judges Rich, Newman, and Michel.

Chief Justice Marshall had it right in *Grant v. Raymond* (31 U.S. 218, 242 (1832)): a patent is "the reward stipulated for the advantages derived by the public for the exertions of the individual, and is intended as a stimulus to those exertions."

There is nothing there about economic equality between industry and agriculture, or a stable body of law investors can rely on, or national prosperity and economic growth (the twenty-first century view).

Even before *Grant v. Raymond*, the Court held in *Pennock v. Dialogue*, (2 Pet. (27 U.S.) 1 (1829)) that an object of our patent laws was "to stimulate the efforts of genius" in support of the primary purpose of promoting the progress of science and the useful arts.

The Court quoted this language from *Pennock* in *Motion Picture Patents Co. v. Universal Film Co.* (243 U.S. 502, 511(1917)), adding "the primary purpose of our patent laws is not the creation of private fortunes for the owners of patents."

The language of *Motion Picture Patents* has, in turn, been quoted recently in *Quanta Computer, Inc. v. LG Electronics, Inc.* (553 U.S. 617, 626 (2008)) and in Justice Stevens concurrence in *Bilski v. Kappos*, 561 U.S. __ , 1390 S. Ct. 3218 (2010).

The musings of Judges Rich, Newman and Michel are not persuasive in view of (1) the plain language of the patent clause of the Constitution; (2) the low regard for master-servant law in the eyes of the survivors of the oppression of indentured servitude and redemptionism; and (3) these six Supreme Court decisions that teach that the purpose of patent laws is to reward inventors, not to reward the masters or investors that brought the much-hated practices of slavery and indentured servitude to the colonies.

Congress believes that patent law is intended to encourage investment as do patent court judges. Congress, in over 220 years, has never by statute secured to authors and inventors the exclusive rights to their writings and discoveries, as authorized by the Constitution.

Instead, Congress has given us 35 U.S.C. §261, which provides that patents "shall have the attributes of personal property," like a car or a squeegee for cleaning the windshield of a car. It also provides that "applicants for patent, patents, or any interest therein, shall be assignable in law by an instrument in writing. The applicant, patentee, or his assigns or legal representatives may in like manner grant and convey an exclusive right under his application for patent, or patents, to the whole or any specified part of the United States." (If the male patent applicant or patentee resides in a community property state, like California, and uses any community property funds to file an application or obtain a patent, it will be community property and cannot be assigned without the consent of the community. If the applicant or patentee has the good fortune to have his rights assigned to his employer as a condition of employment, even before he makes an invention, neither party in the community owns anything. It is nearly universal in the United States to have future inventions assigned to the employer before the employee even begins work.)

The common practice of assigning inventions to the master before an invention even exists and can be owned by the master, flies in the face of the goal of the Preamble to the Constitution to "establish justice."

Nearly every industrialized country in the world provides a right to compensation if the employer takes the employee's invention. Once a value of the invention can be established, the employee and the employer can negotiate fair compensation for the assignment of the employee's invention to the employer. If needed, government agents can determine fair compensation while considering all relevant factors.

In the United States, master-servant law prevails, and any compensation is a gift resulting from the employer's largesse. No law passed by Congress secures to inventors the exclusive rights to their discoveries, nor is that right secured as part of the "blessings of liberty" referred to in the preamble to the Constitution. The contract of adhesion to assign future inventions as a condition of employment is enforceable in the United States. In the U.K., the source of much of this country's law, such contracts are unenforceable.

The taking of the invention by the employer is simple. In 35 U.S.C. §261, we read that any "person authorized to administer oaths within the United States" can sign and seal an acknowledgement of the assignment. If the assignment is not notarized upon employment, the contract may not be enforced in court.

The inventor must sign an oath before a similarly qualified person that he believes himself to be the "original and first inventor" under §115. If the inventor refuses to sign the oath, the employer may file the application without the inventor's oath if the employed inventor "has assigned in writing or has agreed to assign the invention or [the employer] shows sufficient proprietary interest in the matter justifying such action" under §118. It is no defense to show that the inventor did not own the invention and had no rights secured to him under the Constitution when he or she was compelled to assign the invention to his or her employer.

The Plant Variety Protection Act diminishes the creator of a plant variety even more than the patent law does; 57 U.S.C. §2401(a)(2) defines "breeder" as the creator of the variety: "The term 'breeder' means the person who directs the final breeding creating a variety or who discovers and develops a variety. If the actions are conducted by an agent on behalf of a principal, the principal, rather than the agent, shall be considered the breeder." The creator has no say in the matter.

Translating this into master-servant law, upon which it is based, if the servant creates a plant variety, the master "shall be considered the breeder," and no rights shall be secured to the servant. This patent-like statute codifies the master-servant relationship, while the patent statute merely acquiesces in the contracts of adhesion that employers require employees to sign.

The Supreme Court has also acquiesced in the application of master-servant law in patent cases. In *Board of Trustees v. Roche*, 563 U.S. __, 131 S. Ct. 2188 (May 31, 2011), Dr. Mark Holodniy was employed by Stanford University, and signed the usual assignment to Stanford of any future invention he might make during his employment. Stanford sent him to Cetus to learn Polymerase Chain Reaction ("PCR"), a procedure owned by Cetus by reason of an assignment by Dr. Mullin, inventor of PCR, to Cetus. (No rights are secured to creators).

The assignment to Cetus was before Mullin was awarded the Nobel Prize for the PCR procedure. Apparently, Dr. Mullin had his prize secured to him, but his master appropriated the patent for PCR because Congress has never secured to the inventor the exclusive right to the discovery.

Dr. Holodniy was never employed by Cetus. At all times he was employed by his master Stanford. However, before allowing Dr. Holodniy access to the Cetus premises, he was required to make a present assignment ("I do hereby assign") to Cetus of any future invention made while on the Cetus premises. He did not tell Stanford that he had assigned future inventions to Cetus. The assignment to master Cetus was a breach of his prior assignment to master Stanford.

While learning PCR at Cetus, Dr. Holodniy coauthored one or more articles with Cetus employees on how PCR would be used in the Stanford research. It turns out that those papers were a public disclosure of the invention embodied in the Stanford patents taken out after Holodniy had returned to Stanford.

Stanford applied for patents listing Holodniy and his Stanford superiors as inventors. Holodniy had a duty, under 37 C.F.R. §1.56(b)(1), to disclose to the PTO the publications he authored with Cetus employees before filing for patents with Stanford colleagues. He, Stanford, and the preparers of the patent applications had a duty to disclose information "material to patentability." No one met that obligation.

When the patents were granted, Stanford sued Roche, the large Swiss company that had acquired Cetus. Cetus proved that the Stanford patents were invalid because the patented invention was described in the papers authored by Holodniy and Cetus colleagues more than a year before filing for patent, a violation of 35 U.S.C. §102(b).

The Stanford patents were invalid and therefore worthless, and neither Roche nor Cetus had any patents on the invention patented by Stanford. But the issue before the Supreme Court was which assignment of this worthless invention was first? Was it the assignment of future inventions by Holodniy to Stanford, signed before he visited Cetus? Or was it the later assignment that had the words "do hereby assign" to Cetus?

The dispute had no monetary consequences because Stanford's patents are invalid, and Cetus and Roche have no patents on the Stanford procedure using PCR. In litigation in the Northern District of California, in the Federal Circuit, and in the Supreme Court, there were dozens of lawyers representing the two warring elephants fighting for bragging rights, as money damages could not have been awarded. There were dozens of other lawyers representing "friends" of the Supreme Court (including me) that sought to persuade the Court to adopt one view or another.

Jurisdiction over the case of *Stanford v. Roche* was based on 28 U.S.C. §1338(a) for patent infringement. There is no jurisdictional amount in controversy under that section, as there is for diversity cases. When the district court ruled that the Stanford patents were invalid, the amount in controversy between the litigants would not have met the minimum of $75,000 under 28 U.S.C. §1332(a) if the case had been based upon diversity of citizenship.

It seems that the huge amount of billable hours and attorney's fees were expended trying to determine how many angels could dance on the head of a pin, because there could be no damages for infringing invalid patents. Cetus and Roche filed no patent applications on whatever was contained in the papers published by Holodniy and Cetus employees. Those papers invalidated Stanford's patents, but gave no right to exclude to Cetus or Roche.

There were no economic consequences resulting from the issue of whether Holodniy assigned the invention first to Cetus or to Stanford, yet that was the issue that was presented to the Supreme Court. The Federal Circuit decided, and the Supreme Court affirmed, that the later contract-with the words I "do hereby assign" to Cetus-trumps the earlier agreement with Stanford. In both cases, when Holodniy signed the agreements he owned no invention and had nothing whatsoever to sell to anyone. In both cases, Holodniy had no bargaining power and could extract no compensation for the assignment of an invention he had not yet invented and thus did not own. Each was a contract of adhesion– not a bargain at all.

Neither assignment contract was an arm's length transaction between a willing seller and a willing buyer who mutually agreed to a price for the product sold. Instead, we had two masters fighting over an invention the servant never owned because he signed two contracts of adhesion before the invention ever existed.

This farce would never have been performed if Congress had done the job the Constitution assigned to it in 1789: "To promote the progress of…useful arts, by securing for limited times to…inventors the exclusive right to their…discoveries."

If Holodniy secured his patent right for a limited time, he could have negotiated the sale of it once it came into existence, and there would not have been a master-servant relationship with either Stanford or Cetus.

To "hereby assign" something that has never been conceived or reduced to practice, much less patented or even applied for, defies common sense. How could anyone put a value on anything so nebulous? Master-servant law makes the servant's labor the property of the master even when the labor has not been performed. Master-servant law should be banished to the seventeenth Century and before from whence it came. Cutting edge technology in the twenty-first century has no use for such archaic thinking.

At the very least, we should embrace the late eighteenth century thinking of the Constitution and secure to inventors the exclusive right to their discoveries so that a value can be determined by an agreement between buyer and seller. Placing no monetary value upon the indentured servant's labor because it is the property of the Master is not just and should not be the law. We should reward inventors by the patent grant. A tussle between two assignees, Cetus and Roche, over Holodniy's invention is possible in seventeenth century master-servant law, but it is not appropriate in 2012. In this case, the invention was worthless because the two warring masters failed to properly patent the invention.

The patent clause of the Constitution has been distorted by Congress, which has harmed society as a whole by allowing patents to be tools of masters to create private fortunes rather than reward inventors.

The rights that may be secured to authors and inventors by Congress are the only rights specified in the original Constitution. Congress proposed the first ten amendments to the Constitution on September 25, 1789.

The First Amendment barred Congress from establishing religion "or prohibiting the free exercise thereof." Rights to "freedom of speech, [and] of the press," to peaceably "assemble, and to petition the Government for a redress of grievances" were also created.

The Second Amendment said that in order to support a well-regulated militia, "the right of the people to keep and bear arms" was secured. Congress was given the power, in Article 1, Section 8, clause 15 "To provide for calling forth the militia to execute the laws of the union, suppress insurrections and repel invasions." Clause 16 allowed Congress "To provide for organizing, arming, and disciplining the militia." Read in light of Clauses 15 and 16, it seems that the Second Amendment secured to militiamen the right to bear arms pursuant to Congress's power in "arming...the militia." The Supreme Court has, however, held that the amendment allowed all of the nation's people of the nation to be armed, not just the militia.

The Fifth Amendment provides protections for persons charged with crimes, protects all persons against being "deprived of life, liberty, or property, without due process of law." The Fourteenth Amendment echoes this phrase in the language "nor shall any State deprive any person of life, liberty, or property, without due process of law."

Due process of law was the topic of the Federal Circuit case reviewed by the Supreme Court in

*Nelson v. Adams USA, Inc.,* 529 U.S.460 (2000).

In all of the years since 1929, when the first specialist patent court was created, no judge was ever asked to decide whether a person was deprived of property "without due process of law."

Specialist judges had never reviewed any case other than from an administrative agency before 1982, when patent cases appealed from district courts fell within the jurisdiction of the new patent court. Depriving a person of "life, liberty, or property" is a subject district courts encounter often, but not the specialist patent court. The PTO lacks the power to deprive anyone of "life, liberty, or property."

Petitioner Donald Nelson was the president and sole shareholder of the company that owned the patent at issue. His company sued Adams USA for infringing the patent. Adams proved that Nelson had known of prior art that anticipated the Nelson invention, but Nelson had not disclosed the prior art to the PTO. The district court held that the conduct of the patentee was inequitable and deceitful. Not only was the patent infringement charge dismissed, but the district court also granted Adams USA about $180,000 for attorney fees and costs against the patentee company.

After the award was entered against Nelson's company, Adams USA moved to amend the judgment to name Nelson personally liable as a defendant. The district court granted the motion and "allowed the pleading amendment and altered the judgment at a single stroke" (529 U.S, 464).

The Federal Circuit affirmed because Nelson was not prejudiced by the post-judgment joinder of Nelson. Nelson had failed to show that "anything different or additional would have been done" if Nelson had been a party at the outset of the litigation. "[A]dding Nelson as a party and simultaneously amending the judgment to obligate him individually met due process requirements," according to the Federal Circuit (465).

Judge Newman dissented from the Federal Circuit decision, calling it "unprecedented," which of course it was, since no patent court had ever decided a due process issue. She wrote: "The law, at its most fundamental, does not render judgment simply because a person might have been found liable had he been charged" (471).

The Supreme Court unanimously reversed. "Judicial predictions about the outcome of hypothesized litigation cannot substitute for the actual opportunity to defend that due process affords every party against whom a claim is stated" (*id.*).

Federal Rules of Civil Procedure 15(a) and 12 (a)(1) reveal the process. The party charged has the opportunity to respond to a pleading, whether it's an original pleading or an amended pleading. The pleading must be filed and served, and "the party so added is given 10 days after service of the amended pleading to plead a response" (468). Nelson was never afforded a proper opportunity to respond to the claim against him.

The case illustrates that specialist judges trained in PTO proceedings rather than district court litigation governed by the Federal Rules of Civil Procedure and the Federal Rules of Evidence are less familiar with "due process" than judges in regional courts of appeal that deal primarily with reviewing district court decisions in civil and criminal matters.

The Eleventh Amendment was the issue in

*Florida Prepaid v. College Savings Bank*, 527 U.S. 627 (1999).

The Amendment reads "The Judicial power of the United States shall not be construed to extend to any suit in law or equity, commenced or prosecuted against one of the United States by citizens of another State, or by Citizens or Subjects of a Foreign State."

At issue was whether a patent owner could sue a state agency, like a state university, for patent infringement. The state agency is protected by the Eleventh Amendment as part of the sovereign state, and is immune from suit. Congress attempted to strip the state's sovereign immunity in patent infringement cases.

In *Chew v. California*, 893 F. 2d 331 (Fed. Cir. 1989), the patent court held that the state of California was immune from suit for patent infringement because the patent laws contained no statement of intent to abrogate a state's sovereign immunity. State universities were using patented inventions in research without compensating the owners of the patents that otherwise would be infringed.

Congress viewed this as a "loophole," allowing state universities to compete commercially by using patented inventions without paying royalties for using valuable inventions. Congress sought to close the loophole by passing the Patent and Plant Variety Protection Remedy Clarification Act, 35 U.S.C. §§271(h), 296(a), which states that states "shall not be immune, under the Eleventh Amendment of the Constitution," from patent infringement.

The intent to abrogate state's sovereign immunity was clear from the act passed by Congress, but it was not clear that Congress had the power to do so under the "due process clause" of both the Fifth and the Fourteenth amendments to the Constitution.

College Savings sold certificates of deposit to finance future college expenses. It patented its method. Florida Prepaid, a board of the state of Florida, administered tuition prepayment contracts for Florida residents. College Savings sued Florida Prepaid for willful infringement of its patent and inducing infringement. The United States intervened to defend the constitutionality of the statute.

The district court found in favor of College Savings and denied the motion to dismiss. The Federal Circuit affirmed, finding that Florida Prepaid was not immune from suit for infringing on the patent.

The Supreme Court reversed in a 5-4 decision favoring the state's right to immunity.

The majority conceded that the intent of Congress to abrogate was clear, but denied that Congress had the power to compel states to surrender their sovereign immunity under the enforcement clause of section 5 of the Fourteenth Amendment: "The Congress shall have the power to enforce, by appropriate legislation, the provisions of this article."

The majority, in an opinion by Chief Justice Rehnquist, held that "under *City of Boerne v. Flores*, 521 U.S. 507 (1997), the statute cannot be sustained as legislation enacted to enforce the guarantees of the Fourteenth Amendment Due Process Clause, and accordingly reverse the decision of the Court of Appeals" (the decision is at 893 F.2d 331 Fed. Cir. 1989) ( 630).

"Congress does not enforce a constitutional right by changing what the right is. It has been given the power 'to enforce,' not the power to determine what constitutes a constitutional violation" (638, quoting *Boerne* at 519). For section 5 of the Fourteenth Amendment to apply, Congress "must identify conduct transgressing the Fourteenth Amendment's substantive provisions, and must tailor its legislative scheme to remedying or preventing such conduct" (639). "The underlying conduct at issue here is state infringement of patents and the use of sovereign immunity to deny patent owners compensation for the invasion of their patent rights" (640).

Rehnquist continued: "The legislative record thus suggests that the Patent Remedy Act does not respond to a history of 'widespread and persisting deprivation of constitutional rights' of the sort Congress has faced in enacting proper prophylactic §5 legislation...the provisions of the Patent Remedy Act are 'so out of proportion to a supposed remedial or preventive object that [they] cannot be understood as responsive to, or designed to prevent, unconstitutional behavior" (646, quoting *Boerne* at 532).

Justice Stevens dissented for himself and Justices Souter, Ginsberg and Breyer, noting "continuing dissent from the Court's aggressive sovereign immunity jurisprudence; today, this Court once again demonstrates itself to be the champion of States' rights. In this case, it seeks to guarantee rights the States themselves did not express any particular desire in possessing; during Congress' hearings on the Patent Remedy Act, although invited to do so, the States chose not to testify in opposition to the abrogation of their immunity.

In between the Fifth Amendment discussed in *Nelson* and in *Florida Prepaid* and the Eleventh Amendment in *Florida Prepaid* is the Seventh Amendment, dealing with the right to jury trial–"and no fact tried by a jury shall be otherwise reexamined in any court of the United States, than according to the rules of the common law."

The Seventh Amendment was raised in *Markman v. Westview Instruments, Inc.*, 517 U.S. 370 (1996). The case turned on a Rule 50 motion, and it is primarily discussed in the Rule 50 chapter. It is mentioned here briefly because of the insights it provides as to the Seventh Amendment. It also is referred to here because this amendment mandates deference by courts of appeal to facts found by a jury, and the patent courts have failed to honor this deference that is required by the Constitution.

Markman had a patent for keeping track of inventory in a dry cleaning establishment. Markman sued Westview Instruments for infringement. The case went to trial, and the jury found that Westview had infringed the patent. The district court granted

Westview's motion for judgment as a matter of law (Rule 50) because it interpreted the term "inventory" in the patent claims as not covering what Westview kept track of in dry cleaning plants.

In one system, "inventory" referred to items of clothing passing from place to place in the plant. In the other system, pieces of paper with bar codes represented the inventory being tracked. The issue was whether the jury or the district judge was the proper entity to interpret claim terms.

Justice Souter, for a unanimous Court, explained that it is for the trial court, not the jury, to construe terms used in written documents like patents. The right to jury trial is preserved, but "a mongrel practice (like construing a term of art following receipt of evidence)" is best left to the court to decide. At pages 387-88, both Walker, *Patent Laws* and Robinson, *Law of Patents* were quoted in support of the proposition that expert testimony may be received by the trial judge to assist in interpreting terms of art for instructing the jury.

The opinion is thorough, well supported by authority, and persuasive. What is troubling is the message that the Federal Circuit took from the Supreme Court opinion. The Court concluded: "Accordingly, we hold that the interpretation of the word 'inventory' in this case is an issue for the judge, not the jury, and affirm the decision of the Court of Appeals for the Federal Circuit" (517 U.S. 370 (1996), 391).

The message was clear that a "mongrel" question, part fact and part law, is best determined by the trial judge, and the court of appeals should defer to the trial judge's decision unless it is clearly erroneous.

What the patent court believed was that its *opinion* was affirmed, not its decision to abide by the district court's decision to grant the Rule 50 motion. Its "own law," before and after its decision in *Markman*, was that claim terms are "devoid of fact content," and present solely a question of law. Further, under its "own law," the patent court need not defer to the district court decision on any claim term, and is free to substitute its view of the meaning of the claim term for that of the trial court. The patent court overrules trial court claim constructions most of the time that they are presented to it on appeal.

The Supreme Court has never approved of this peculiar Federal Circuit view, which is contrary to the Federal Rules of Civil Procedure, what *Markman* actually decided, and common sense. Rule 52 requires an appellate court to defer to the district court's decision on mixed questions of law and fact unless clearly erroneous. The Supreme Court deferred to the district court's interpretation, which the Federal Circuit also adopted as its own. Claims define the invention, as a matter of fact. It is nonsense to state that claim terms are devoid of fact content.

Perhaps someday the Court will sort this out, but it has declined to do so in many petitions for certiorari presented in the past. For its part, the Federal Circuit abides by its "own law," even though it is contrary to *Markman* and other Court precedents, the federal rules, and common sense.

# CHAPTER 5

# PATENTABLE SUBJECT MATTER UNDER 35 U.S.C. §101

A surprising number of the Supreme Court reviews of patent court decisions have dealt with the issue of whether the invention embodied in the patent or patent application is patentable subject matter. This issue was the focus of five of the first six patent decisions of the CCPA that were reviewed by the Supreme Court, which were discussed at length in chapter 2 in relation to the omniscience of the patent courts. More recent decisions of the Federal Circuit have also discussed whether the subject matter at issue fell within §101. The tendency has been for the Supreme Court to leave the door open to new areas of technology to be included in patentable subject matter. But the pace of Court review of patent court decisions is accelerating. Six years elapsed between the first and second reviews of CCPA decisions. In the 2010 Term, the Court decided three entirely different appeals from the Federal Circuit.

What is important about the first six CCPA decisions that were reviewed by the Supreme Court is not that four were reversed and only two were affirmed, as indicated in chapter 2. Rather, the important message is that the Supreme Court follows the *teachings* of its precedents, not just the final holding of whether the decision below is affirmed or reversed. What the law *is*, requires reasoning (*judgment*, as Judge Hand put it), not whether the lower tribunal was right or wrong.

Even where the Court holds that the subject matter is patentable under Section 101, it often cites with approval its precedents holding that other subject matter is not patentable. For example, *Chakrabarty* held that genetically modified Pseudomonas were patentable and affirmed the CCPA decision. It also cited its opinion *American Fruit Growers, Inc. v. Brogdex Co.*, 283 U.S. 1, 12 (1931), which taught that soaking oranges in borax to make the rind resistant to blue mold decay was not a "manufacture." The treated oranges were still oranges. "There is no change in the name, appearance, or general character of the fruit. It remains a fresh orange fit only for the same beneficial uses as theretofore."

Chakrabarty, on the other hand, created an organism that was not natural and had a new use for treating oil spills, an important teaching. Whether *Chakrabarty* was affirmed or reversed was irrelevant to that teaching.

*Chakrabarty* also cited with approval *Benson* and *Flook* that held the subject matter was not patentable under section 101. It also cited with approval *Funk Brothers Seed Co. v. Kalo Innoculant Co.*, 333 U.S. 127, 131 (1948), which held that selecting and isolating several species of root-mold bacteria was not patentable subject matter. The various species would inhibit some legumes from fixing nitrogen from air but would not inhibit other legumes. For example, a species that works well with clover may not work well with alfalfa. By selling a mixture of six different species, all legumes could be protected from the root-mold bacteria.

*Kalo Innoculant* sued *Funk Brothers* for infringing its patent on the use of the mixture. The district court held the patent invalid, but the Seventh Circuit reversed, finding the patent valid. The Supreme Court reversed, finding that the discovery in the patent was the mixture's qualities of non-inhibition. The Court concluded that the discovery was no more than the discovery of some of the handiwork of nature and hence is not patentable.

"Each of the species of root-module bacteria contained in the package infects the same group of leguminous pants which it has always infected. No species acquires a different use. The combination of species produces no new bacteria, no change in the six species of bacteria, and no enlargement of the range of their utility. Each species has the same effect it always had. The bacteria perform in their natural way. Their use in combination does not improve in any way their natural functioning. They serve the ends nature originally provided and act quite independently of any effort of the patentee (131)."

It is worth noting that *Funk Bros.* was authored by Justice Douglas, the Supreme Court justice most hated by Judge Rich, the pro-patent advocate who claimed to have authored the pro-patent 1952 patent act. If one compares *Funk Bros.* with *Bergy*, the difference between anti-patent and pro-patent becomes clear.

Yet another Supreme Court precedent cited with approval by the Supreme Court in *Chakrabarty* is *Hartranft v. Weigmann*, 121 U.S. 609, 615 (1887). Ornamental shells that had been cleaned with acid to remove their outer layer, then ground with an emery wheel to remove a second layer in order "to expose the brilliant inner layer," were not articles of manufacture. "They were still shells. They had not been manufactured into a new and different article, having a distinctive name, character or use from that of a shell."

The Court in *Chakrabarty* approved, and did *not* overrule, the 1887 *Hartranft* case, the 1931 *Brogdex* case, the 1948 *Funk Bros.* case, the 1972 *Benson* case, and the 1978 *Flook* case. All of these cases held that the products involved were the work of nature, not works of man. This shows that the Supreme Court honors its precedents for what they teach, and not for the holding of each case.

Patent courts, in contrast, focus on the holding and ignore precedents that say, for example, that products of nature are not patentable. *Chakrabarty* held that genetically modified Pseudomonas were patentable, but the Court continued to follow its precedents, including these five, that did *not* hold that the products were man-made.

This lesson is also taught by the last CCPA decision on patentable subject matter that was reviewed by the Supreme Court.

*Diamond v. Diehr*, 450 U.S. 175 (1981)

The Supreme Court in *Diehr* cited *Flook*, *Benson*, and *Funk Bros.* with approval, among others, even though the holdings in those cases conflicted with the holding in *Diehr*.

The lesson should not be forgotten for future decisions of the patent courts that will be reviewed by the Supreme Court. As this was being written, the Federal Circuit has reversed the district court decision in *Association for Molecular Pathology v. Myriad Genetics, Inc.* "653 F. 3d 1329, Fed. Cir. 2001." The Supreme Court granted the petition for certiorari, but it immediately remanded the case to the Federal Circuit to consider the Court's March 12, 2012, decision in *Mayo v. Prometheus*, and did not decide the matter on its merits. (The Court followed the same procedure in *Bergy* a generation ago, that ultimately led to *Chakrabarty*).

The *Mayo* decision did not involve a genetically modified organism, as *Myriad* did, but the Federal Circuit would be wise to carefully assess the unanimous decision in *Mayo* on remand. The product of nature cases going back more than a century, which have not been overruled by the Supreme Court or by Act of Congress, will be central to the ultimate outcome in *Myriad*.

The lead opinion in the Federal Circuit's *Myriad* case, said that an isolated genetic sequence is patentable subject matter because it is chemically different from the organism from which it is taken. That argument is misplaced because a genetic sequence taken from an organism is not a separate chemical compound. Rather, it is a part of an organism that has its own natural features. The step pf separating a piece of the organism that expresses a particular trait in the organism, such as hair color, does not create something other than the trait by the isolation step. If one wants to introduce the genetic sequence that expresses a hair color trait into another organism, a person having ordinary skill in the art can readily accomplish that routine step.

The organism having the new trait in its genetic makeup may sexually reproduce the trait in its offspring for generations to follow. A chemical compound does not enter the genome of an organism the way a genetic trait does. The chemical compound does not sexually reproduce itself in future generations of an organism.

This fundamental difference in the natural process makes the fact of a chemical bond in a genetic sequence irrelevant to the expression of a trait.

A chemical reaction, such as hydrolysis of an organic compound to make an ester and an alcohol is a one-off reaction. Though the chemical compound may be called "organic," it does not sexually reproduce itself for generations of esters and alcohols.

The difference between sexual reproduction and asexual reproduction is the difference between Court reviews in chapter 2 and those in chapter 5. *Mayo v. Prometheus* is primarily discussed in chapter 2, where *Diehr* and *Flook* are discussed. The syllabus in *Mayo* states that *Diehr* and *Flook* are the "cases most directly on point" (3). Sexual v. asexual reproduction is not the dispositive issue.

Sexually reproduced seeds were the subject in

*Asgrow Seed Co. v. Denny Winterboer*, 513 U.S. 179 (1995).

Plants were not protectable by patents until 1930, when Congress passed the Plant Patent Act, which allowed the Patent Office to grant patents for "asexually" reproduced plants. Sexually reproduced plants (that is, from seeds that have genes from one parent as well as genes from another parent, just like humans and animals) were deemed to be products of nature.

In 1970, Congress created a patent-like certificate for sexually reproduced seeds. The bar against patenting products of nature was preserved. Instead of patents, Congress created a certificate, not a patent, granted by the Plant Variety Protection Office in the Department of Agriculture, not the Patent Office in the Department of Commerce.

The protection by the certificate was to bar the sale of seed purchased from the seed company holding the certificate, or progeny from those seeds, for reproductive purposes. Seed could be used to grow food, or as feed for animals, but no more than half of a farmer's crop of seeds could be sold to another farmer as seed.

In other words, the Department of Agriculture could grant a seed company a monopoly for a new variety for sexually reproducing plants and seeds derived from the protected seeds. The buyer of the seeds from the seed company could propagate the protected seeds and sell the products for food for consumers or as animal feed. The buyer could also sell up to half of the next generation of seed to another farmer for nonreproductive purposes.

The goal was clear: the owner of the certificate could fix prices for the protected seeds for eighteen years. Buyers of the seeds could not resell them at lower prices than the seed company.

Winterboer bought seeds from Asgrow, planted them, harvested the plants, and then sold the next generation of seeds to other farmers at half the price charged by Asgrow. When sued by Asgrow, Winterboer defended itself on the basis of 7 U.S.C. §2543: "A bona fide sale for other than reproductive purposes . . . of seed produced on a farm either from seed obtained by authority of the owner for seeding purposes or from seed produced by descent on such farm from seed obtained by authority of the owner for seeding purposes shall not constitute an infringement."

Denny Winterboer claimed the sales to other farmers were bona fide, and he had no control over what his buyers did with the seeds. Winterboer grew crops for sale as food and livestock feed, which is exempt from infringement. He also sold "brown bags" of seeds to other farmers, but did not market them as Asgrow seeds and did not direct buyers to plant them as crop seeds or for any other purpose.

Asgrow had a farmer visit Winterboer to purchase seed. Winterboer assured the farmer that the seeds were "just like" Asgrow seeds and sold them to the farmer. The farmer returned some seeds to Asgrow, which had them tested and found they were indeed the protected variety.

The district court granted Asgrow's motion for summary judgment. The Federal Circuit reversed, finding that Winterboer could sell half his crop as seeds, so long as the other half was sold as food or feed, and Winterboer was not "marketing" Asgrow seeds in his sales of the brown bags to neighbors.

The Supreme Court reversed. It noted that the PVPA statute was intended to "yield for the public the benefits of new varieties." The statute "extends patent-like protection to novel varieties of sexually reproduced plants (that is, varieties grown from seed) which parallels the protection afforded asexually reproduced plant varieties (that is, varieties reproduced by propagation or grafting) under Chapter 15 of the Patent Act" (513 U.S. 179 (1995), 180).

Justice Scalia, for the majority, noted "that it is quite impossible to make complete sense of the provision [§2543] at issue here (185-86). The Court made no mention of the reason why "patent-like" protection under the agriculture code was enacted instead of patent protection under the patent law. It was not congressional whimsy; it was because Congress acknowledged that sexually reproduced organisms were not patentable because they were products of nature. The Supreme Court precedents held that products of nature, such as sexually reproduced seeds, were not patentable, and Congress respected the Court precedents. That is why the PVPA was not part of patent law.

Patents are infringed where a person "makes, uses, offers to sell, or sells any patented invention (§271(a)). PVPA, on the other hand, raised the issue in *Asgrow* of "whether the Winterboers' planting and harvesting were conducted 'as a step in marketing' Asgrow's protected seed varieties for growing purposes." The majority in *Asgrow* found that the sale of the brown bags of seeds by Winterboer were steps in marketing a novel seed to provide "for the public the benefits of new varieties" of seed as the PVPA intended. Winterboer was liable for reselling seeds at a price below Asgrow's price.

Justice Stevens dissented, claiming that brown bag sales were intended to be outside the scope of the PVPA and were not what stores did when marketing a product. The dissent also pointed out that restraints on alienation of property are viewed with disfavor. An owner may dispose of even patented products without any obligation to the owner of the patent. Once a protected product is sold, the rights of the owner of the protection end.

Neither the majority nor the minority in *Asgrow* addressed the question of whether sexually reproduced offspring of any organism may be "owned" by anyone having a right to exclude. If products of nature cannot be patented, according to Supreme Court precedent, then products of nature should not be "owned" by another patent-like right to exclude.

A step in marketing by an alleged infringer should not be the same as an "exclusive right" secured to an inventor under the Constitution. That founding document cannot justify granting a company marketing a product of nature the right to exclude others from marketing the product of nature.

The *Asgrow* case did not involve 35 U.S.C. §101, but *J.E.M. AG Supply, Inc. v. Pioneer Hi-Bred International, Inc.*, 534 U.S. 124 (2004) did. Pioneer owned plant patents on asexually reproduced inbred and hybrid corn. Farm Advantage (the d.b.a. of J.E.M. Ag Supply) bought Pioneer seeds and sold them for growing crops without Pioneer's permission, a violation of the license on the package. Pioneer sued for infringement.

Farm Advantage did not contend that seeds are products of nature because they are the offspring of a male plant component and a female plant component, even though one or both parents may have been asexually reproduced plants. Seeds, by definition, are sexually reproduced.

Instead, the defendant counterclaimed, seeking a declaration that the patents were invalid because the 1930 Plant Patent Act and the 1970 Plant Variety Protection Act were the exclusive statutory provisions for protecting plants. Farm Advantage argued that seed patents could not be utility patents under §101 because plant protection under that section was repealed by implication when the Plant Patent Act of 1930 was enacted and when the act was codified in §161 in 1952.

The facts regarding sexual reproduction were not stressed and the Supreme Court precedents holding that products of nature are not patentable subject matter were not the focus of Farm Advantage's presentation. Instead, it stressed the legal argument of repeal by implication.

Pioneer defended the counterclaim by pointing out that its patents were utility patents, not plant patents or PVPA certificates. Living things were patentable under §101, according to *Chakrabarty*. The district court granted summary judgment in favor of Pioneer on the basis of the *Chakrabarty* decision. The Federal Circuit affirmed, as did the Supreme Court.

Like *Asgrow*, *Pioneer* involved seeds, which are the sexually reproduced offspring of a male parent and a female parent. However, the seeds in *Pioneer* were said to be patentable subject matter under an expansive reading of 35 U.S.C. §101 in *Chakrabarty*.

The product-of- nature doctrine should have been the defense of Farm Advantage, not a counterclaim for patent invalidity. Under that doctrine, plants were not patentable subject matter because they were products of nature. Supreme Court precedents had long held that products of nature could not be patented. In 1930, Congress added to the patent statute a provision for patenting asexually reproduced plants because such plants were made by man, not by nature. Plant breeders had succeeded in grafting a plant part exhibiting a trait not found in a host plant into a host plant so that the host plant exhibited that trait.

Because man had grafted one plant part into another plant, the modified plant was said to be "man-made," and not a product of nature. However, the "man-made" plant was capable of sexually reproducing offspring the same way that Adam and Eve did: a male component mated with a female component to naturally produce an offspring having genes of both parents. The offspring was certainly a product of nature–a sexually reproduced plant having genetic sequences derived from both parents.

The offspring does not have 50 percent of the male parent's genes and 50 percent of the female parent's genes. Nature does not work that way. Rather, some traits are more dominant than others. For example, in humans, the offspring of a blue-eyed parent and a brown-eyed parent is more likely to have brown eyes than blue eyes. This has nothing to do with gender, hair color, or any other genetic trait of either parent.

If a rose breeder grafts a plant part exhibiting a red rose into a plant exhibiting a white rose, the offspring may have a red rose, a white rose, a pink rose or some other color, depending upon the dominant expression. The rose offspring is still a rose, and it is still a sexually reproducible rose; that is, its offspring is a product of nature. The sexual reproduction is not a patentable "process." The offspring is not a "machine," a "manufacture," or a "composition of matter" under 35 U.S.C. §101.

Without explaining how a genetically modified corn fit into the four Section 101 categories of process, machine, manufacture or composition of matter, the district court, the Federal Circuit and the Supreme Court held that Pioneer's patents were drawn to patentable subject matter under 35 U.S.C. §101.

To my mind, the *Pioneer* case is a monumental failure of counsel for the alleged infringer to pursue a strong, straight-forward fact presentation. Instead, a dubious legal proposition of "repeal by implication" was pursued and rejected.

The four categories of inventions–process (originally "art"), machine, manufacture, and composition of matter–have been in the patent statute since 1793. Sea shells were held to be products of nature and not "manufactures" in *Hartranft*, 121 U.S. 609 (1887). Oranges were held to be products of nature, not manufactures in *Brogdex*, 283 U.S. 1, (1931). A microorganism was not a manufacture or a composition of matter in *Funk Bros.* 333 U.S. 127 (1948).

Sexually reproduced plants were excluded from patent protection in 1930 when Congress limited plant patents to "asexually reproduce[d]" plants. The Senate report accompanying the 1930 act expressly said the patent right "does not include the right to propagate by seeds" (534 U.S. 135, note 7). Congress repeated this limitation in 35 U.S.C. §161 in 1952.

Notwithstanding the clearly expressed intent of Congress not to include seeds as a category of patentable subject matter, the majority in *Pioneer* held that §161 fails to state that "plant patents are the exclusive means of granting intellectual property protection to plants" (133).

There are two problems with this assertion. First, since 1790, Congress has never granted "intellectual property protection" to *anything*. The term does not exist in any act of Congress, so how could the Court construe §161 as allowing an alternative "intellectual property protection" to patents? (Elsewhere, I contend that "intellectual property" is a misnomer; a sophism intended to portray persons not qualified to be called "patent lawyer" as being grander than they might otherwise be if properly described.)

Second, Congress said the patent right "does not include the right to propagate by seed," which surely bars propagation of Pioneer's seeds. 35 U.S.C. §101 has no category for patents on seeds, which are not processes, machines, manufactures or compositions of matter. The Supreme Court may not enact an expansion of §101 to include seeds.

Justice Thomas, for the majority, quoted the Senate report on the Plant Patent Act–the "patent right...does not include the right to propagate by seeds" (135), but then concluded that utility patents may be granted for seeds (143-44), because (1) "there is no 'positive repugnancy' between the issuance of utility patents for plants and [plant patents] for plants; (2) §101 and §161 can mutually coexist; and (3) "the 'plain meaning' of §101, as interpreted by this Court in *Chakrabarty*, clearly includes plants within its subject matter."

These three reasons are fallacious. If the patent right "does not include the right to propagate by seeds," then §101 cannot be interpreted to include propagation by seeds. Section 101 and 161 can only coexist if §101 does not include seeds. The "plain meaning of §101" is that sexually reproduced plants are *not* a category of patentable subject matter. §101 was rewritten by legerdemain to include sexually reproduced seeds in the majority opinion.

Justice Breyer, joined by Justice Stevens, dissented in *Pioneer*, noting "*Chakrabarty* said nothing about the specific issue" of whether plants from sexually reproduced seeds are a "manufacture" or a "composition of matter." Whether a bacterium that is "not nature's handiwork" (*Chakrabarty*, 310) is patentable subject matter does not determine that sexually reproduced seeds are not nature's handiwork. No clearer example of nature's handiwork can be found than in sexually reproduced seeds.

Judge Rich, co-author of the 1952 act with Pat Federico, knew that plant patents were limited to asexually reproduced plants to get around the product-of-nature prohibition. He wrote in *In re Bergy* 596 F. 2d 952, 981 (CCPA 1979), which was affirmed by the Supreme Court in *Chakrabarty*, that "the product of nature rejection...by the Patent Office" in plant patent applications was only a "legal nicety" to be overcome.

It was the primary purpose of the Plant Patent Act, he wrote (982), to afford agriculture "the same opportunity to participate in the benefits of the patent system as has been given industry." A "secondary purpose...was to avoid the judicial interpretation which had been placed on then-existing patent laws that *products of nature* are not statutory subject matter." This suggests that the legal nicety that existed in 1930 had been overcome or "avoided" somehow by 1979, and products of nature were no longer non-statutory.

The implication from Judge Rich's writing in *Bergy* is that the 1952 act had eliminated the hated legal nicety of holding that products of nature were unpatentable subject matter. The new law that replaced this legal nicety was "the identical statement in the House and Senate reports accompanying the 1952 reenactment... that 'a machine, or a manufacture' may include *anything under the sun that is made by man*" (987, emphasis Rich's). How that statement, probably written by Rich or Federico, could be deemed a congressional rejection of the definition of machine or manufacture as including any man-made thing under the sun in the 1952 act. Senate and House reports are not acts of Congress.

I believe the words "anything under the sun that is made by man" went from Rich-drafted congressional reports to Rich-authored *Bergy* opinion of the Federal Circuit to the Supreme Court decisions in *Chakrabarty* (which affirmed *Bergy*) and *Pioneer* (which repeatedly cites *Chakrabarty*).

In *Bergy* (984), Judge Rich added another reason why the product-of-nature bar had gone away. The Plant Patent Act of 1930 applied "only to plants propagated by asexual reproduction." By the time of the 1970 Plant Variety Protection Act, Congressman Wiley Mayne of Iowa said "Those plants which reproduce asexually such as by budding and grafting have been covered by the patent law since 1930. There is no justification for not extending the same coverage to sexually reproduced plants." Such an extension was not specifically included in the 1970 Act. If Congress wanted to reject the product-of-nature ban for sexually reproduced plants in PVPA, more evidence must be presented that a comment from a Congressman from a farm state.

The Supreme Court precedents that hold products of nature inappropriate for patenting were not overruled by the PVPA, which is not a *patent* law. This seed problem v. asexual reproduction problem needs clarification.

The last Supreme Court case involving the issue of patentable subject matter in this book is *Bilski v. Kappos*, 130 Sup. Ct 3218

(2010). All of the Supreme Court reviews of decisions of the CCPA were on petition from the Patent Office seeking reversal of the patent court decision. *Bilski* was, for the first time in a patent-eligible subject matter case, before the Court on petition from a patent applicant instead of a petition by the PTO agency. *Bilski* was brought by inventors dissatisfied with the decision of the Office rejecting the application. There had been a debate in the patent courts regarding whether business methods could be patented. Judge Rich, always seeking to broaden patent protection beyond the original industrial "useful arts," had succeeded in extending patent protection to microorganisms that did not exist in nature in the CCPA decision in *In re Bergy*, the first patent court decision to have been affirmed (as *Diamond v. Chakrabarty*).

Judge Rich, near the end of his life, again succeeded in broadening 35 U.S.C. §101 to cover business methods if they produced a "useful, concrete, and tangible result" (*State Street Bank & Trust Co. v. Signature Financial Group, Inc.*, 149 F. 3d 1368 (Fed. Cir.1998)). After his death, the Federal Circuit backed away from expansive interpretations of §101, and instead created a new "definitive test" called the "machine-or-transformation test," first announced in *Bilski*. The Supreme Court once more chose to enter the field of patent-eligibility under §101.

Claim I of the Bilski application recites the steps of "(a) initiating a series of transactions between said commodity provider and consumers of said commodity wherein said consumers purchase said commodity at a fixed rate based upon historical averages, said fixed rate corresponding to a risk position of said consumers; (b) identifying market participants for said commodity having a counter-risk position to said consumers; and (c) initiating a series of transactions between said commodity provider and said market participants at a second fixed rate such that said series of market participant transactions balances the risk position of said series of consumer transactions."

The Board of Patent Appeals and Interferences held it was an abstract idea, not a process within Section 101. The Federal Circuit affirmed, but on different grounds than the PTO relied on, namely, that the claim was not tied to a particular machine and did not transform the commodity or anything else into a different state.

The Supreme Court affirmed, but it rejected the broad rule, as it frequently has in recent years. The Court prefers to decide each case on its merits, rather than issue broad rules that will govern future cases, as the Federal Circuit does. Congress can pass laws with a "definitive test," but courts should not.

A business method might be patentable as a "process" under Section 101, but the *Bilski* method is an abstract idea. "Hedging is a fundamental economic practice long prevalent in our system of commerce and taught in any introductory finance class." 545 F. 3d, at 1013 (Rader, J. dissenting).

Although the last sentence of the majority Supreme Court opinion in *Bilski* is "The judgment of the Court of Appeals is affirmed," the new "definitive test" of the Federal Circuit was rejected.

Justice Stevens dissented, contending that business methods should not be patent-eligible.

The tally for the six CCPA cases involving patentable subject matter was four reversals and two affirmations. For the four Federal Circuit cases involving the issue of patentable subject matter, two were affirmed and two were reversed. But as previously noted, just because a judgment is affirmed, that doesn't mean the reasoning of the patent court will not be criticized–sometimes severely.

CHAPTER 6

# NOVELTY UNDER 35 U.S.C. §102

The ten Supreme Court decisions involving statutory subject matter under 35 U.S.C. §101 in chapter 5 can be compared to the much more frequently litigated issue of novelty in lower courts. Novelty under 35 U.S.C. §102 has been before the Supreme Court on appeal from a patent court only once:

*Pfaff v. Wells Electronics, Inc.*, 525 U.S. 55 (1998).

The relevant part of 35 U.S.C. §102 reads: "A person shall be entitled to a patent unless—

–(b) The invention was in public use or on sale in this country more than one year prior to the date of application for patent in the United States."

This exclusion of the right to a patent is called the "on-sale bar." The one-year limitation is a grace period during which an inventor may test the conception to be sure it works as intended. The inventor may publicly disclose or sell an embodiment of the invention and have one year from such a public act to file for a patent.

Most other nations do not have a grace period and the inventor must file a patent application *before* public disclosure or sale of the invention. The harmonization of patent laws in all countries–whether to include or exclude a grace period–has been studied for years. Harmonization of sorts was achieved recently by the United States patent law being changed to grant a patent to the first person to file a patent application, instead of the first person to make the invention.

Pfaff began work on his invention in November, 1980, when Texas Instruments asked him to develop a carrier for computer chips. Pfaff prepared detailed drawings of the carriers (called "sockets") and sent the drawings to a manufacturer to make the sockets. The drawings were also sent to Texas Instruments, and on March 17, 1981, it ordered thirty thousand sockets in an oral purchase order. The oral order was confirmed in writing on April 8, 1981.

More than a year later, on April 19, 1982, Pfaff filed a patent application.

The order was not filled until July 1981 because the manufacturer had to make special tools for manufacturing the sockets.

Pfaff did not make prototypes to test the sockets. The one-year grace period is often used to make prototypes from sketches and test them in a commercial environment. Pfaff, however, had done work for Texas Instruments previously, and he was confident that the drawings were precise enough for the final product to be made without testing prototypes.

A patent was granted to Pfaff on January 1, 1985. Pfaff sued Wells Electronics, a competitor, for patent infringement on two occasions. The first was in the Northern District of Indiana. Wells counterclaimed for a declaration of invalidity on several grounds, one of which was that the invention was on sale more than a year before the patent application was filed.

For an invention to be "on sale" under section 102(b) usually means that the invention exists in some form of embodiment. An invention is "conceived," meaning that the inventor has a mental idea of a problem and a proposed solution to that problem. The progression typically involves preparing drawings or written explanations of the perceived problem and the contemplated solution to that problem.

Next, the inventor usually proceeds to make something that solves the problem. For a "process," each step is performed to make sure that the step is carried out in the manner intended. Sometimes a step may not perform as predicted and must be revised to accomplish the intended result.

For a manufacture, something is built to constitute the manufacture, which is called "reducing the concept to practice." Almost always, the inventor must tweak the manufacture to ensure that it performs in the manner intended. The same is true of a machine. The reason for the grace period is to provide time for an inventor to perfect the machine to properly do the work it is supposed to do.

A composition of matter is often a mixture or a chemical reaction among two or more ingredients. Like a recipe, sometimes a dash of salt or a splash of vinegar will improve the composition substantially. Again, it takes time to experiment in order to achieve the best results.

The on-sale bar in patent law has long had an exception for "experimental use." The classic example of experimental use, as distinguished from commercial use, is *City of Elizabeth v. Pavement Co.*, 97 U.S. 126 (1877). There, the inventor, Samuel Nicholson, had laid down wooden pavement on a Boston toll road that was used by the public for six years before he filed for a patent. The public road "belonged to the Boston and Roxbury Mill Corporation, which received toll for its use, and Nicholson was a stockholder and treasurer of the corporation" (133). (Current United States patent law, which rewards the first to file rather than the first to invent, would not allow public use for six years).

Thus, the company of which Nicholson was treasurer received tolls from public users for the use of the road for six years. Still, the use was held to be experimental, not commercial.

Pfaff did not make commercial use of his invention by selling a commercial product to an unrelated buyer. The concept was merely described on paper in the form of mechanical drawings before the critical date, and there was no machine or product in existence. Wells failed to show that a device (socket) incorporating the invention existed and was on sale commercially before the critical date.

Usually, drawings are part of the conception, not the reduction of the invention to practice. Usually, providing drawings, without a prototype, to an existing customer who has purchased other products from the inventor, is not a commercial sale. Usually, a purchase order is not a commercial sale. The sale takes place when the product is delivered and paid for, which occurred after the critical date. Usually, whether a sale has occurred is an issue to be determined by state law, not federal law.

The Indiana district court decided that Pfaff had failed to prove infringement by Wells, and that Wells had failed to prove that the Pfaff socket was in commercial use before the critical date. Both Pfaff and Wells Electronics appealed to the Federal Circuit. In an unpublished decision, the Federal Circuit affirmed the district court's decision that Pfaff failed to prove that Wells infringed the patent, but it vacated the decision that Pfaff had not placed a commercial product on sale.

Either the sockets were on sale or they were not on sale. That fact issue was for the district court to decide, not the court of appeals. In *Pfaff*, the Federal Circuit substituted its view of the facts for that of the trier of fact, a violation of its duty under Rule 52(a)(6): "Findings of fact...must not be set aside unless clearly erroneous."

The Supreme Court had scolded the Federal Circuit in *Dennison Mfg. Co. v. Panduit Corp.*, 475 U.S. 809 (1986) for not deferring to facts found below. But the Federal Circuit repeated its error in the Indiana *Pfaff* case.

The second suit brought by Pfaff against Wells was in Texas, where the identical issue of the on-sale bar was raised again–with the opposite result in the district court *and* in the Federal Circuit. The only difference that I can discern between the two cases is that in the second bite at the apple given to Wells was that Pfaff was deposed and asked about whether his pre-filing acts constituted a commercial offer for sale.

The first case was tried before the district court sitting without a jury. The district judge found, as a matter of fact, that "the Wells device does not literally infringe upon Mr. Pfaff's patent and that the doctrine of prosecution history estoppel precludes Mr. Pfaff from resorting to the doctrine of equivalents to support his contention of infringement" (9 USPQ2d 1367). As to the on-sale bar, the facts found "to comply with the requirements of Fed. R. Civ. P. 52(a)" (*id.*, 1366) were that the "claims were not reduced to practice before April 19, 1981. Reduction to practice refers to the physical fact of producing the desired result by the means conceived by the inventor. The information was merely described on paper in the form of mechanical drawings before the critical date. No component parts had been manufactured or assembled; no testing was done until after delivery, well after the critical date. Wells has shown only that a concept of the invention existed before the critical date; that showing is insufficient under 35 U.S.C. §102(b)" (1375).

Both parties appealed to the Federal Circuit. It affirmed the district court holding on infringement in an opinion designated as "one that 'has not been prepared for publication in a printed volume because it does not add significantly to the body of law and is not of widespread legal interest. It is a public record. It is not citable as precedent'" *Pfaff v. Wells Electronics, Inc.*, 12 USPQ2d 1158, 1159 (Fed. Cir. 1989).

The Federal Circuit did not find the facts found by the district court to be "clearly erroneous," as it must under Rule 52(a)(6). Nevertheless, it vacated the district court's finding of patent validity, based on its decision in *Vieau v. Japax, Inc.* 823 F. 2d 1517 (Fed Cir. 1987). The Supreme Court overruled *Vieau* four years later in *Cardinal Chemical Co. v. Morton Int'l Inc.*, 508 U.S. 83 (1993).

It is not clear why the Federal Circuit and the Supreme Court purported to rewrite the law. The statute indicates that if an invention is on sale more than a year before the patent application is filed, the patent is invalid. Case law said that an invention that is not reduced to practice cannot be on sale. The Federal Circuit in *Pfaff* said that "reduction to practice" is not the test; the test is whether the invention is "substantially complete," which is not in section 102. The Supreme Court held in *Pfaff* that the Federal Circuit rewrite of "substantially complete" was too vague, and wrote its own law that the correct test is when the invention is "ready for patenting," which is also not in section 102.

Congress should write patent laws– not the Federal Circuit and not the Supreme Court. When the Indiana district court held that the invention was not reduced to practice, and therefore was not on sale, no court said that was "clearly erroneous" under Rule 52.

When I first read *Pfaff v. Wells Electronics*, I was impressed that the Court was unanimous in supporting the opinion by Justice Stevens, a rare occurrence. Besides, "reduced to practice" is an extremely nebulous test for determining the precise date when an invention is "made." "Ready for patenting" is a better way to fix a date on a calendar.

Now I know that the two parties participated in two trials in which the opposite results were reached, and the Supreme Court affirmed the second Federal Circuit decision in the same case (but not the first, which did not reach the Court).

What seems like a fairly straight-forward decision by the Supreme Court in *Pfaff* hides a complex mess from trials in Indiana and Texas, appeals resulting in inconsistent conclusions, reliance on a doctrine of the Federal Circuit that had been over-ruled by the Supreme Court five years before the *Pfaff* decision in the Supreme Court, and rewriting section 102 by both the Federal Circuit and the Supreme Court in ways quite unlike that section in the 1952 act. The apparently wise and simple decision glosses over a huge pile of twisted wreckage below.

For example, in the second trial in Texas, Wells produced Pfaff's deposition, in which he testified that he and Texas Instruments "had a 'deal' prior to the critical date," and that his "arrangement with TI was purely commercial, with no experimentation or additional development involved" (43 USPQ2d 1928, 1931). Assuming that testimony is relevant to the fact question of whether it was more probable that the invention was reduced to practice before the critical date, it was not presented in the Indiana trial, and the final judgment in Indiana, which was not set aside as clearly erroneous, is *res judicata* as between Pfaff and Wells. Apparently, Pfaff's new counsel did not raise the issue of whether that issue had already been determined in his favor.

Another example is the issue of "substantially complete," a test under the Federal Circuit's "own law," which replaced the test of reduction to practice used in the Indiana trial and was not rejected as "clearly erroneous" under Rule 52(a) in the first Federal Circuit appeal. In the second appeal, it said "the appropriate question is whether the invention was substantially complete at the time of sale, such that there was 'reason to expect that it would work for its intended purpose upon completion'" (43 USPQ2d, 1932).

The Supreme Court rejected the "substantially complete" test on appeal of the second Federal Circuit decision. In its place, the Court advanced its own test of "ready for patenting" in the *Pfaff* case. No precedent had ever advanced that test for determining whether an invention was on sale. Instead of remanding the case to the Federal Circuit to determine whether Pfaff met the new test, the Court decided that Pfaff had not shown that his invention was not ready for patenting when there was an offer for sale and a purchase order.

An offer for sale is not a sale because it contemplates future acceptance of the offer, delivery of the product sold, and payment for the purchase before the act of selling is complete. An offer for sale and a purchase order from the prospective buyer to the prospective seller surely cannot constitute a sale. Webster's *Third New International Dictionary* (1968) defines "sale" as "a contract transferring the absolute or general ownership of property from one person or corporate body for a price (as a sum of money or other consideration)." There is no "transfer" in an offer for sale and a purchase order.

Likewise, there is no transfer in "ready for patenting." The seller has not given up dominion over the property being sold when it does not exist. The product being sold by Pfaff had not yet been made, so it was impossible to transfer the property to a buyer who had sent a purchase order for a product yet to be made.

All three of the tests (reduced to practice, substantially complete, and ready for patenting) contemplate something that exists and can be transferred. It is impossible to deliver something that does not exist. Future acts by both sides were expected with the offer for sale and the purchase order. The act of selling was by no means complete.

Accordingly, I believe the judicial legislation is inadequate in that (1) on-sale means "reduced to practice" as the Indiana court held; or (2) it does not mean reduced to practice because "this court has held, however, that reduction to practice is not necessarily a prerequisite to application of the on-sale bar" (43 USPQ2d, 1931); or (3) it means "substantially complete" as the Federal Circuit held in the second appeal; or (4) it means "ready for patenting" as the Supreme Court framed the test.

This dilemma was resolved by analyzing the text of the Supreme Court decision in *Pfaff* to find that the case was wrongly decided. At 525 U.S. 58, the Court noted "Pfaff showed a sketch of his concept to representatives of Texas Instruments...Pfaff did not make and test a prototype of the new device before offering to sell it in commercial quantities. n3." Footnote 3 quotes from Pfaff's deposition which was taken by the counsel for Wells Electronics. These quotations show that Pfaff lost the case because his lawyer was not as skilled as the lawyer for Wells. I will call the lawyer for Wells the "good lawyer," and the lawyer for Pfaff the "poor lawyer."

The good lawyer is quoted in note 3 as asking Pfaff whether, before he gave a drawing to Wells, he had "any prototypes developed or anything of that nature, working embodiment." Pfaff's answer was "No."

The good lawyer knew that he was permitted to ask leading questions of the inventor in a deposition, so he asked "It was in a drawing, is that correct?" Pfaff's answer was "Strictly a drawing; went from the drawing to hard tooling. That's the way I do my business."

The poor lawyer representing Pfaff had failed to prepare the inventor for the question and the failure led to losing the case. The facts were that Pfaff was unable to go from his "drawing to hard tooling," because Pfaff did not make the "hard tools" needed to make the sockets shown in the drawing. His lawyer should have prepared Pfaff to explain that there was a long delay in progressing from a sketch until a finished product was made and delivered.

The very next sentence in the *Pfaff* opinion following note 3 in the Supreme Court opinion reads: "The manufacturer took several months to develop the customized tooling necessary to produce the device, and Pfaff did not fill the order until July 1981."

Had Pfaff been properly prepared by the poor lawyer, he would have testified that he did not go from drawing to finished product.

Instead, he made the sketch, and then gave it to a manufacturer who was unable to make the sockets from just the sketch. The manufacturer had to have "customized tooling" constructed before the patented product could be made. Pfaff's testimony about how he did business was simply wrong in the particular case of making the sockets for Texas Instruments. The Pfaff invention certainly was not "ready for patenting" when the sketch was made.

The good lawyer followed up on Pfaff's egotistical, but wrong, explanation of how he did his business. He asked whether the drawing led directly to finished product as "Boom-boom?" with no intermediate steps like "customized tooling" that actually were required. Pfaff's ego responded that "Boom-boom" was indeed the sequence: "You got it."

The good lawyer nailed the coffin shut with: "You are satisfied, obviously, when you come up with some drawings that it is going to go—'it works'?" Pfaff responded: "I know what I'm doing, yes, most of the time." The truth is that Pfaff did not know what he was doing and it took months to transform a sketch into the "customized tooling" needed to make the sockets.

The poor lawyer could have saved the day by cross-examining his witness to show that in the particular situation, having a drawing did not "work," and months passed before the sockets could be made. Either the poor lawyer did not know the facts (which made him a poor lawyer), or he did not want to show that his client did *not* know what he was doing in the particular case.

In any event, the Court was mistaken in holding that the invention was "ready for patenting" when the sketch was prepared. Footnote 2 in the opinion quotes *Corona Cord Tire Co. v. Dovan Chemical Corp.*, 276 U.S 358,383 (1928): "A manufacture is reduced to practice when it is completely manufactured."

The critical date was April 19, 1981, and the sockets were completely manufactured in July 1981 (525 U.S., 58), less than one year later. The case was wrongly decided because of poor lawyering.

The Federal Circuit was wrong in holding that "in public use of on sale in this country, more than one year prior to the date of the application for patent" (the words in section 102(b)) means "substantially complete."

The Supreme Court was wrong in interpreting those words of Section 102(b) to mean "ready for patenting."

Both errors of judicial legislation in the *Pfaff* appeals were mooted because the United States has abolished the "first-to-invent" rule and has joined the rest of the world in granting patents to the "first-to-file" a patent application. Section 102(b) no longer exists; the Federal Circuit concept of "substantially complete" is irrelevant; and the Supreme Court concept of "ready for patenting" is irrelevant. This chapter is largely irrelevant because *Pfaff v. Wells* is ancient history.

*Microsoft Corp. v. i4i Ltd. Partnership* is primarily discussed in chapter 12 because the primary issue was the presumption of validity. A secondary issue, relevant to this chapter, is the on-sale bar issue raised (unsuccessfully) by Microsoft. This case related to the on-sale bar becomes irrelevant because it relates to first-to-invent, and first-to-file is now the law. A brief discussion of the section 102(b) issue is presented here for completeness of coverage of the thirty-three reviews of patent court decisions.

More than a year before filing for a patent, the founders of i4i had sold a product called S4, which had some of the attributes of the patented product. Whether S4 was an embodiment of the patented invention was an issue never resolved in the *i4i* case because the creators had destroyed the software and could not recall what it did. They had advertised the fact that S4 was a predecessor to the patented invention, but that was insufficient proof that the invention was on sale more than a year before filing.

CHAPTER 7

# OBVIOUSNESS UNDER 35 U.S.C.§103(a)

B y far the most litigated section of the patent law is the provision on obviousness in Section 103(a). It reads:

"A patent may not be obtained though the invention is not identically disclosed or described as set forth in section 102 of this title, if the differences between the subject matter sought to be patented and the prior art are such that the subject matter as a whole would have been obvious at the time the invention was made to a person having ordinary skill in the art to which it pertains. Patentability shall not be negatived by the manner in which the invention was made."

Before this addition in the 1952 patent act, there was no statutory requirement for "the general level of innovation required to sustain patentability," a principle announced by the Supreme Court in *Hotchkiss v. Greenwood*, 52 U.S. (11 How.) 248 (1851). *Graham v. John Deere Co.*, 383 U.S. 1, 3 (1966) concluded that the principle of the *Hotchkiss* case was codified in section 103.

In the century between *Hotchkiss* and the 1952 act, the Industrial Revolution brought great change to the landscape of technology. The advances in technology led to more patents, which, in turn, led to more patent infringement cases. The Supreme Court decided a great number of patent cases between 1851 and 1952. The pace of determining patent cases began to slow when Theodore Roosevelt became president in 1901and the federal government began enforcing the Sherman Act against monopolies.

The growth of Court review of anti-trust cases corresponded to the decline of Court review of patent cases, even though patents are not, *per se*, illegal monopolies. When Justice Douglas, a former anti-trust official, and Justice Black came to the Supreme Court, the pace of Court review of patent cases slowed as the pace of anti-trust cases increased. The decline in patent cases came gradually to a dead stop in 1950, when *Great Atlantic& Pacific Tea Co. v. Supermarket Equipment Corp.*, 340 U.S. 147 (1950) was decided.

The Supreme Court did not decide any patent cases at all from December 1950, when *A & P* was decided and February 1966, when *Graham* was decided. During those sixteen years, district courts and federal courts of appeal were left without Supreme Court guidance on what Congress intended in its codification of the 1850 *Hotchkiss* case, as well as any other provisions of patent law.

One month after *Graham* was decided, the Supreme Court decided, for the first time, a case from the CCPA (*Brenner v. Manson*, 383 U.S. 519 (1966). The pace of review of patent court decisions has gradually increased in the years since 1966.

The addition of section 103 was probably the most substantial change in patent law in more than a century. It was intended to bring more precision to the vague concept of "invention" as the additional requirement for patentability beyond novelty and usefulness.

"Nonobviousness" was the brainchild of Giles Rich, co-author of the 1952 act. Rich's motivation in seeking more precision in defining the "invention" requirement was to overcome what he perceived as "anti-patent" views promoted by Supreme Court justices who favored strong antitrust laws. Rich knew that the 1623 Statute of Monopolies treated anti-competitive monopolies differently than patents. Patents were promoted while monopolies were condemned, and that English law was adopted by the United States.

The Douglas concurring opinion in *A & P* stated:

"Every patent is a grant of a privilege of exacting tolls from the public. The Framers plainly did not want those monopolies freely granted. The invention, to justify a patent, had to serve the ends of science—to push back the frontiers of chemistry, physics, and the like; to make a distinctive contribution to scientific knowledge."

A Nobel Prize is supposed to recognize "a distinctive contribution of scientific knowledge," as Justice Douglas put it, not a patent. Rich thought that small steps forward can "promote the progress" of the useful arts, as the Constitution says, without pushing "back the frontiers" of chemistry of physics. A cardboard box can be patented without pushing back the frontiers of physics. Rich believed that the Constitution intended a much lower standard for patentability–allowing more than one prize per year for medicine, for example, as with the Nobel Committee grants.

The Rich goal in formulating the "nonobvious" standard was precisely to overrule the *A & P* language of Justice Douglas. However, the 1952 act has not been interpreted as overruling the Douglas concurring opinion in *A & P.* It has never been rejected. On the contrary, the concurrence by Justice Douglas is frequently cited with approval in Supreme Court opinions.

For example, in *Microsoft Corp. v. i4i Limited Partnership*, 564 U.S. __ (2011)." the Court cited the Douglas concurring opinion for the proposition that the "standard of patentability is a constitutional standard and the question of validity of a patent is a question of law." Although that does not specifically approve the assertion that the "standard written onto the Constitution" is "to push back the frontiers," it certainly does not overrule it.

Congress, in the 1952 act, restated the judge-made requirement for "inventive genius" as "nonobvious" to one of ordinary skill in the art. Congress did not, in section 103, expressly overrule the Douglas language of pushing back the frontiers of chemistry and physics. Overruling must be explicit, and cannot be by simply by implication, as the *Pioneer* case in chapter 5 teaches.

After Judge Rich was appointed to the CCPA in 1956, he had occasion to explain whether the standard of section 103 that the "differences between the subject matter sought to be patented and the prior art...would have been obvious" (by definition a prospective view, not a retrospective view) was broad enough to encompass the "obvious to try" solution contemplated in the prior art.

I was a law clerk (later retroactively called "technical advisor") at the CCPA in 1963, when Judge Rich explained what Congress intended with regard to "obvious to try" (as its unidentified author and explainer). In the case of *In re Papesch*, 315 F. 2d 381, 391 (CCPA 1963), Judge Rich indicated that patentability is not to be determined on the basis of structure alone, and a compound may be patentable if properties not known in the prior art are found in the claimed compound. The reason given was that "from the standpoint of patent law, a compound and all of its properties are inseparable."

Another Rich opinion relevant to "obvious to try" is *In re Huellmantel*, 324 F. 2d 998, 1003 (CCPA 1963). The invention combined two known anti-inflammatory agents, salicylate and prednisolone. The claims were rejected, based on a reference showing cortisone combined with salicylate and prednisolone were as superior as anti-inflammatory agents, as cortisone. The Board said "It would be obvious at least to try to substitute prednisolone for cortisone in combinations in which cortisone has been employed."

The CCPA affirmed the rejection, but Judge Rich, for the court, complained about the "obvious to try" language. The statute says "the subject matter as a whole would have been obvious." "Nothing is said about 'obvious to try'" (note 3).

This is another example of the patent court writing its "own law" to interpret what Congress intended by a statute. The patent court can change its "own law" by overturning it *en banc*. Congress can change the statute to overturn patent court interpretations. The only other way to correct the patent court's "own law" is by Supreme Court review. This last way is the path reviewed here.

Fast forward forty-four years after *Papesch* and *Huellmantel* to 2007, and we learn what the Supreme Court thinks of this part of the patent court's "own law." *KSR Int'l Co. v .Teleflex, Inc.*, 550 U.S. 398 (2007) was critical of the patent court's effort to achieve more "uniformity and consistency" as intended when Congress created the Federal Circuit. The patent court rewrote section 103 to have the obviousness test changed to "an approach referred to by the parties as the 'teaching, suggestion or motivation' test (TSM) test" (407). The Supreme Court found the test to be a "helpful insight," but no substitute for the congressional test of section 103. The TSM test was "contrary to §103 and our precedents" (*id.*).

The examples of the patent courts' "own law" are a series of rules devised by the specialist courts without the authority of Congress or the Supreme Court. Rather, the rules are just manifestations of the patent court's perceived omniscience (see chapter 2). That perceived omniscience took a hit when the Court in *KSR* said "When a court transforms a general principle into a rigid rule that limits the obviousness inquiry, as the court of appeals did here, it errs" (*id.*) Rules related to other inquiries of the patent court's "own law," besides the obviousness inquiry, should be examined through the *KSR* lens.

The Federal Circuit found that the district court in *KSR* had failed to follow a corollary of the TSM test–that the prior art must be addressed to solve the same problem as that addressed in the patented invention. The district court had failed to make findings regarding the "'specific understanding or principle within the knowledge of the skilled artisan that would have motivated one with no knowledge of [the] invention' to attach an electronic control to the support bracket of the Asano assembly" (414). The prior art addressed "the constant ratio problem," which was not the problem addressed by the patent's inventor.

The Federal Circuit conceded that it might have been obvious to try the prior art solution, but "obvious to try has long been held not to constitute obviousness" (*id.*) under section 103, according to the Federal Circuit's "own law." The Supreme Court struck down this aspect of the patent court's "own law,"

In its place, the Supreme Court resurrected "obvious to try." "When there is a design need or market pressure to solve a problem and there are a finite number of identified, predictable solutions, a person of ordinary skill has good reason to pursue the known options within his or her technical grasp. If this leads to the anticipated success, it is likely the product not of innovation but of ordinary skill and common sense. In that instance the fact that a combination was obvious to try might show that it was obvious under §103" (429).

In other words, "ordinary skill" under section 103 includes "common sense" from the perspective of the Supreme Court. The patent court's "own law" must give way to the Supreme Court's interpretation.

An issue that has gained little attention by commentators on the *KSR* decision is the Federal Circuit's reversal of the district court's decision on summary judgment under Federal Rule of Civil Procedure 56. The testimony of an expert on the facts of the case was heard by the district court and adopted as its findings of fact. The Federal Circuit reversed the district court's findings because it disagreed with them. It did not find clear error in the findings, as required by Rule 52. The Supreme Court reversed the Federal Circuit decision, stating that "Nothing in the declarations proffered by Teleflex prevented the District Court from reaching the careful conclusions underlying its order for summary judgment" (427). The "careful conclusions" cannot be set aside without finding clear error.

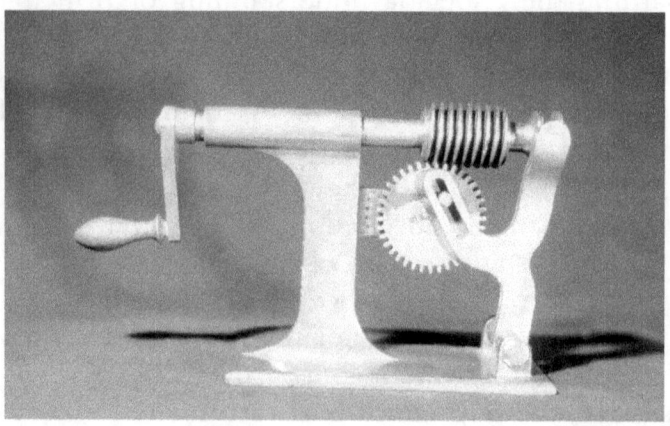

# CHAPTER 8

# BAYH-DOLE ACT 35 U.S.C. §200-212

Chapter 18 of the patent code is entitled "Patent Rights in Inventions Made with Federal Assistance." The two sponsors of the act, Senators Birch Bayh and Bob Dole, sought to facilitate the technology transfer from universities, where government grants led to inventions made by academics, to entrepreneurs and small businesses, where inventions could be commercialized.

The first section of the act, which is now 35 U.S.C. §200, sets forth the policy and objective of the 1980 enactment: "to use the patent system to promote the utilization of inventions arising from federally supported research or development." This is the 1980 congressional variation of the constitutional mandate in 1789: "To promote the progress of...the useful arts," as applied to federally funded research.

Section 200 continues, indicating that Congress wanted "to encourage maximum participation of small business firms–to promote collaboration between commercial concerns and nonprofit organizations, including universities" and five other objectives. None of the objectives that Congress sought to achieve in 1980 included the one specified in the Constitution: "securing for limited times to...inventors the exclusive right to their...discoveries."

Nearly two hundred years on, Congress still has not secured to inventors the exclusive right to their discoveries. Instead, Congress in the new federally funded enactment wanted to protect "inventions made by nonprofit organizations and small business firms" and make sure "the Government obtains sufficient rights in federally supported inventions." That is, the act is intended to preserve rights of nonprofit organizations and small business firms, on the one hand, and the Government, on the other hand. There is no hand for the inventors who created the inventions to promote progress of the useful arts.

The founding fathers were well aware of the British treatment of the colonists in America. The patent system in England began as royal largesse to favorites of the monarch. Patents began in England as royal monopolies to import technology invented elsewhere into England to promote progress. The grant was to the importer of the invention to England, not to the inventor, who was in a foreign country. The royal grant of a patent was intended to "promote the utilization of inventions," just as the 1980 Bayh-Dole act intended.

The term "utilization of inventions" meant, then as now, encouraging investment in commercializing inventions. Both patents of importation in England and rights under the Bayh-Dole act were inducements to commercialize by investment. Neither was intended to reward inventors for coming forth with new inventions that promote the progress of the useful arts.

The common law in England came to abhor monopolies given to favorites of the monarch. In 1623, Parliament passed the Statute of Monopolies, prohibiting monopolies as hindering competition. Patents, which had evolved from royal grants of monopolies into rewards for inventors, were expressly excluded from the Statute of Monopolies because they were pro-competition, not anti-competition.

The two primary English colonies in America, Jamestown in 1607 and Plymouth in 1620, preceded the enactment of the Statute of Monopolies. As a result, the colonies were intended to be sites for investments in monopolies. For example, monopolies like cotton, tobacco, and rum, came to be exported from the colonies to England and Europe.

The primary investments were for land for growing agricultural products and people to populate the colonies. Land was allocated by muniments of title or land patents granted by the government. People were brought to the colonies by investors.

Indentured servants comprised perhaps the largest number of people originally brought to the colonies. An investor would provide passage to the New World by ship. In return, the servant signed an indenture that required service for a period of years, typically four, in return for passage, food, clothing and shelter for the entire period. The fruits of the servant's labor belonged to the master—the investor. Master-servant law was well established in England in the eighteenth century.

Later, investors imported slaves, largely from Africa, to work the land. The term of service for a slave was as long as the master wished. Slaves were property, unlike indentured servants. Other categories of people were redemptioners (who paid back the price of passage to the colony) and convicts (who were let out of prison and shipped to the New World so they would not have to be cared for in England).

Excluding Puritan migrations of the 1630's, "not less than one-half, nor more than two-thirds of all white immigrants to the colonies were indentured servants or redemptioners or convicts" (Smith, 1947, 336).

The impact of the pre-Independence master-servant law was profound. It allowed owners of indentures and employers of convicts and redemptioners to appropriate inventions and discoveries made by immigrant workers in America. The founders of the new nation wanted to be sure that this oppressive law, which so many of their ancestors were subjected to, was abolished. The constitutional mandate, that progress of the useful arts required securing to inventors the exclusive right to their discoveries, becomes clear when this history of indentured servants is understood. Instead of allowing masters to appropriate the fruits of the labor of servants, the founding fathers really meant what the Constitution says: the exclusive right was to be "secured" to inventors, and not to their masters.

The unfairness, indeed the injustice, of masters taking rights to inventions made by servants was apparent to the people seeking independence from colonizers. That half or more of the migrants, whose descendants were the "People...form[ing] a more perfect Union, establish[ing] justice,...and secur[ing] the Blessings of Liberty to ourselves and our Posterity" by the Constitution, were the servants in this master-servant relationship that led to the provision that the exclusive right to an invention was secured to the inventor.

Has the clear intent expressed by the founders been recognized by the Supreme Court? It appears from *Board of Trustees of Stanford v. Roche*, that the answer is "no." The patent right was not secured to the inventor. The battle was between Stanford, a prominent American university that employed Dr. Mark Holodniy, and Roche, a large Swiss company prominent in chemical research, each of whom induced Dr. Holodniy to assign rights to the invention to it. The assigning inventor got nothing for his invention as a result of the Court decision.

Chief Justice John Roberts, writing the majority opinion in *Stanford v. Roche*, decided June 6, 2011, began: "Since 1790, the patent law has operated on the premise that rights in an invention belong to the inventor." That beginning would appear to signal that the exclusive right was secured to Dr. Holodniy and his two co-inventors. Unfortunately, that was not the signal sent by the opinion, which favors one master over another master, with nothing secured to the servant inventor.

The facts in the case are fairly straight-forward. PCR (polymerase chain reaction) is a way to make huge numbers of copies of a genetic sequence from a very small sample. It was invented by Dr. Kary Mullis, an employee of Cetus who won the 1993 Nobel Prize in Chemistry for his discovery. Mullis assigned his invention to Cetus as required by his employment agreement. No rights in the invention were secured to the Nobel Prize-winner.

Stanford University received funds from the National Institutes of Health (NIH) under the Bayh-Dole act to do research in efficacy of drugs for treating HIV, a life-threatening organism not well understood in 1985. Two senior research scientists in charge of the NIH project at Stanford used some of the NIH funds to hire Dr. Holodniy, a junior researcher inexperienced in the use of PCR, to help on the project. All three of the Stanford researchers had signed the standard agreement that any fruits of the research in the form of patentable inventions would be assigned to Stanford, their employer.

It was apparent that PCR would be useful for the drug research being conducted by Stanford, but the three researchers did not know how to use it. It was agreed that Holodniy, the new addition to the Stanford team, would collaborate with Cetus in order to use PCR in the Stanford project. Cetus agreed that it would teach Dr. Holodniy the PCR process on the condition that he sign a standard contract that any invention made during the collaboration belonged to Cetus. Dr. Holodniy was not an employee of Cetus, and was not in what historically would be regarded as a master-servant relationship with Cetus. He was an employee of Stanford, and had agreed to assign any invention he made as an employee to Stanford.

Both the contract that Dr. Holodniy signed with Stanford and the one he signed with Cetus were intended to assign to master Stanford and to master Cetus, respectively, any future inventions made by Dr. Holodniy during his work on the project. Servant Holodniy was secured no rights to his inventions. The Supreme Court was to determine which of the two masters had superior rights to his inventions. The rights of his superiors at Stanford were not at issue, because they had not agreed to assign anything to Cetus.

The two Holodniy assignments are relics from the English master-servant law of the seventeenth century. They exist today simply because Congress has never done what the patent clause of the Constitution intended—namely, to secure to inventors the exclusive right to their inventions. Instead, Congress has only required in the patent law that the inventor be named in the patent.

Congress has never, in over two hundred years, secured to the inventor the exclusive right to the invention. The patent right is almost universally assigned to the master by contract signed by the servant as a condition of employment. (Nearly every other industrialized country in the world secures rights to inventors, usually by fair compensation for the assignment.)

The first sentence of the majority opinion in *Stanford v. Roche* is wrong as a matter of fact. The first patent act in 1790 did not operate "on the premise that rights to an invention belong to the inventor." Contracts under the ancient master-servant law allow the master to contractually bind the servant to surrender any patent rights in the servant's invention (initially under the contract of indentured servitude). For 220 years, Congress, by its silence, has permitted masters to frustrate the intent of the Constitution to secure exclusive rights in discoveries to the inventors.

Worse, Congress has relegated the servant to the bottom of the hierarchy rather than to the top. The Bayh-Dole act states the pecking order this way: the government must obtain "sufficient rights in federally supported inventions" ( 35 U.S.C. §200); the master "that is a party to a funding agreement" has rights "to any invention [owned by the master] conceived or first actually reduced to practice in the performance of work under a funding agreement (§201(e)). The servant that conceives the invention and presumably participates in the reduction to practice is in last place: "If a contractor does not elect to retain title to a subject invention... the Federal agency may consider and after consultation with the contractor grant requests for retention of rights by the inventor" (§202(d).

That is, if the government does not receive the right to exclude, the contractor may do so. Only if the government and the contractor agree might the right to exclude pass to the servant who created the invention. That is upside down; not the arrangement contemplated by the founding fathers in the Constitution.

Congress has continued the injustice of master-servant law in its treatment of discoverers of seed varieties. In 7 U.S.C. §2401(a)(2), the Plant Variety Protection Act provides that where a discovery is made "by an agent on behalf of a principal, the principal, rather than the agent, shall be considered the breeder." "Master," "principal" and "employer" are synonyms, as are "servant," "agent" and "employee." Congress secured the patent right to the master in the PVPA, contrary to the intent expressed in the Constitution to secure the right to exclude to the servant if the servant is the discoverer.

The Supreme Court, in *Asgrow Seed Co. v. Winterboer*, 513 U.S. 179 (1995) said that the "whole purpose of the [PVPA] statute is to create a valuable property in the botanical research by giving the developer the right to 'exclude others from selling the variety.'" In this context, "developer" is another synonym for "master." Instead of securing to the inventor the right to exclude others from using the discovery, Congress again ignored the constitutional mandate. The Supreme Court appears in *Asgrow*, to have approved of Congress securing a patent-like right to the master rather than the servant. In *Stanford*, the Court appears to have ignored the constitutional mandate, just as Congress has.

The Supreme Court had previously characterized a patent as a "reward" for the "exertions" of artisans (*Grant v. Raymond*, 31 U.S. 318 (1832)). *Graham v. John Deere Co.*, 383 U.S. 1, 9 (1966) said a patent "was a reward, an inducement, to bring forth new knowledge." That message has not reached the Roberts Court.

In *Stanford v. Roche*, the Court treats patents under the Bayh-Dole act as tools to protect the rights of nonprofit organizations, small businesses, and the government. There were two contracts of adhesion in the case. (A contract of adhesion is between two parties that have uneven bargaining powers. It is sometimes called a "take-it-or-leave-it" contract because there is no room for negotiation. If the servant wants the job, the servant assigns future inventions to the master).

Stanford sued Roche for infringement of the patents on inventions made by Holodniy and his superiors. Roche defended the charge by proving that the Stanford patents were invalid because it was obvious to try PCR in determining efficacy of HIV drugs.

Stanford appealed the district court holding of invalidity to the Federal Circuit. The appellate court found that a later contract of adhesion signed by Dr. Holodniy that assigned any future invention to Cetus gave superior rights to Cetus, not to Stanford. The reasoning was that the first adhesion contract promised to assign future inventions to Stanford; and the second adhesion contract used present tense—that Holodniy stated "I do hereby assign" future inventions to Cetus. The present tense assignment to Cetus trumped the future tense assignment to Stanford, according to the Federal Circuit. The second assignment did not erase the first assignment; it just "deprived Stanford of standing" to sue its co-owner.

This reasoning overlooks several important facts. First, the lead inventors of the Stanford invention did not assign anything to Cetus. Holodniy was the junior-most of the three inventors and lacked the power to assign all rights to the invention to Cetus. Theoretically, if one inventor assigned rights to Cetus and the other two inventors assigned their rights to Stanford, both Cetus and Stanford would share non-exclusive patent rights. The Federal Circuit had no jurisdiction to strike down the assignment of patent rights to Stanford by the two senior inventors.

In the majority opinion, the Court indicates that Roche asserted "that it was a co-owner of the HIV quantification procedure, based on Holodniy's assignment of his rights." That seems to indicate that Roche did not claim to own the rights of the other two inventors and shared ownership with them.

Second, Holodniy had promised Stanford, in the first adhesion contract, that he "will not enter into any agreement creating . . . patent obligations in conflict with this agreement." Holodniy breached that Stanford agreement by signing the Cetus agreement. How could the Cetus agreement that violated the prior contract supersede the prior agreement? An assignment of at most one-third of the patent rights cannot void the prior agreement.

Third, the invention was not in existence when the two adhesion contracts were signed. How could Holodniy "hereby assign" something that had not even been conceived? Neither party could put a value on an invention that did not exist, so there could have been no consideration for a present assignment of property that was not even imagined yet.

Fourth, Holodniy was an employee of Stanford. He had skills and experience (including a Ph. D. degree) useful to Stanford in its NIH research. Cetus did not employ Holodniy. As far as the record shows, Holodniy gave nothing of his experience and skills to Cetus, and Cetus did not provide salary, benefits, health insurance, and other consideration to Holodniy. A "Visitor's Confidentiality Agreement" is not an employment agreement. Where is the quid pro quo?

Fifth, Cetus opted to publish the results of the work done by Holodniy and his colleagues at Cetus. Cetus did not seek to patent any invention that Holodniy might have assigned to it in the second (present tense assignment) agreement. It was long after Stanford had filed patent applications, patented the invention, and sued Roche for patent infringement that the afterthought occurred. If Cetus truly believed that the invention Holodniy was said to "hereby assign" to Cetus, it would have filed a patent application, just as it had for the PCR invention of Dr. Mullis.

Patent law has for centuries in this country provided for inter partes proceedings to determine which one of two or more claimants is the true and first inventor. The proceedings are called "interferences," and rival claimants introduce evidence to show priority of invention. Because Cetus and Roche never filed a patent application on the Holodniy invention allegedly assigned to Cetus, no interference could have been declared.

Sixth, Roche chose to challenge the validity of the Stanford patents by showing that it was obvious to try PCR to develop assays. It was an afterthought that followed the successful challenge to the Stanford claim of ownership based solely upon the present tense used in the assignment of the future invention. Roche did not claim ownership of the invention that was assigned before it existed. Rather, Roche only claimed that it had "'an ownership interest in the patents-in-suit' that was not extinguished by the Bayh-Dole Act" (slip op. at 5-6). The Federal Circuit agreed that the "ownership interest" meant that Stanford could not sue Roche. It did not hold that Roche had priority. If priority was intended to be established, interference is the way to prove priority, not the present tense of the verb "to assign" an invention that did not exist, was never patented, and was never held to be Roche property in the district court.

As Justice Breyer put it in dissenting, "the slight linguistic differences in the contractual language [in the first and second adhesion contracts] seems to make too much of too little...." "Copying the precise words blessed by the Federal Circuit... remains a technical drafting trap for the unwary" (slip op. at 7-8).

The Supreme Court went further than the Federal Circuit did. Whereas the district court held that Bayh-Dole protects "any invention of the contractor conceived or first actually reduced to practice in the performance of work under a funding agreement," as the statute reads, the Federal Circuit held that Roche was a co-owner with Stanford and Stanford could not sue its co-owner. That decision did not hold that Roche was a prior owner and therefore had superior rights to Stanford.

The majority opinion held that "the general rule [is] that rights in an invention belong to the inventor" who is "vested by law with an inchoate right to its exclusive use" (7, quoting *Gayler v. Wilder*, 10 How.477, 493 (1851). The Bayh-Dole Act does not "expressly deprive [inventors] of their interest in federally funded inventions" (8).

The act permits contractors to "elect to retain title," but it "does not vest title" in the contractor. "You cannot retain something unless you already have it" (11). Stanford did not have title because it did not "already have" the future invention when the first adhesion contract was signed. But Cetus did not "already have" the Holodniy invention when he purported to "hereby assign" a future invention.

The Supreme Court held that the second adhesion contract was prior to the first one because the present tense "hereby assign" was used instead of a promise to assign (the promise to assign to Stanford was fulfilled and the patents were in fact assigned to Stanford). The Federal Circuit did not decide priority. It only held that Bayh-Dole did extinguish the co-ownership of Stanford and Roche, both of whom traced ownership to Holodniy. But Stanford had assignments from all three inventors and Cetus did not. It was error to hold that "co-ownership" meant "priority" in the junior-most of the three inventors simply because the present tense was used in his promise to assign a future invention.

Justice Sotomayor, in a concurring opinion, concluded that the points made in the Breyer dissent could be raised in future cases because they were not presented in the court of appeals. Let us hope that the difference between priority of invention and the co-ownership resulting from two adhesion contracts signed by one of the three inventors will be explored in a future case.

CHAPTER 9

# 35 U.S.C. §271(b) INDUCED INFRINGEMENT

Infringement of a patent is the topic of section 271 of the patent statute. Subpart *a* deals with acts of infringement. Subpart *b* deals with inducing infringement by one who is not an actual infringer. A few words about jurisdiction over acts of infringement in general are appropriate. The CCPA had no jurisdiction over patent infringement cases because it was created as an administrative court, and patent infringement is a judicial proceeding, not an administrative proceeding. Before 1982, judicial courts, namely federal district courts and regional courts of appeal, considered cases and controversies. The CCPA only considered appeals from the PTO, and not appeals from district courts. Patent infringement cases were the domain of judicial courts. Appeals from district court decisions went to the regional courts of appeal in which the district courts were located.

In contrast, PTO decisions were made as an administrative agency under the procedures specified in the Administrative Procedure Act rather than the federal rules governing procedure in judicial cases. Appeals from the Patent Office agency went to the CCPA. The CCPA became a judicial court in 1958 by an act of Congress. The CCPA still had no jurisdiction over patent infringement cases, even though it was a judicial, rather than an administrative, court.

The Federal Circuit had jurisdiction over appeals from every patent case in every United States district court, beginning in 1982. Patent infringement cases in district courts were governed by 35 U.S.C. §271. A person believing that he has been damaged by a patent infringement could seek declarative relief in district court. But even in such a declaratory judgment case, the plaintiff had to allege that the risk of a lawsuit for patent infringement under §271 was imminent.

Today, the overwhelming majority of cases before the Federal Circuit involve charges of infringement under this section. They rely upon direct infringement under subsection *a*, active inducement of infringement under subsection *b*, or contributory infringement under subsection *c*. These subsections were present in the 1952 patent act. All issues that relate to the meanings of these subsections were initially resolved in district courts, appealed to regional courts, and reached the Supreme Court on petitions for certiorari during the thirty years between 1952 and the creation of the Federal Circuit in 1982. Section 271(b) simply states: "Whoever actively induces infringement of a patent shall be liable as an infringer."

Criminal law has a doctrine of "willful blindness," which is not a familiar term in the patent law. The obligation of a patent owner to mark the patented product with the patent number has been in the patent law for a very long time. It is now embodied in 35 U.S.C. §287(a).

That section states that "patentees, and persons...importing any patented article into the United States, may give notice that the same is patented....In the event of failure to so mark, no damages shall be recovered by the patentee in any action for infringement, except on proof that the infringer was notified of the infringement...Filing of an action for infringement shall constitute such notice."

Another kind of notice is implied notice. It is implied in Section 271(b) that if one actively induces infringement of a patent, it is implied that the inducer knew of the patent. The criminal law doctrine of "willful blindness" implies that the party would have had knowledge of the fact if he had not been willfully blind to the fact.

The patent statute does not use the term "willful blindness" of the patent by the infringer, but the Supreme Court introduced the term in its only decision addressing induced infringement. On May 31, 2011, the Supreme Court decided *Global-Tech Appliances, Inc. v. SEB S.A.*, 131 S. Ct. 458 (2011), the only time that the Court has reviewed a decision of a patent court interpreting section 271(b). The Court did not address the patent marking statute, which has been a limitation on damages for failure to mark since 1861. It is a limitation on damages awarded under §284, as is §285, which bars damages for infringement more than six years before the filing of the complaint. Damages and limitations on damages are in the patent code as "remedies for infringement of patent," which had their beginnings in the nineteenth century. Inducing infringement was added to the patent code in 1952.

It is arguable that the section 271 concepts of inducing infringement and contributory infringement were intended to counter antitrust doctrines that limit the scope of patent law protection. Without getting deeply into antitrust law, some have argued that patent law should not prohibit either inducing infringement (§271(b)) or contributory infringement (§271(c)). The argument is that only direct infringement should be actionable, because giving patent owners protection beyond direct infringement impinges upon competition law that allows competitors to perform acts that are not clear infringements.

Giles Rich, co-author of the 1952 act, was staunchly pro-patent and wanted to be sure that antitrust doctrines did not trump patent law doctrines. Hence, inducing infringement and contributory infringement were expressly made actionable under the 1952 Patent Act.

The Supreme Court in *Global-Tech* made no reference to the history of the 1952 act because no anti-trust claim was raised in the case. The sole issue was whether the alleged infringer knew, or should have known, that the deep fryer it asked to be copied was protected by patent. As stated in the first sentence of the Supreme Court opinion, to actively induce infringement a party "must know that the induced acts constitute patent infringement." (The first sentence of the opinion also states that SEB "obtained a U.S. patent for its design." (It was not a design patent; it was a utility patent).

Respondent *SEB* is a French maker of appliances. It patented a new deep fryer with external surfaces that remain cool during frying. Sunbeam, a competitor of SEB, asked Pentalpha, a subsidiary of *Global-Tech*, to make a deep fryer meeting certain specifications. Pentalpha bought an SEB fryer and copied it. Pentalpha retained an attorney to do a patent search without revealing that it had copied the SEB fryer. The attorney opined that the Pentalpha fryer did not infringe any patents found in the search, but the search did not reveal the SEB patent (it was an inadequate search). Pentalpha had no notice of the patent from the inadequate search, and there was no public notice by the patent owner on the copied fryer (such as the patent number).

SEB sued Sunbeam for patent infringement, and the parties settled short of trial. Other appliance sellers bought Pentalpha fryers and SEB sued Pentalpha for those sales in another case. That case went to trial, and a jury found that there was direct infringement under §271(a), as well as induced infringement under §271(b).

Pentalpha filed post-trial motions contending that it did not know of SEB's patent when it copied the SEB fryer. The district court denied the motions. Pentalpha appealed. The Federal Circuit affirmed: "Pentalpha deliberately disregarded a known risk that SEB had a protective patent."

Pentalpha petitioned for certiorari, claiming that actual knowledge of the patent is needed. The Court affirmed the Federal Circuit holding of induced infringement.

"Although the text of §271(b) makes no mention of intent, we infer that at least some intent is required." The dictionary definition of "actively" suggests that "the inducement must involve the taking of affirmative steps to bring about the desired result."

Because induced infringement was included in "contributory infringement" before 1952, the Court analyzed its pre-1952 contributory infringement cases to conclude that §271(b) and §271(c) both require knowledge of the patent for infringement. The Court agreed with Pentalpha that "deliberate indifference to a known risk that a patent exists is not the appropriate standard under §271(b)" (slip op. at 10). But deliberate indifference did not describe the situation presented. Instead, the Court found "the evidence in this case was plainly sufficient to support a finding of Pentalpha's knowledge under the doctrine of willful blindness" (id.)

It concluded: "Given the long history of willful blindness and its wide acceptance in the Federal Judiciary, we can see no reason why the doctrine should not apply in civil lawsuits for induced patent infringement under 35 U. S. C. §271(b)."

In the absence of Congress amending patent law to include "the doctrine of willful blindness," there should be a reason given as to why a criminal law doctrine, where proof must be beyond a reasonable doubt, should be used in civil cases where the lesser standard of preponderance of the evidence is required.

The Court failed to address the apparent favoritism of patent owners as claimants of rights proved by a mere preponderance of evidence, rather than beyond a reasonable doubt. Normally, when a new theory is developed in the Supreme Court, the case is remanded for the court of first instance and the court of appeals to apply the new law to the facts of the case. There was no remand here, only the insertion of a criminal law doctrine into patent law.

The Court referred to willful blindness of "clear evidence of critical facts that are strongly suggested by the circumstances," which certainly sounds like an issue for a trier of fact. If there were a reason why a criminal law doctrine should not be extended to patent law, it would be appropriate for the Federal Circuit to decide whether it should do so after a full briefing by the parties.

The jury in *Global-Tech* was not asked about "high probability," or taking "deliberate steps to avoid knowing" a fact, nor was an instruction given to the jury regarding the duty of a patentee under 35 U.S.C. §287(a) to give notice of the patent to the world by placing the word "patent" (or "pat.") and the patent number on the fryers.

On the other hand, if a jury found Pentalpha did *not* have that subjective belief, did *not* take those deliberate steps, and was *not* given notice of the patent, then "the right to trial by jury shall be preserved, and no fact tried by a jury, shall be otherwise reexamined in any Court of the United States, than according to the rules of the common law" (Seventh Amendment). How specific did the jury instructions have to be?

Justice Kennedy, often the deciding vote when the remaining justices are evenly divided, was alone in dissenting. He urged remand to the Court of Appeals for "examining the sufficiency of the evidence" in the first instance. Presumably, this would include Pentalpha's subjective belief, Pentalpha's deliberate steps to avoid knowing, and whether notice by the owner of the patent was placed on the copied fryer.

When the patent court uses the wrong standard, the case should be reversed and remanded for application of the correct standard. If application of the correct standard requires findings of additional facts, the motion for a new trial should be granted.

I believe that Justice Kennedy's dissent showed the wisest course to follow in order to have a district court decide, in the first instance, what evidence should be admitted, and a trier of fact, in the first instance, finding what the facts are. Those are tasks that should not be determined in the Supreme Court.

In my view, substantial justice was obtained by the majority decision. Buying a competitor's product and faithfully copying all of its important features, then undercutting the selling price of the genuine product, is conduct not to be condoned (but it is not a crime). The copier did not have to do research and development or any of the other "exertions" that are rewarded by the grant of a patent (*Grant v. Raymond*, 31 U.S. 218 (1832)).

At the very least, copying a superior product in order to reap where one has not sown, is not fair competition. If the originator of the superior product intentionally dedicated the invention to the public domain, there may be no unfair competition claim. But outright theft is not in the best interests of society.

It is curious that the same verb "to induce" is used in §271(b) and in the rebirth (after a hiatus of fifteen years) of Supreme Court interest in patent cases: *Graham v. John Deere Co.* (The patent monopoly "was a reward, an inducement, to bring forth new knowledge" (383 U.S., 9)). The difference is that in §271(b) inducing is an act of wrong-doing, and the grant of a patent is a reward for the patentee.

A patent is a right to exclude for a limited time, and the Court honored that exclusive right in *Global-Tech*. The copier knew that he had copied the original. Whether the copier knew of the patent is not relevant to the issue of whether the exclusive right was violated. Willful copying should not be forgiven simply because the copier did not know the patent number.

The *Global-Tech* case, when it reached the Supreme Court, turned on the question of the "state-of-mind element" of a claim under 35 U.S.C. §271(b) (according to "The Question Presented" in docket no. 10-6). The Court found the Federal Circuit test lacking in proving willful inducement of infringement.

Other regional courts of appeal had "articulate[d] the doctrine of willful blindness" as having "two basic requirements: (1) the defendant must subjectively believe that there is a high probability that a fact exists and (2) the defendant must take deliberate actions to avoid learning of that fact" (*Global-Tech* slip op. at 13, citing criminal law authorities).

"The test applied by the Federal Circuit in this case departs from the proper willful blindness standard [of criminal law] in two important respects. First, it permits a finding of knowledge when there is merely a 'known risk' that the induced acts are infringing. Second, in demanding only 'deliberate indifference' to that risk, the Federal Circuit's test does not require active efforts by an inducer to avoid knowing about the infringing nature of the activities" (*id.*, 14).

As we have seen time and again, the mere fact that the Supreme Court opinion ends with the word "affirmed," does not mean the Federal Circuit's reasoning in a case has not been rejected by the Court. Here, as in so many other affirmances, the Federal Circuit may have reached the right result for the wrong reasons.

If the patent code is to have an amendment taken from the penal code to define who "actively induces infringement" of a patent, the legislation should come from Congress, not from the Supreme Court. Infringement is not a crime, so lifting the criminal law term "willful blindness" and moving it to patent law without the benefit of hearings and studies by the political branches of government seems unwise.

We learned at the end of the 2010 term that "clear and convincing evidence" is required to overcome the presumption of validity (*Microsoft v. i4i*, see chapter 13). Criminal law requires an even higher standard of proof–"beyond a reasonable doubt." Should we mix up criminal law and patent law doctrines?

Moreover, Congress has already legislated on the proper notice a patent owner must provide to the public. "Letters patent" means the patents are open for inspection.

The marking statute requires more than just being open for inspection. Since 1861, failure to mark put a limit on the collection of damages.

The district court and the Federal Circuit in *Global-Tech* aired the issue of whether the patentee properly marked the deep fryers with the patent number as required by 35 U.S.C. §287(a). But the Supreme Court ignored the marking statute and instead applied a criminal law doctrine regarding the conduct of the defendant, not the patent owner who had a duty to mark.

Not only did the patentee in *Global-Tech* collect damages before the suit was filed, but it was awarded enhanced damages as well. There was no penalty for not marking.

The copier willfully copied the original and attempted to reap where he has not sown. Surely a failure to mark a fryer sold in Hong Kong with a U.S. patent number should not forgive outright theft of the invention.

CHAPTER 10

# 35 U.S.C. §271(e)(1) INFRINGEMENT OF DRUG AND MEDICAL DEVICE PATENTS

T he infringement statute of 1952 was fine for addressing direct infringement, inducing infringement, and contributory infringement, but complications arising from acts of Congress that allowed for patent extensions required attention to these new statutes.

The problem was that Congress decided that a patent could not be granted for products requiring approval by the federal Food and Drug Administration (FDA) until the approval was final. The drug industry flourished after passage of the 1952 patent act, but the grant of a patent did not allow the patent owner to sue for patent infringement merely because competitors could not market copies of the patented drugs without FDA approval.

For example, if it took two years from filing an application until a patent was granted, and it took five years for the FDA to approve marketing a new drug after testing for safety and efficacy, then the life of the patent was in reality only fourteen years (seventeen year normal life less three more years of delay for FDA approval). Because it takes longer than fourteen years for a new drug to become obsolete, drug makers felt they were at a disadvantage, compared to all other patentees who enjoyed seventeen years of patent life.

There were two obvious solutions to the problem facing drug makers: increase FDA funding so that approval could be obtained in two years, as in approval of other kinds of patents, or delay granting the patents until FDA approval was obtained. Clearly, the wisest solution was to speed up FDA approval, so that all patents would expire seventeen years after patent grant. Delaying the patent grants would mean delaying patent expirations and the entry of the inventions into the public domain.

The whole purpose of the patent system is to encourage inventors to come forward with new knowledge that will enter the public domain for others to build upon at the end of the limited time during which the inventor had a right to exclude. This is called "promoting the progress of the useful arts" in the Constitution.

Congress, however, seldom follows the wisest course and instead follows the money. Investors had the money, not inventors. The Constitution authorizes Congress to grant a right to exclude others from using an invention for limited times. From the beginning of our nation, the investors who owned the indentures for servants and slaves had the money, and Congress overlooked the obligation to "secure to inventors" the exclusive right of a patent. Instead, those with the money (who could support congressional election and reelection campaigns) were allowed to appropriate the exclusive right under master-servant law.

Likewise, the investors wanted to extend the life of a patent to seventeen years from the beginning of marketing a drug, not the grant of a patent. Congress obliged, not just to oblige sponsors, but also to save all that money that would be needed to speed up drug approval. Speeding up drug approval might save lives and benefit society, but money comes first.

The problem is that extending the date of patent grant meant that the date of expiration had to be extended also. Not extending the expiration date would mean that investors in non-drug patents had a competitive advantage over investors in drug patents.

Another complication was that a thriving generic drug industry wanted to be able to sell copies of patented drugs as soon as the patents expired. Because it took time for FDA approval of copycat drugs, those investors wanted to be able to get FDA approval by starting the process before the patents expired.

Yet another complication was that investors in medical devices that also needed government approval before marketing did not want to be treated differently than were the drug companies. The investors in makers of pacemakers would not stand for less of a deal that a heart drug maker got.

The net result of all of the demands of these special interests was section 271(e), which delays entry of inventions into the public domain to the detriment to society. No one has calculated the costs to society of all of this special-interest legislation, as compared to beefing up FDA to approve drugs and medical devices faster. Sadly, that is how the sausage of legislation is made.

*Eli Lilly & Co. v. Medtronic, Inc.*, 496 U.S. 661 (1990).

This is the first of the two cases in this chapter, one involving the expiration of a medical device patent and the other involving the expiration of a drug patent. Lilly acquired a company that had two patents on an implantable cardiac defibrillator. The predecessor sued Medtronic for infringement of the patents. Medtronic claimed that its device was used in order to test and obtain approval from the FDA for selling its version of a patented product when the patents expired. Medtronic defended itself on the ground that it was allowed to prepare for expiration of the patent under 35 U.S.C. §271(e)(1), which covers both drugs and medical devices, at the end of the extended patent term.

The district court held that the section was limited to drugs, so the fact that the case involved a medical device was not a defense against the infringement claim. The case went to trial and the jury found one patent infringed, and the district court directed a verdict for Lilly on the second patent. The trial court entered an injunction against the sale of the Medtronic medical devices. Medtronic filed an appeal to the Federal Circuit.

The patent court disagreed with the district court's view that the infringement statute was limited to drugs and reversed. However, "because it is unclear that all of Medtronic's activities fall within the section 271(e)(1) exception, we leave it for the court on remand to decide" how to proceed (872 F.2d, 403).

The district court found that "a genuine issue of material fact exists as to whether Medtronic's use of its devices was 'solely for purposes reasonably related to submission of information' to the FDA" (872 F. 2d, 406). The Federal Circuit remanded the case to the district court to determine that fact issue.

Lilly petitioned for Supreme Court review. The Court granted the petition and wrestled with the language of §271(e)(1). Justice Scalia was the author of the *Lilly* majority opinion (as he was author of the earlier *Pioneer* decision in chapter 5) which had equally obscure language. The statutory section reads: "It shall not be an act of infringement to...use...within the United States...a patented invention...solely for uses reasonably related to the development and submission of information under a federal law which regulates the manufacture, use, or sale of drugs."

The term "patented invention" is not limited to drugs. But "federal law which regulates...use...of drugs" appears to be limited to drugs. Lilly contended that "federal law" related to regulating drugs. Medtronic contended that "patented invention" was the key term, which was not so limited. Justice Scalia resolved the dispute by finding (496 U.S. 661, 667): "The centrally important distinction in this legislation (from the standpoint of the commercial interests affected) is not between applications for drug approval and applications for device approval, but between patents relating to drugs and patents relating to devices."

The analysis in the Scalia opinion of arguments on both sides goes on for pages in the usual lawyerly style ("on the one hand," then "on the other hand"). Finally, "we conclude that we have before us a provision that somewhat more naturally reads as the Court of Appeals determined, but that is not plainly comprehensible on anyone's view" (872 F. 2d, 669). This reluctant acceptance of the patent court view would appear to be a plea for Congress to explain what it intended by the legislation, but Congress has not responded to that plea in recent decades.

While it counts as an affirmance of the patent court decision, it is clearly not enthusiastic.

What I found most striking about the *Lilly* case is that the Federal Circuit and the Supreme Court seemed to describe different case histories. The patent court said that Medtronic brought "an interlocutory appeal from a permanent injunction entered by" the district court (872 F. 2d, 403). "Interlocutory," according to *Black's Law Dictionary* (1951) means "Something intervening between the commencement and the end of a suit which decides some point or matter, but is not a final decision of the whole controversy."

The Supreme Court, however, summarized the district court proceeding as final: "Following a jury trial, the jury returned a verdict for petitioner [*Lilly*] on infringement of the first patent and the court directed a verdict for petitioner on infringement of the second patent. The court entered judgment for petitioner and issued a permanent injunction against infringement of both patents. On appeal, the Court of Appeals for the Federal Circuit reversed" (496 U.S. 664).

If the issue before the Federal Circuit was an interlocutory appeal regarding the meaning of §271(e)(1), as the Federal Circuit said, then it was appropriate to construe the statute and to remand the case to the district court for trial with the district court instructing the jury as to what the law is.

If the case had been tried and the jury had decided, as a matter of fact, that Medtronic had infringed, as the Supreme Court said, then the remand would have to be for a new trial with proper instructions on what the law is. It may be a fine point that makes no difference in the outcome, but the Seventh Amendment takes seriously the fact of infringement that has been tried before a jury.

The Federal Circuit seems less certain that patent infringement is a fact, or that deference must be paid to facts determined by the trier of fact.

*Merck KGaA v. Integra Lifesciences I, Ltd*, 545 U.S. 193 (2005)

This is the other §271(e)(1) case in this chapter, decided fifteen years after the first decision. Justice Scalia was author of the majority opinion in *Lilly*, and wrote for a unanimous Court here.

Integra owned five patents for RGD peptides, possibly useful as drugs for inhibiting angiogenesis, a condition in which existing blood vessels sprout new blood vessels. A crude oversimplification of the goal is "to shrink tumors."

Merck contracted with Scripps Research Institute and asked Dr. David Cheresh to conduct research into the use of RGD peptides provided by Merck as potential drug candidates. Tests of various candidates for efficacy, specificity, and toxicity were carried out to determine the peptide most promising for human testing. The RGD peptides were used as "positive controls" to measure efficacy as an inhibitor of angiogenesis.

Merck submitted its research findings to the FDA, and the National Cancer Institute agreed to sponsor clinical trials. Integra sued Merck and Scripps for patent infringement for using the patented RGD peptides in experiments related to angiogenesis. Merck claimed that its use of RGD peptides fell within the §271(e)(1) safe harbor.

At trial, the jury found that Merck, Dr. Cheresh and Scripps infringed the patents, as a matter of fact, and that Merck had failed to prove that the activities were protected by §271(e)(1). In post-trial motions, the district court dismissed the suit against Dr. Cheresh and Scripps, but affirmed the fifteen million dollar damage award against Merck because "any connection between the infringing Scripps experiments and FDA review was insufficiently direct to qualify for the §271(e)(1) exemption" (201).

On appeal, the Federal Circuit panel majority affirmed the denial of judgment as a matter of law because "the Scripps work sponsored by Merck was not clinical testing to supply information to the FDA, but only general biomedical research to identify new pharmaceutical compounds" (331 F. 3d, 866). The majority of the Federal Circuit panel reversed the damage award and remanded for further proceedings. On remand, the damage award was reduced from $15 million to $6.375 million.

The Supreme Court granted Merck's petition for certiorari and reversed. Citing its earlier *Lilly* decision, the Court held that the §271(e)(1) exemption "extends to *all* uses of patented inventions that are reasonably related to the development of *any* information under the" Federal Food, Drug, and Cosmetic Act. "This necessarily includes preclinical studies of patented compounds that are appropriate for submission to the FDA in the regulatory process, There is simply no room in the statute for excluding certain information from the exemption on the basis of the phase of research in which it is developed or the particular submission in which it could be included" (202).

The pro-patent patent court held that the "Scripps-Merck experiments did not supply information for submission to the [FDA], but instead identified the best candidate to subject to future testing under the FDA processes" (331 F. 3d, 865).

The pro-competition Supreme Court conceded that "basic scientific research on a particular compound, performed without the intent to develop a particular drug or a reasonable belief that the compound will cause the sort of physiological effect the researchers intend to induce, is surely not 'reasonably related to the development and submission of information' to the FDA. It does not follow from this, however, that §271(e)(1)'s exemption from infringement categorically excludes either (1) experimentation on drugs that are not ultimately the subject of an FDA submission or (2) use of patented compounds on experiments that are not ultimately submitted to the FDA. Under certain conditions, we think the exemption is sufficiently broad to protect the use of patented compounds in both situations" (206).

The Court cited *Lilly* again for the proposition that the exemption from infringement extends to "*all* uses of patented compounds 'reasonably related' to the process of developing information for submission under *any* federal law regulating the manufacture, use, or distribution of drugs" (*id.*, the Court's italics).

It quoted the government's *amicus curiae* brief, which states "that the use of patented compounds in preclinical studies is protected under §271(e)(1) as long as there is a reasonable basis for believing that the experiments will produce 'the types of information that are relevant to an IND or NDA" (id., 208).

It vacated the judgment of the patent court and remanded for further proceedings related to the sufficiency of the evidence under a proper construction of §271(e)(1).

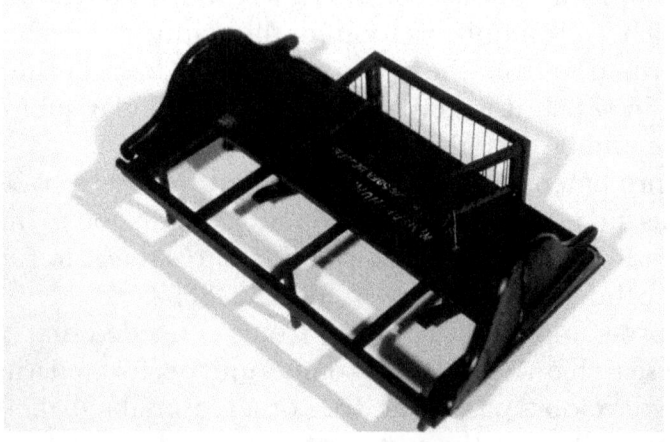

CHAPTER 11

# 35 U.S.C. §271(f) COMBINATIONS MADE OUTSIDE THE UNITED STATES

O ur study of the infringement statute ends with a look at §271(f), which addresses assembling a patented combination outside the United States "in a manner that would infringe the patent if such a combination occurred in the United States."

This section was added to chapter 28 of the patent code which discusses what constitutes infringement of a patent and was conceived to overrule the earlier Supreme Court decision in *Deepsouth Packing Co., Inc. v. Laitram Corp.*, 408 U.S. 518 (1972).

Laitram owned two patents for machinery that deveined shrimp, and sued Deepsouth for infringement of the patents. The district court found infringement and enjoined Deepsouth from making and selling machines to devein shrimp.

Deepsouth sought approval from the district court to make the parts for the machines in the United States, and sell the parts to foreign buyers who would assemble the parts and use the machines abroad. The district court found that the combination patents were not infringed when the components of the combinations were not assembled in the United States.

Laitram appealed to the Fifth Circuit, which reversed the district court's approval of the off-shore assembly, finding that the substantial manufacture of the parts of the machine in the United States was a direct infringement and should be enjoined.

The Supreme Court granted certiorari, conceding that Deepsouth was "barred from the American market by Laitram's patents," in order to consider the question of whether Deepsouth was "also foreclosed by the patent laws from exporting its deveiners, in less that fully assembled form, for use abroad?" (408 U.S., 519).

Justice White, for the 5–4 majority, reversed the Fifth Circuit decision. Ample precedent was cited for both of the key points: (1) combinations are not infringed if the complete combination is not used, and (2) patents have no extraterritorial reach.

"The 'combination, composed of all the parts mentioned in the specification, and arranged with reference to each other, and to no other parts of the [machine] in the manner therein described, is stated to be the improvement, and is the thing patented.' *Prouty v. Ruggles*, 16 pet. 336, 341 (1842)" (408 U.S., 520-21).

He continued: "The [Laitram] patents were warranted not by the novelty of their elements but by the novelty of the combination they represented. Invention was recognized because Laitram's assignors combined ordinary elements in an extraordinary way— a novel union of old means was designed to achieve a new end. Thus, for both inventions 'the whole in some way exceed[ed] the sum of its parts.' *Great A. & P. Tea Co. v. Supermarket Equipment Corp.*, 340 U.S. 147, 152 (1950)…A 'patent on a combination is a patent on the assembled or functioning whole, not on the separate parts.' *Mercoid Corp. v. Minneapolis-Honeywell Regulator Co,*, 320 U.S. 680, 684 (1944)" (408 U.S., 526).

Further: "Our patent system makes no claim to extraterritorial effect; 'these acts of Congress do not, and were not intended to, operate beyond the limits of the United States.' *Brown v. Duchesne*, 19 How., at 195" (408 U.S., 531).

The dissent by Justice Blackmun stated that the majority read the statutes too narrowly. "The result is unduly to reward the artful competitor who uses another's invention in its entirety and who seeks to profit thereby. [Deepsouth's literature] reveals the very iniquitous and evasive nature of Deepsouth's operations" (id. 532-33).

The dissent agreed with the Fifth Circuit opinion that the constitutional promotion of "the Progress of Science and the useful arts" is subverted by the majority decision that "would allow an infringer to set up shop next door to a patent-protected inventor whose product enjoys a substantial foreign market and deprive him of this valuable business" (534).

The majority had addressed this point of the dissenters on page 531: Congress intended that the patent owner should seek patents "in countries where his goods are being used. Respondent holds foreign patents; it does not adequately explain why it does not avail itself of them."

*Microsoft Corp .v. AT&T Corp.*, 550 U.S. 437 (2007)

Two important events occurred between 1972, when *Deepsouth* was decided and 2007, when *Microsoft v. AT&T* was decided (because Microsoft was a party in two of the 33 Supreme Court decision that are the core of this book, this case is referred to as "*AT&T*" to distinguish it from the other case, referred to as "*i4i*").

In 1982, the Federal Circuit was created, and given jurisdiction over all appeals of patent infringement cases decided in district courts, replacing the jurisdiction of regional courts of appeal.

In 1984, Congress amended the patent law provision on what constitutes infringement to include supplying "in or from the United States all or a substantial portion of the components of a patented invention, where such component parts are uncombined in whole or in part, in such manner as to actively induce the combination of such components outside of the United States in a manner that would infringe the patent if such combination occurred within the United States, shall be liable as an infringer" (§271(f)(1)).

The purpose of this amendment was to incorporate the concept of inducing infringement (from §271(b))–the assembling of components outside the United States to avoid liability for infringement, as happened in *Deepsouth*– into §271(f)(1). A similar addition was made in §271(f)(2) to incorporate the concept of contributory infringement from §271(c) into the infringement statute in cases in which the component is "especially made or especially adapted for use" in the invention.

The idea was to use these two concepts from the 1952 patent act to include what Deepsouth did with the Laitram inventions as acts of infringement under the statute. For Congress to overrule a Supreme Court decision is always messy and difficult. Congress tried instead to make an end-around to accomplish proof of infringement by inducing or contributing to infringement. Deepsouth sold the components of the combination along with instructions as to how to assemble the components to make the whole patented combination abroad, which would infringe the Laitram patents assembled in the United States. Congress intended §271(f)(1) to cover the *Deepsouth* fact pattern.

The issue in *AT&T* was whether §271(f)(1) or §271(f)(2) covered the Microsoft Windows fact pattern. Windows is an operating system for personal computers. Microsoft sells personal computers in the United States that run on the Windows operating system. In foreign countries, Microsoft sells Windows software separately to foreign computer makers for installation into their computers. The foreign computer makers then sell computers with the Windows operation system to the public.

Unlike Deepsouth, which made all of the components for deveining machines in a single package for the foreign buyer to assemble, Microsoft sends a master version of Windows, either on a disk or electronically via encrypted transmission. The foreign maker did not install anything made by Microsoft onto its computers. Rather, it installs copies of the software sent by Microsoft. Accordingly, in foreign countries, the buyer acquires a personal computer from one maker with a copy of software purchased from Microsoft, a different maker. No hardware components made by Microsoft are in the combination sold by the foreign manufacturer.

AT&T had a patent on digitally encoding and compressing recorded speech with a computer. Microsoft provided "Windows" software for use in computers all over the world. When Windows software is installed on a computer, the computer has the capacity to encode and compress recorded speech in the manner claimed in the patent.

AT&T sued Microsoft for infringement of its patent, asserting that Windows was a "component" supplied from the United States for installation in a "combination" that would induce infringement if done in the United States. This inducement of infringement was, AT&T claimed, a violation of §271(f)(1). The district court found that Microsoft was liable for infringement, and a divided Federal Circuit panel affirmed. The majority of the Federal Circuit found that software inscribed on a disk supplied from the United States is a component of AT&T's patented combination. The fact that the software in the combination is copied from the disk does not make the combination any less of a component when the software is combined with a computer. The combination is the same whether a disk is combined or a copy is combined. It accomplishes infringement under §271(f). In short, the pro-patent majority of the Federal Circuit panel found infringement.

The pro-competition Supreme Court reversed, holding that no "component" was supplied from the United States. The majority opinion by Justice Ginsburg did not agree with Microsoft's view that even if a disk were sent to the foreign computer maker and copied onto the computer, there would have been no infringement if the disk were removed after the software was loaded onto the computer.

Justice Alito, joined by Justices Thomas and Breyer, concurred in the majority opinion but indicated that if a physical disk has been sent by Microsoft and inserted into a foreign computer there would have been infringement, but the master disk was copied by the foreign company and nothing from Microsoft was combined with the foreign equipment.

Justice Stevens dissented, believing that indirect transmission from Microsoft to its customer, followed by the customer loading the software into the computer, was within Congress's intent in enacting §271(f).

No one appears to have raised the argument that the Paris Convention, a treaty that the United States agreed to many years ago, governs whether acts in one country can be an infringement of a patent in another country. Ordinarily, if acts that might be an infringement of a patent granted in one country are performed entirely in another country where no patent has been granted, the acts are not infringing because no patent covers the acts performed in that country. Congress simply lacks the power to legislate activities outside the United States.

The distinction between "abstract" and "concrete" is interesting, as Justice Ginsburg explained it, but I think a stronger argument is that assembling a machine entirely in a country where the machine or process is not patented cannot be an infringement of a United States patent. This is not a problem of interpreting an act of Congress; it is a problem of interpreting a Treaty signed by the United States regarding the infringement of a patent in another country.

Article 4bis of the Paris Convention relates to "Independence of Patents Obtained for the Same Invention in Different Countries." It follows that infringement of a patent requires that a patent must exist for the invention where the infringement takes place.

Microsoft did not make this argument to the Court. I did raise it in an *amicus curiae* brief I filed on behalf of an international federation I belong to, but it was ignored, presumably because neither Microsoft nor AT&T addressed the issue.

# CHAPTER 12

# 35 U.S.C. §281 REMEDIES FOR INFRINGEMENT

This section of the patent law is simple, yet profound: "A patentee shall have remedy by civil action for infringement of his patent." It is profound not because it is gender-specific (females may receive patents), but because it embodies the constitutional provision of "the exclusive right to [an inventor's] discover[y]."

Its importance in this book is that it differentiates the two patent courts. The first one, the CCPA, never had jurisdiction to address the issue of infringement of a patent during its existence from 1929 to 1982. That issue was, and is, decided in the first instance by United States district courts. From 1890 to 1982, appeals of infringement actions were to the regional United States Courts of Appeal across the country. While the CCPA was a Court of Appeal of the same rank as the regional courts, it never had jurisdiction over patent infringement disputes.

The change in the appellate process from appeals from district courts to twelve different courts of appeal staffed by generalist judges who were experts in the judicial appellate process to a single court of appeal staffed by patent specialists unfamiliar with the judicial process of dispute resolution was profound.

The change was made because Congress perceived that there were conflicts in the jurisprudence among regional courts of appeal in reviewing district court decisions in patent infringement cases on appeal. The judicial branch resolved conflicts between regional courts of appeal by petition to the Supreme Court (without limitation on the subject matter being appealed).

The judicial branch had addressed conflicts between regional circuits in patent infringement decisions on appeal since 1890, when regional circuits were created as intermediate courts of appeal between the district courts and the Supreme Court. A conflict between regional circuit courts of appeal was a judicial problem to be addressed by the judicial branch of government.

However, the legislative branch, at the urging of the executive branch, sought to resolve the judicial problem of conflicts between two different courts of appeal by transferring jurisdiction over appeals of all district court decisions in patent infringement cases in the United States to a new court of appeals, the Federal Circuit. The new court was staffed by judges with limited or no experience resolving judicial disputes related to patent infringement cases.

In the fifty-three years that the CCPA existed, only two of its judges had ever had experience in trying cases: Judge Almond was a state court trial judge, and Judge Lane was a trial judge at the US Court of Federal Claims). Both were deceased by 1982, when the Federal Circuit was created.

In retrospect, it was unwise for the legislative branch to intrude upon the judicial branch's procedure for resolving conflicts among regional circuit courts. It was equally unwise to create a specialist patent court inexperienced in judicial procedures in resolving patent infringement disputes.

The fact that most appeals from the Federal Circuit to the Supreme Court are either overturned or criticized for poor reasoning attests to the unwise solution enacted by the executive and legislative branches. This book shows that two-thirds of the patent courts' decisions have been overturned by the Supreme Court. Of the rest, many find fault with the reasoning of the patent court's view of its "own law."

"Remedies for infringement," the topic of this chapter, is an issue of fact, and whether the remedy is warranted is to be determined by the trier of fact. There have been no Supreme Court decisions interpreting §281 specifically, but every patent infringement suit involves the remedy of a civil action, so in that sense most patent court decisions since 1982 have involved that remedy.

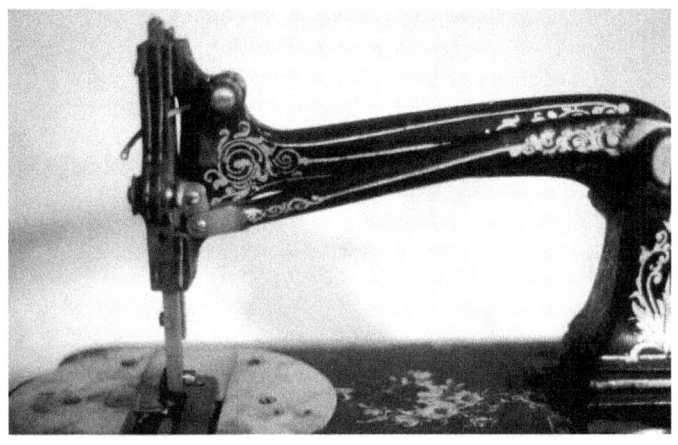

# CHAPTER 13

# 35 U.S.C. §282 PRESUMPTION OF VALIDITY

*Microsoft Corp. v. i4i Ltd Partnership*, 10-290

This is the last of the three patent cases decided in the 2010 term. All of the 2010 term reviews were affirmances of the Federal Circuit's decisions, which is a record. Because Microsoft was the petitioner in an earlier case (against AT&T), I shall refer to this case by the respondent's name, i4i.

I believe that the Court made a mistake when it stated that its opinion in *Radio Corp. of America v. Radio Engineering Laboratories*, 293 U.S. 1 (1934) controlled the outcome of the *i4i* case. It did not, because the 1934 case held that there was no bright-line test to overcome the presumption of validity. Rather, the standard of proof required to overcome the presumption depended upon whether the Patent Office resolved an issue within its expertise.

*Radio Corp.* was an interference proceeding among four different patent applicants. The Patent Office weighed the evidence presented by each one of the four claimants, and decided that Lee

De Forest (the last one of the four to file a patent application) was in fact the first inventor.

As the Court said, "there were four claimants to priority of title. All four, acting independently, had made the same or nearly the same discovery at times not widely separate. The prize of an exclusive patent falls to the one who had the fortune to be first.... The others gain nothing for their toil and talents....Langmuir filed an application for patent October 29, 1913. Armstrong filed an application on October 29, 1913....Meissner filed an application on March 16, 1914. De Forest filed an application on March 20, 1914." ( 3).

Under the first-to-file regime that became US law in legislation enacted in 2011, De Forest would lose as the last to file a patent application. However, the law was different in 1934 when *Radio Corp.* was decided. De Forest was able to fix "the date of his invention [as] August 6, 1912, the earliest date of all, [which made] him the first inventor."

The Patent Office found, as a matter of fact, that De Forest was the first inventor and was therefore granted the patent. The other three received no patent.

In contrast, *i4i* was a patent infringement case, not an interference proceeding. The Patent and Trademark Office did not decide whether the same invention was publicly disclosed in Defendant's S4 system and in the patent. Microsoft sought to prove that i4i had sold the invention of the patent in suit when it sold the S4 system more than a year before the filing of a patent application. The PTO never considered when the S4 system was invented. The inventors of S4 had no duty to reveal to the PTO when it first sold the S4 system. The issue to be determined by the examiner was whether the S4 system was patentable, not which one of four patent applicants was first, the issue before the De Forest patent interference tribunal.

Microsoft was not a party to the *ex parte* proceeding of the i4i patent application in the PTO. The inventors in the *ex parte* proceeding in the PTO were the same as the creators of the S4 system. They never disclosed S4 to the PTO, although they were required to do so under 37 C.F.R. §1.56(a): "Duty to disclose information material to patentability." The PTO was unable to decide whether S4 was the same invention as claimed in the patent application because it never knew about the prior work of the inventors.

It was undisputed in the *i4i* case that the inventors had sold the S4 system more than a year before filing a patent application. The presumption of validity did not extend to S4 simply because it was not raised in the examination process and the PTO could not apply its expertise in considering S4.

This is a fundamental difference between the *Microsoft v. i4i* patent infringement case and the *Radio Corp.* patent interference case. The interference case did not decide whether there was infringement, so it could not determine the 2012 *i4i* case. There was no doubt in *Radio Corp.* that the same invention was made by four different rival claimants. The Patent Office made the presumptively valid decision that De Forest was first. In *i4i*, the PTO never decided whether S4 was or was not first. There was no PTO decision regarding priority.

The Court was simply mistaken on page 2 of the *i4i* slip opinion: "The same factual questions underlying the PTO's original examination of a patent application will also bear on an invalidity defense in an infringement action." The original examination of the patent application did not decide the factual question whether S4 was the same invention as in the patent application. Nor was the issue of priority of S4 the same factual question in the PTO and in the infringement litigation.

The solicitor general was asked to file an amicus brief giving its view of the question. The government did so, and the Supreme Court adopted much of the solicitor general's brief which supported the respondent's position on the question presented. The government argued that *Radio Corp.* decided that clear and convincing evidence was essential to overcome the presumption of a patent's validity.

What *Radio Corp.* decided was that "the presumption of the validity of the patent is such that the *defense of invention by another* must be established by the clearest proof—perhaps beyond reasonable doubt" (293 U.S., 8, quoting *Austin Machinery Co. v. Buckeye Traction Ditcher Co.*, 13 F. 2d 697, 700 (6th Cir. 1926), italics added). The *i4i* case did not present the defense of invention by another. The district court found that Vulpe and Owens invented both S4 and the patented invention. There was no "other" inventor, as in the De Forest contest.

The Court in *Radio Corp.* pointed out that the *Austin Machinery* case, in context, was "not defining a standard in terms of scientific accuracy or literal precision, but [was] offering counsel and suggestion to guide the course of judgment....The common core of thought and truth [is] that one otherwise an infringer who assails the validity of a patent fair upon its face bears a heavy burden of persuasion, and fails unless his evidence has more than a dubious preponderance."

In other words, the burden of persuasion is not "beyond reasonable doubt," nor is it a "dubious preponderance." There is no bright-line test objectively applied as a matter of law. Rather, it is what the trier of fact finds persuasive, not what the judge believes is persuasive and certainly not what the Supreme Court believes the facts to be.

*Morgan v. Daniels*, 153 U.S. 120, 123 (1894) is quoted in *Radio Corp.* at 293 U.S. 6: "where the question decided in the patent office is one *between contesting parties as to priority of invention*, the decision there made must be accepted as controlling upon that question of fact in any subsequent suit *between the same parties*, unless the contrary is established by testimony which in character and amount carries thorough conviction" (italics added). Counsel for i4i and the solicitor general knew that Microsoft was not a party to the PTO decision and that the PTO decision to grant the *ex parte* patent application was not related to an interference that determined priority of invention.

The true message of *Radio Corp.* is that the fact the trier of fact's determination is entitled to deference unless clearly erroneous. In *Radio Corp.*, the trier of fact was the Patent Office. In i4i, the jury was the trier of fact, but the jury was never asked whether S4 did or did not contain the Vulpe and Owens invention. Instead, the jury was asked whether Microsoft proved by clear and convincing evidence that the patent was invalid, a question far different from whether Vulpe and Owens' testimony was credible.

There was a credibility issue in *Radio Corp.*, unlike *i4i*. The rival claimants made much of De Forest's "failure to perfect his invention or to apply promptly for a patent, the delay being extraordinary, it is argued, if a conception so important in its possibilities was present in [De Forest's] mind" (293 U.S., 13–14).

The Court addresses the responses to these arguments in *Radio Corp.*, which concluded that there was no clear error in the Patent Office decision, so deference to the trier of fact was given. In *i4i*, the PTO made no assessment of the credibility of the inventors as to what was disclosed in S4 because the inventors failed to disclose their prior work. The PTO never judged the credibility of the i4i inventors, as it had in *Radio Corp.* There is no live testimony in an interference, but the PTO may determine the credibility of an inventor's written testimony. Without the "body language" of live testimony; the power of cross-examination before the trier of fact; and the solemnity of a trial setting; it is much more difficult to assess the truth in PTO proceedings.

The solicitor general's brief acknowledged that *Radio Corp.* was an interference, not a patent infringement case. But it argued that deference to the PTO decision to grant a patent should be accorded for two reasons. First, the law is clear that an inventor and the drafter of the patent application have a duty to disclose to the PTO any information material to patentability. But S4 was not disclosed to the PTO, so the first reason was not present because material facts were not disclosed to the PTO. If S4 did indeed use the patented invention, the patent would be invalid under 35 U.S. §102(b), as Microsoft argued. The trial court posed the question to the jury whether Microsoft proved by clear and convincing evidence that the patent was anticipated. That question fails to address whether the jury believed the testimony of the inventors that S4 did not incorporate the patented invention.

The unanimous opinion of the Federal Circuit panel was that inventor Vulpe was "impeached" when he denied that S4 used the invention. Vulpe had written that the patented invention had its beginning in S4. The credibility of witnesses is a jury determination, not a court of appeals determination. It was inconsistent for the Federal Circuit to hold that the witness was impeached and at the same time affirm the jury damage award based upon that impeached testimony. The Federal Circuit should have remanded for the credibility issue to be put to a jury.

Either S4 did or did not use the patented invention. It is a fact for a trier of fact to decide.

The second argument advanced by the solicitor general for deferring to the PTO is that Congress has instituted reexamination proceedings that permit the PTO to decide validity issues in adversarial controversies. As an alternative to expensive patent infringement litigation in district court, PTO may determine the validity of an issued patent. Before the reexamination statute was enacted, the only *inter partes* disputes that could be determined were interferences, such as those in *Radio Corp.* Now one can challenge an issued patent in proceedings before the PTO.

The argument fails here, as it does in many patent infringement suits, because the reexamination statute is too narrow–35 U.S.C. §301 applies only to "prior art consisting of patents and printed publications." Microsoft could not possibly have initiated a reexamination proceeding because S4 was not disclosed in a "patent or a printed publication," as the statute requires. The software used in S4 probably was never published. It may have existed as a confidential writing, but the inventors testified that it had been destroyed, and that they could not recall whether it performed the same functions as the patented invention.

The Supreme Court did not adopt either the duty-to-disclose argument or the reexamination argument made by the solicitor general. Instead, it relied primarily upon the fact that "PTO examiners must make various factual determinations—for instance, the state of the prior art in the field and the nature of the advancement embodied in the invention," citing *Dickenson v. Zurko*, 527 U.S. 150, 153 (1999).

The examiner in the *i4i* application made no fact determination regarding S4 because i4i failed to disclose S4, in violation of its duty to disclose. Nor could the examiner determine the nature of the advancement of the invention of the application over S4. S4 was not before either the PTO expert or an expert at trial testifying for either the plaintiff or the defendant. S4 simply did not exist as a fact proven either at trial or in the PTO examination.

The Court heavily relied upon the dictum of Judge Rich in *American Hoist v. Sowa*, 725 F. 2d 1350, 1360 (Fed Cir. 1984) that "§282 creates a presumption that a patent is valid and imposes the burden of proving invalidity on the attacker." This much is correct and statutory. What is not correct and in keeping with the statute is the dictum that the "burden is constant and never changes and is to convince the court of invalidity by clear evidence."

The added sentence is wrong in two respects. First, the court does not weigh the evidence to determine facts; the trier of fact does. While obviousness is an issue of law, it is dependent on fact determinations (*Graham v. John Deere Co.*). Either S4 did or did not publicly reveal the invention more than a year before the patent application was filed. That issue has nothing to do with obviousness and everything to do with fact. It is therefore not for the court to decide unless it is sitting without a jury or with an advisory jury.

Second, the burden varies depending upon the evidence, as *Radio Corp.* teaches. It is not "constant and never changes." Those words were not included in the statute passed by Congress. They were the words of the author of §282, written thirty-two years after the statute was enacted. They are the words of a pro-patent advocate who wished they had been written into the statute. The advocate loved bright-line tests like "constant and never chang[ing]" during his more than four decades on the patent court benches.

Judge Rich was my hero and mentor, but bright-line tests do not make good law. *Radio Corp.* did not state that the presumption of validity was "constant and never changes." After citing a case that suggested that proof that was "perhaps beyond a reasonable doubt" might be a suitable test, the Supreme Court said in *Radio Corp.* that the "context suggests that, in these and like phrases, the courts were not defining a standard in terms of scientific accuracy or literal precision, but were offering counsel and suggestion to guide the course of judgment. Through all the verbal variances, however,...one otherwise an infringer who assails the validity of a patent fair upon its face bears a heavy burden of persuasion, and fails unless his evidence has more than a dubious preponderance" (8).

Clearly, there is no bright-line test. "Verbal variances" are allowed, and "constant and never changes" does not allow verbal variances. The standard of proof required is somewhere between 'perhaps beyond reasonable doubt" (*Austin Machinery*) and "more than a dubious preponderance." The Court in *i4i* quoted the "dubious preponderance" language (7), but not in the context of the paragraph in which it appears. Both "verbal variances"–"perhaps beyond reasonable doubt" and "dubious preponderance"– have the common concept of doubt, and do not express bright-line tests. The Federal Circuit in *American Hoist* said that the burden on one challenging the validity of a patent is to produce "clear and convincing" evidence, and the burden is "constant and never changes." The Supreme Court said, "In the nearly thirty years since *American Hoist*, the Federal Circuit has never wavered in this interpretation of §282" ( 3).

This unwavering definition of the term "presumption of validity" in the statute brings to mind the debate between Alice and Humpty Dumpty in Lewis Carroll's *Through the Looking-Glass*, chapter 6:

"There's glory for you!" "I don't know what you mean by 'glory.'" "I meant, 'there's a nice knock-down argument for you.'" "But 'glory' doesn't mean 'a nice knock-down argument,'" Alice objected. "When *I* use a word," Humpty Dumpty said in a rather scornful tone, "it means just what I choose it to mean, neither more nor less."

The Federal Circuit chooses to interpret "presumed valid" to mean that overcoming it requires "clear and convincing evidence" that is "constant and never changes," neither more nor less.

Bright-line tests have always been the choice of the patent courts, but in recent years the Supreme Court has rejected them. In *Bilski v. Kappos*, 129 S. Ct. 2735 (2010), the bright-line test for patentable subject matter was rejected. In *Quanta Computer v. LG Electronics*, 553 U.S. 617 (2008), the bright-line test for exhaustion by sale was rejected. In *KSR v. Teleflex*, 550 U.S. 398 (2007), the bright-line test for obviousness was rejected. In *eBay Inc. v. MercExchange, LLC*, 547 U.S. 388 (2006), the bright-line test for an injunction in cases in which a patent is valid and infringed was rejected. In *Festo Corp. v. Shoketsu Kinzoku Kogyo Kabushiki Co.*, 535 U.S. 722 (2002), a bright-line test for prosecution history estoppel was rejected.

The bright-line test of "clear and convincing" or "constant and never changes" is not supported by the 1934 *Radio Corp.* precedent or the post-2000 precedents. It is only supported by Humpty Dumpty.

Accordingly, the case before the Court in *i4i* was a garden variety-patent infringement case (even though the "parties collectively spent nearly $30 million" in the trial court (670 F. Supp. 2d, 604). It had nothing to do with an interference proceeding to determine priority among rival claimants. It therefore must "be sustained by a mere preponderance of evidence."

The "clear and convincing evidence" rule applies only to adversarial proceedings in interferences assigned to the executive branch, which is not this case. This Court's precedents since 1894 are consistent with this distinction.

*Morgan v. Daniels*, 153 U.S. 120 (1894) said "Where the question decided in the patent office is one between contesting parties as to priority of invention, the decision here must be accepted as controlling upon that question of fact in any subsequent suit between the same parties, unless the contrary is established by testimony which in character and amount carries thorough conviction."

In *i4i*, the Patent Office was not a party to either S4 or to the patent infringement case. It decided no issue between contesting parties. Microsoft was not a party in any Patent Office proceeding. Vulpe and Owens were the *same parties* in both S4 and the patented invention, not contesting parties.

The distinction between the mere issuance of a patent in an *ex parte* examination and a patent interference adversarial proceeding went unnoticed in the case of *Williams Co, v. United Shoe Machinery Corp.*, 316 U.S. 364 (1942). *Williams* was a patent infringement case, not a patent interference between two rival claimants of the same invention.

United Shoe had a patent for improvements in automatic heel lasting machines used in making shoes. The district court found the patent valid and infringed. The defendant bought exact copies of the patented machines and did not dispute the findings that the patent was infringed if it was valid. Williams claimed that the patent was invalid in view of two Supreme Court decisions barring extensions of the patent monopoly. The court of appeals affirmed.

The defendant petitioned for certiorari on the ground that *Bassick Mfg. Co. v. Hollingshead*, 298 U.S. 415 (1936), and *Lincoln Engineering Co. v. Stewart-Warner Corp.*, 303 U.S. 545 (1938) "forbid any such extension of the patent monopoly" (316 U.S., 368).

The Court affirmed, distinguishing the two cases relied upon by the petitioner as contributory infringement cases. "The present suit for infringement is not for the use of an automatic bed lasting and tacking machine as such. It is for the use in such a machine of improvements of certain features of the machine" (316 U.S., 370).

Justice Black, joined by Justices Douglas and Murphy, dissented. The patent does not "particularly point out and distinctly claim the part, improvement, or combination which he claims as his invention or discovery." The patent had 137 claims and twenty-five thousand words. "Remarks of Judge Learned Hand, made with respect to a patent much shorter than the one before us, are pertinent here: 'Such claims violate the very purpose of any claims at all, which is to define the forbidden field. In such a waste of abstract verbiage...it takes the scholastic ingenuity of a St. Thomas with the patience of a yogi to decipher their meaning, as they stand'" (316 U.S., 375).

On page 392, the dissent addressed the "*presumption of validity arising from issuance.*" It did not address the presumption arising from adversary interference proceedings for determining priority by the executive branch of government, as in the *Radio Corp.* case. Instead, the dissent quoted *Radio Corp.* for the test that a court must "give consideration to the rule that 'one otherwise an infringer who assails the validity of a patent fair upon its face bears a heavy burden of persuasion, and fails unless his evidence has more than a dubious preponderance .'"

Justice Black saw that as a proper measure of the presumption of validity, nothing more. His reasoning was that a "patent is a grant of exclusive privilege" that is "normally issued in a non-adversary proceeding" conducted in secret. The "patent examiner, unlike the court in an infringement suit, does not have the benefit of the researches of opposing counsel upon the state of the prior art." Even where the Patent Office conducts interference proceedings for the purpose of determining priority of invention, a contestant is not permitted to prove that a stranger to the proceedings was the first inventor.

Accordingly, the dissent would not apply a heightened burden of proof even in an adversarial proceeding in the Patent Office between rival claimants because no one represented the public interest in establishing that someone other than the rival claimants was the true and first inventor.

The Court in *i4i* never adopted the view of the dissent in *Williams*. But the Court never adopted the view that mere grant of a patent in an *ex parte* proceeding placed a heightened burden in the accused infringer of "clear and convincing evidence."

How, then, did the Federal Circuit apply the heightened burden when the patent at issue was not determined in an adversarial proceeding in the Patent Office? I suggest that it was error to apply the heightened standard. All of the twelve regional courts of appeal had rejected the heightened burden when the prior art in question was not before the patent examiner. Why did one court of appeals differ from all of the others?

One answer is that the Federal Circuit, in its very first decision, held that only CCPA and Court of Federal Claims decisions would be binding precedents on patent law (*South Corp v. United States*, 690 F. 2d 1368 (Fed. Cir. 1982)) . Regional circuit court precedents would be ignored in order to have the specialist court develop its own law without regard to nearly a century of regional court decisions in patent infringement cases.

The specialist patent court also ignored Supreme Court precedents, including those that deferred to adversarial proceedings in patent interferences. It chose to apply the heightened standard to *ex parte* grants of patents even though no precedent required it.

My guess is that Giles Rich, before he became judge, disagreed with the reluctance of the Court to extend the presumption of validity to *ex parte* grants of patents by the PTO, as suggested in the Black dissent in the 1942 *Williams* decision, The dissent attempted to raise the bar by placing the "burden of establishing invalidity of a patent or any claim thereof . . . on the party asserting such invalidity." This led to the higher standard applied by the Federal Circuit in the *i4i* case.

The language "constant and never changing," though not in section 282, was an added Rich fillip to enhance the pro-patent presumption of validity. This is pure speculation on my part, from observing Rich's animosity towards the "pro-competition" (if not "anti-patent") expressions of Justices Black and Douglas.

The Supreme Court, in *Microsoft v. i4i*, accepted the Rich view of a strong presumption of validity in its entirety. It mistakenly deferred to the PTO's quest for deference to PTO decisions by assuming that *Radio Corp.* was a patent infringement case, like *i4i*, when it was not. *Radio Corp.* was an interference proceeding; an adversarial proceeding, not an *ex parte* examination. The difference is between dispute resolution between adversaries and solicitation of a government grant.

# CHAPTER 14

# 35 U.S.C. §283 INJUNCTION

This chapter follows the chapter on the presumption of validity simply because §283 of the patent code follows §282. But both sections follow §281, which provides the remedy of civil action for infringement of a patent. The presumption of validity greatly strengthens the civil action remedy, as the *i4i* case illustrates. However, the Supreme Court decision that dominates this chapter greatly diminishes the civil action remedy.

I argued in the last chapter that the interpretation of the presumption of validity as being "constant and never changing" was the product of Giles Rich and was not necessarily the will of Congress. As Judge Rich, the senior patent court judge, the constant and never changing presumption became part of the patent courts' "own law" that was accepted by the Supreme Court in *i4i*.

In similar fashion, the patent courts developed as part of their "own law" a presumption that if infringement of a patent is found, the patent owner has the remedy of a permanent injunction. Unlike the presumption of validity, which is part of patent law exclusively, the presumption of an injunction bumps up against centuries of equity decisions here and in England applicable to much more than patent law.

The Federal Circuit's "own law"–that if infringed, a presumptively valid patent is usually enforced by a permanent injunction– did not fare as well in the Supreme Court as the presumption of validity did.

### *eBay, Inc. v. MercExchange LLC*, 547 U.S. 388 (2006)

This is the only Supreme Court decision that considers the remedy of permanent injunction for the infringement of a patent. MercExchange owned patents for online auction technology that was used by eBay. MercExchange sought to license its patents to eBay, but eBay refused.

MercExchange then sued eBay in district court for infringing the patents. eBay was found liable for infringement and damages were awarded. However, the district court refused to grant an injunction against future use of the MercExchange patents on the ground that the damage award was substantial and the remedy at law was adequate. Equitable relief is only to be granted where the remedy at law is not adequate. MercExchange showed that the remedy at law was adequate because it offered to license its patents to eBay. eBay argued that MercExchange did not practice the inventions of the patents it owned, so the remedy of an injunction against the use of inventions it did not use was a windfall that MercExchange was not entitled to. If a reasonable remedy was adequate before suit was filed, the remedy of thirty million dollars awarded at trial must have been adequate. If eBay continued to infringe in the future, then the remedy at law was still adequate and MercExchange could recover further money damages.

MercExchange appealed the district court's denial of an injunction to the Federal Circuit, which reversed the district court decision because the Federal Circuit rule was that when infringement has been found, a permanent injunction should ordinarily be granted to bar future infringement.

EBay petitioned the Supreme Court to review the Federal Circuit decision, which it believed was contrary to the four-factor test long established to determine whether a permanent injunction is appropriate. The Court granted the petition, overturned the Federal Circuit's rule in favor of the four-factor test, and criticized the district court holding that because the patentee did not use the patented inventions it was not entitled to an injunction.

The four factors that a plaintiff must establish to warrant a permanent injunction are: (1) that it has suffered an irreparable injury; (2) that the remedies available at law are inadequate to compensate for that injury; (3) that considering the balance of hardships between the plaintiff and defendant, a remedy in equity is warranted; and (4) that the public interest would not be disserved by a permanent injunction. The decision to grant or deny such relief is an act of equitable discretion by the district court, and is reviewable on appeal for abuse of discretion.

The Federal Circuit failed to consider these time-honored equitable principles, and the district court abused its discretion in denying the injunction simply because the plaintiff was not practicing the patented inventions.

The message I take from the *eBay* decision is that a patent court making up its "own law" as it goes along, disregarding the development of the judicial branch of government over centuries, is a mistake. In England, the rigidity of the judiciary led to a more flexible ecclesiastical court called the equity or chancery courts. Equity courts were a separate system from common-law courts, and addressed remedies other than judicial remedies, such as injunctions.

The United States adopted the principles of equity as well as the rules of law in a merged judicial system headed by one Supreme Court. The single judicial system applied both equitable principles as well as legal principles according to the two separate sets of rules. A judicial court could preside over a jury trial, for example, according to the rules of law. A jury trial is a judicial, not an equitable proceeding. But the judicial court had to follow the rules of equity in granting an injunction, because the common law did not provide for injunctions.

It was not until 1937 that Federal Rules of Civil Procedure provided for one form of action allowing both judicial and equitable remedies. While the first patent court (CCPA) was created in 1929 (before those Federal Rules were established), it was neither a judicial court nor an equitable court in the judicial system. Rather, the CCPA was a legislative court within the legislative branch of government until 1958, when Congress transformed it into a judicial court.

Even after 1958, the CCPA never dealt with equitable remedies like injunctions, because it had no jurisdiction over judicial proceedings. Its jurisdiction was limited to administrative matters appealed from agencies within the executive branch of government.

It was not until 1982, when the Federal Circuit was created, that the judges from the CCPA and the Court of Federal Claims (which heard administrative proceedings appealed from claims against the government) reviewed decisions by federal district judges. Overnight, the judges of the new patent court became responsible for reviewing every patent infringement case on appeal in the entire nation.

None of the judges in the new patent court had ever considered the judicial remedy of injunction on appeal (the government could not be enjoined; only the judicial remedy of damages could be awarded). It is not surprising that the difference between judicial courts and equitable courts, and the difference between law and equity, were not within the everyday fare of the judges of the new court.

It follows that the new court lacking that background, and perceiving itself as the new fountainhead of patent law, would develop its "own law" without regard to the difference between law and equity.

And that is precisely what happened. The judicial branch, consisting of district courts and courts of appeal, under the guidance of the Supreme Court, had developed a multi-factor test for granting injunctions in view of the merged rules of law and equity in the "one form of action" required by Rule 1 of the Federal Rules of Civil Procedure.

The new patent court, on the other hand, had a "pro-patent" orientation, grounded on the obviousness test in section 103, the presumption of validity under section 182, and what I call a "presumption on steroids," the "rule" that a patent held by the district court to be valid and infringed must be given the added protection of a permanent injunction against further infringement.

Whatever the reason was, the patent court revealed a serious lack of understanding of the difference between law and equity. Treating section 182 as a presumption that one found to have infringed should be enjoined from infringing in the future is improper judicial behavior.

The primary issue in *eBay* was the four equity factors to be considered in granting a permanent injunction, and on this the eight justices (Justice Samuel Alito did not participate) were united. But two concurring opinions revealed a division over when to grant an injunction.

Chief Justice Roberts wrote for himself, Justice Scalia and Justice Ginsberg, that courts have long issued injunctions in cases in which infringement has been found by applying the four factor test. Thus, the Federal Circuit reached the correct result, but relied upon its own interpretation rather than the four-factor test.

Justices Kennedy, Stevens, Souter and Breyer wrote in another concurring opinion that the district court's concern about non-practicing entities was worthy of comment. The issue they were concerned about was whether injunctive relief was appropriate when the patents related to "an industry...in which firms use patents not as a basis for producing and selling goods but, instead, primarily for obtaining licensing fees." Legal damages may be sufficient to compensate for infringement and an injunction may not serve the public interest (factor 4 in the four-part test).

It may be argued that four justices are concerned about "patent trolls" that use patents to squeeze exorbitant fees from infringers. One more vote would have permitted the Court to address the problem that had concerned the district court in *eBay*.

Reading the tea leaves in a concurrent opinion is a tenuous proposition at best, but there might be further inquiry into this development by the Court. The difference between law and equity might be surfaced in a "patent troll" case.

CHAPTER 15

# ADMINISTRATIVE PROCEDURE ACT, 5 U.S.C. §706(2)

W e depart from the patent code for consideration of whether the Administrative Procedure Act governs judicial review of findings of fact made by administrative agencies.

The Administrative Procedure Act (APA) was enacted in 1946 to provide standardized procedures for all federal administrative agencies. Before the APA, there was an array of different procedures that depended upon the nature of the agency. One of the oldest federal administrative agencies was the Patent Office. Since 1929, its decision on whether a patent should be granted to a patent applicant could be reviewed by appeal to the CCPA, a specialized federal court assigned jurisdiction over appeals of customs cases and patent cases from two different agencies, the Customs Bureau and the Patent Office. The CCPA was a legislative court of appeals that heard administrative appeals from these administrative agencies. Its judges did not have lifetime tenure as did judges in the judicial branch of government. In 1958, Congress made CCPA judges judicial judges with lifetime tenures.

Because the procedure in patent appeals was well established in 1946, the Patent Office and the CCPA paid little attention to the new APA. The Patent Office did not alter the Manual of Patent Examining Procedure in response to the APA, apparently believing its procedures were "grandfathered."

One peculiar feature of patent law was, and is, that a patent applicant dissatisfied with the decision of the Patent Office (now the Patent and Trademark Office) has two options for review. By far the most common option is to appeal to the CCPA (now the Federal Circuit). Since the 1952 patent act, the appellate path is defined in 35U.S.C. §144 for a review of "the record before the Patent and Trademark Office" by the patent court.

An alternative path is defined in §145: "by civil action against the Director in the United States District Court for the District of Columbia." That statute was first enacted when the Patent Office was in the District of Columbia. The jurisdiction of district courts and federal courts of appeal is geographic; the civil action must be filed in the district where the defendant is located. The statute, 28 U.S.C. §1391(e), provides that "a civil action in which a defendant is an officer or employee of the United States or any agency thereof acting in his official capacity...may...be brought in any judicial district in which (1) a defendant in the action resides."

The Patent and Trademark Office now resides in Alexandria, Virginia, so venue properly lies in the Eastern District of Virginia. The patent statute conflicted with the venue statute. Fortunately, section 9(a) of the recent America Invents Act has corrected section 145 to specify that the civil action must be filed in the Eastern District of Virginia instead of the District of Columbia, effective in 2011.

Correcting the venue problem does not address the more fundamental problem of having a choice between (1) appeal governed by the APA, and (2) appeal governed by the Federal Rules of Civil Procedure.

If the §144 route is followed, the Federal Circuit "shall," under 5 U.S.C. §706A(2) "hold unlawful and set aside...findings [by the agency] found to be...arbitrary, capricious, [or] an abuse of discretion, or unsupported by substantial evidence" (There is no provision for oral testimony in administrative proceedings).

If the §145 route is followed, the applicant for patent may file a civil action in district court (now in Virginia), and demand trial by jury instead of findings by administrative experts. The jury findings cannot be set aside on appeal to the Federal Circuit unless they are unsupported by substantial evidence. If no jury is demanded, findings by the district court "whether based on oral or other evidence, must not be set aside unless clearly erroneous and the reviewing court must give due regard to the trial court's opportunity to judge the witnesses' credibility" (Rule 52(a)(6)).

The strategic choice between the administrative path via APA and the judicial path via district court trial seems unnecessary and an opportunity to game the patent granting system, distorting the pursuit of truth and justice.

For example, because the patent applicant cannot depose and cross-examine a patent examiner to establish arbitrary or capricious decision-making by the examiner, and cannot ask the examiner about the evidence relied upon, many trial lawyers would shun the administrative route and seek a jury trial at which the inventor could tell his story of the inventive process and the greatness achieved by the invention. An expert could opine at trial about the importance of the invention and the weakness of the rejection of the application. The government would be hard-pressed to refute this evidence, because the ban on discovery of the examiner's rejection precludes the government from calling the examiner as a witness.

Juries respond emotionally to witnesses, sometimes to the point of not facing the truth (the O.J. Simpson trial for the death of his wife comes to mind). I am a great believer in the jury system because the collective wisdom of multiple people from different backgrounds, sworn to do their civic duty and uphold the law, stacks up better than a single person's subjective assessment of the facts at trial. But no human endeavor will always be perfect.

A jury in a civil action against the Director of the PTO, in these days of dissatisfaction with many of the activities of government, could well be impressed by a sincere, knowledgeable, articulate inventor, supported by one or more qualified, charming, persuasive experts and a thoroughly experienced jury trial lawyer, and might find, by a preponderance of the evidence, that the Director of the PTO erred.

In the real world, however, the §144 path is almost always followed, and the §145 path is rarely followed. Primarily, this is an economic decision. An appeal based on the record before the PTO in the Federal Circuit costs a tiny fraction of the cost of a jury trial with experts, *voir dire*, delays, and huge expenses from both a jury trial and a Federal Circuit appeal, make the choice an obvious one.

The only party who could afford to pursue the §145 path is one that would seek a judgment in the millions of dollars in a jury trial in a patent-friendly forum (see *i4i v. Microsoft* in chapter 13). The risk of an unjust result when the financial stakes are so high leads me to believe that it is a mistake to offer a choice between an administrative path and a judicial path. Society is better served by allowing the appeal from an administrative agency under §144 and not allowing a trial *de novo* in a district court under §145. Such a procedure is consistent with the APA and the judicial trial option is not consistent with the APA.

*Dickinson v. Zurko*, 527 U.S. 150 (1999)

The only Supreme Court review of a Federal Circuit decision under the Administrative Procedure Act was a reversal of the PTO decision rejecting a patent application by Zurko. All six of the CCPA cases reviewed by the Supreme Court were on petitions from the PTO. *Zurko* is the only Federal Circuit decision that the PTO has ever sought to overturn.

Mary Zurko invented a method of improving computer security and applied for a patent. The examiner held the method to be obvious to one having ordinary skill in the art. The Board of Patent Appeals and Interferences affirmed the examiner's decision. Zurko appealed to the Federal Circuit, where a panel held that the PTO decision must be reversed if it is "clearly erroneous" under Rule 52(a).

Three prior Federal Circuit cases were cited to show its reliance on the "clearly erroneous" test. In all three, the PTO had contended that a PTO decision of obviousness had to be affirmed unless it was found to be "arbitrary or capricious" under the APA. The Federal Circuit rejected the PTO argument, preferring its view that the PTO holding may be set aside if clearly erroneous.

Rule 52(a) would apply if the §145 path was followed and a civil action was filed. But the §145 path was not followed in any of the three cases; the administrative procedure of the §144 path was followed. The patent court's "own law," ignoring the APA and instead applying the "clear error" test of Rule 52(a), was clearly wrong.

Justice Breyer, for the six-justice majority, distinguished what it called "court/agency review" under the APA from "court/court review" in which a court of appeals reviews a district court decision under Rule 52(a). The Court analyzed eighty-nine patent court decisions and dozens of other precedents before concluding that the APA controls, and there should not be an exception for court/agency reviews of decisions denying the grant of a patent.

Among the extensive points analyzed by the Court is the §145 path compared to the §144 path discussed above, and the difference between interference proceedings in the Patent Office and the decision to grant or refuse a patent by the Patent Office, discussed in chapter 13 with many citations, such as *Morgan v. Daniels* common to both the *i4i* case and the *Zurko* case.

The majority found no reason to except patent grant cases from the APA coverage. The PTO is an administrative agency governed by the APA.

Chief Justice Rehnquist, joined by Justices Kennedy and Ginsburg, dissented on the ground that that "clearly erroneous" standard was "recognized by law" in 1946, which qualifies as an exception to the scope of the APA.

# CHAPTER 16

# FED. R. CIV. P. 50(a), JUDGMENT AS A MATTER OF LAW

W e now turn from constitutional and statutory enactments to Federal Rules of Civil Procedure promulgated by the judicial branch of government. The first rule addressed is Rule 50(a), for Judgment as a Matter of Law (JMOL).

Historically, when a trial court is satisfied that an issue raised in a jury trial is so clear that a reasonable jury would not have a sufficient evidentiary basis to rule in favor of a party, the opposing party can move for the trial court to direct the jury to enter a verdict in its favor on that issue.

The term "directed verdict," the original name of the motion, is somewhat misleading, because the jury decides fact issues and the court decides law issues. When the court grants a motion for directed verdict, it decides the issue as a matter of law, and the jury has no fact issue to decide. Telling the jury how it must rule on an issue in a verdict the jury did not reach as a result of its own deliberations serves no useful purpose, and may offend the jury.

Accordingly, in 1963, the rule was changed to more accurately state what it is: a motion for judgment as a matter of law. The judge decides the motion and no action is needed from the jury.

The historical term "directed verdict" was retained in the 1963 amendment to Rule 50 "in the interest of simplicity."

In the 1991amendment, the language "direction of verdict" was abandoned for, among other reasons, being misleading in describing the relationship between judge and jury. "The expressed standard [for granting of a motion for judgment as a matter of law] makes clear that action taken under the rule is a performance of the court's duty to assure enforcement of the controlling law and is not an intrusion on any responsibility for factual determinations conferred on the jury by the Seventh Amendment or any other provision of federal law."

The *Verdegaal Brothers* case before the Federal Circuit was a Rule 50 decision. It is discussed in detail in chapter 2, and will not be revisited here beyond noting that the district court denied the Rule 50 motion, meaning that the district court believed substantial evidence supported the jury's verdict that the defendant infringed, which is a question of fact. The district judge, who also heard the evidence, deferred to the jury decision on the fact issue. Instead of deferring to the fact finding by the jury that Union Oil infringed, which the district court accepted, the Federal Circuit substituted its view of the facts for that found by the jury and concurred in by the district court. The Supreme Court did not review the Federal Circuit's decision which violated Rule 50 "as a matter of law."

*Markman v. Westview Instruments, Inc.*, 517 U.S. 370 (1996)

A Rule 50 motion that *was* reviewed by the Supreme Court is the *Markman* case. Although the *decision* of the Federal Circuit was affirmed because the district court decision was given deference (unlike *Verdegaal*), the Federal Circuit's reasoning was found to be erroneous. The Federal Circuit has misinterpreted the Court's decision to affirm *Markman* for the last sixteen years, preferring to believe that the Court's conclusion that the Rule 50 motion was correctly decided meant that the Federal Circuit can determine what claims mean as a matter of law, and trial judges need not determine what evidence is admissible to prove what claims mean and juries need not decide what claims mean as a matter of fact. The Federal Circuit is simply wrong in its interpretation of *Markman*.

Markman invented a system for keeping track of garments passing through a dry cleaning plant. When a garment arrived at the plant, a label with a bar code was affixed to the garment. At each step in the dry cleaning process, a bar code reader indicated where the garment was located in the plant. Markman claimed his invention as a method of keeping track of inventory.

Westview made use of a bar code and a bar code reader to keep track of the cost of cleaning the garment in dollars and cents. Westview did not keep track of where the garment was in the plant, just what the cost quoted to the customer for cleaning the garment was from the beginning of the process to the end.

Markman's independent claim called for "a description of each of said articles" and a "means to maintain an inventory total." The Westview Instruments system had cost, but not a description of the garments. The Westview system did not show how many garments were in the plant.

This should be a message to claim drafters: do not recite superfluous add-ons in your main independent claim, because it makes it easy to avoid infringement of a claim full of extras that are not essential to the invention. Claiming too much in the independent claim doomed Markman's infringement case.

Markman sued Westview Instruments for patent infringement. Markman demanded a jury trial, which is often wise for a patent owner. Juries are more sensitive to perceiving who wears the white hat and who wears the black hat. The property owner is sometimes viewed more sympathetically than the accused infringer who is said to have "stolen" the invention.

Westview pointed out that it did not describe the garments on the bar code slip, and there was no record of the plant's inventory total on the bar code slip. The jury apparently did not sense that this excused the "wrong" of taking the bar code invention. The jury decided, as a matter of fact, that Westview Instruments had infringed.

Westview filed timely motions for judgment as a matter of law, alleging that there was no substantial evidence to support the finding of infringement because there was no description of the garments and no means to determine the total inventory of garments in the plant using Westview Instruments' system.

The district court granted the JMOL motion, holding that "inventory" meant garments, not dollar amounts.

Markman appealed to the Federal Circuit, claiming that the district court erred (1) in allowing the jury to interpret the claims, an issue exclusively for the court; and (2) in finding that "inventory" did include the bar code slips on each garment.

The Federal Circuit held that claim construction was a matter strictly for the district court to decide, not the jury. The majority opinion wanted the issue of judgment as a matter of law to be assigned to the trial judge under Rule 50. That was not because the Federal Circuit defers to decisions of district judges; it rarely does. We have seen, time and again, that the Federal Circuit goes out of its way to substitute its view of the meaning of claim terms for that of the district court.

Rather, the motivation for characterizing claim construction as an issue of law was part of a "turf war." Rule 52(a)(6) mandates that deference be paid to the district court findings unless they are "clearly erroneous." But that deference only applies to findings of fact, not conclusions of law. If the Federal Circuit can fairly declare claim interpretation to be a conclusion of law, and not a finding of fact, then on appeal the Federal Circuit can ignore the decision of the district court and substitute its view for that of the district court without deference.

The Federal Circuit zealously protects its "turf," claim construction, by claiming that patent claims are "devoid of facts" and may be reviewed *de novo* without deference to anything decided in the district court. This warped view of the omniscience of the Federal Circuit has never been tested in the Supreme Court, although many efforts have been made to have the Court review it.

The Federal Circuit maintains that it alone can interpret claims, without deference to any determinations made in district courts. In *Markman,* the Supreme Court did not correct the Federal Circuit's assertion that all things relating to claims rest on the Federal Circuit's turf, and that deference is not owed to those who receive the evidence, weigh witness credibility, and decide cases in the first instance.

The Supreme Court, apparently unaware that the Federal Circuit claims that its "turf" includes anything involving claims, pointed out that claims do indeed have facts. Unfortunately, the Court did not state that the Federal Circuit must defer to findings of fact by the district court unless clearly erroneous, as Rule 52 requires.

Instead, the Supreme Court decision stated that construing terms of art used in patent claims is a "mongrel practice" in a jury trial. Although the jury decides fact issues, the trial judge is better qualified to interpret documents. That includes the judge, not the jury, "construing a term of art [in a patent] after receiving evidence" from a qualified expert (517 U.S., 378).

It should have been clear, though left unsaid in the Supreme Court opinion, that the "mongrel practice" is limited to a proceeding in the trial court, and has nothing to do with appeals. That is, the trial judge, not the jury, construes terms of art. The "mongrel" is the offspring of the jury as one parent and the judge as the other parent.

Justice Souter, a former trial judge, elaborated on the meaning of "construing a term of art after receiving evidence" at trial. The Court, quoting *Bischoff v. Wethered*, 76 U.S. 812 (1870), stated that documents describing "mechanisms and complicated machinery, chemical compositions and other manufactured products, which have their existence *in pais*, outside of the documents themselves; and which are commonly described by terms of the art or mystery to which they respectively belong; and these descriptions and terms of art often require peculiar knowledge and education to understand them aright" (517 U.S., 385-86).

*Bischoff* acknowledged that the law requires that "the construction of written instruments is the province of the [trial] court alone" (id., 386) and "addressing the ultimate issue of mixed fact and law, it was for the [trial] court to 'lay down to the jury the law which should govern them,'" (*id.*, quoting *Tucker v. Spalding*, 80 U.S. 453 (1872)).

The Court moved on from its precedents to treatises on patent law. Walker's, *Patent Laws*, was quoted at 387: "As it cannot be expected, however, that judges will always possess the requisite knowledge of the meaning of terms of art or science used in letters patent, it often becomes necessary that they shall avail themselves of the light furnished by experts relevant to the significance of such words and phrases."

The other important treatise on patent law, Robinson's, *Law of Patents*, was quoted at 388: where "data necessary to the comprehension of the language of the patent are unknown to the trial judge, the testimony of witnesses may be received on these subjects."

It is important to note that the issue in the Supreme Court review of *Markman* was whether the trial judge or the jury considered the evidence. It is not an issue between the trial judge and the appellate judges. The trial judge receives the evidence and construes the patent, not the appellate judges.

It is appropriate at this point to stress that the trial judge makes determinations of the admissibility and relevance of evidence. The Federal Circuit is wrong in assuming that it can decide what expert testimony is to be admitted and how relevant that testimony is. The appellate court has limited power to reverse trial court rulings on admissibility.

"Whether a witness is shown to be qualified or not is a preliminary question to be determined in the first place by the court, and the rule is that if the court admits the testimony, then it is for the jury to decide whether any, and if any what, weight is to be given to the testimony. Cases arise where it is very much a matter of discretion with the court to receive or exclude the evidence; but the appellate court will not reverse in such a case, unless the ruling is manifestly erroneous" *Spring Co. v. Edgar*, 99 U.S. 645, 658 (1878).

Nearly a century after that decision limiting appellate court power to second-guess the trial judge, the Federal Rules of Evidence provided a modern codification, in Rules 702–06, of what *Spring*, the Walker treatise, and the Robinson treatise have stated:

Rule 702. If scientific, technical, or other specialized knowledge will assist the trier of fact to understand the evidence or to determine a fact in issue, a witness qualified as an expert by knowledge, skill, experience, training, or education, may testify thereto in the form of an opinion or otherwise.

Rule 703. Bases of Opinion Testimony by Experts.

Rule 704. Opinion in Ultimate Issue.

(a) Except [for issues regarding the mental state of a defendant in a criminal case], testimony in the form of an opinion or inference otherwise admissible is not objectionable because it embraces an ultimate issue to be decided by a trier of fact.

The Federal Circuit has ignored nearly all of the wisdom contained in the Supreme Court opinion in *Markman*. It steadfastly continues to believe that it alone can decide the meaning of claim terms, and district judges cannot. The only words that the Federal Circuit has relied upon in the Supreme Court's *Markman* decision are: we "affirm the decision of the Court of Appeals for the Federal Circuit." The teaching in *Markman* that deference must be paid to a trial court's admission of evidence is lost on the Federal Circuit. Affirmance of the Federal Circuit's *Markman* decision is perceived to be approval of the omniscience of the Federal Circuit as the sole determiner of the meaning of claim terms. That is not what the Supreme Court decision stands for.

Just six months after the *Markman* decision, the Federal Circuit decided *Vitronics Corp .v. Conceptronic, Inc.*, 90 F. 3d 1576 (Fed. Cir. 1996). It repeatedly cited its own decision in *Markman* as though the Supreme Court had not modified it. It flatly held that expert witness testimony should rarely be considered, because it is outside the "intrinsic evidence" of the patent application and prosecution history.

This view is contrary to the Court's decisions in *Markman*, *Spring* and *Bischoff*, to the Federal Rules of Civil Procedure, and to the teachings of Walker and Robinson. It is another example of the Federal Circuit making up its "own law" without regard to Court precedents and approved authorities.

*Vitronics* criticized the trial judge for considering "expert testimony and other extrinsic evidence, such as the paper written by a former Vitronics employee." The patent court substituted its view of the facts for that of the trier of fact. Deciding the admissibility of evidence, and the credibility of witnesses, whether experts or former employees, is a task reserved for the trial court, not assigned to the court of appeals.

The patent court has promulgated a rule that generally only intrinsic evidence will be considered on appeal. The Federal Circuit, contrary to the rules of all other courts, ignores expert testimony, inventor testimony, and other extrinsic evidence beyond the file wrapper. Though wrong, that is precisely the Federal Circuit's rule from *Vitronics* and its progeny.

The Federal Rules of Evidence determine the admissibility of evidence, not the rules of the patent court. "All relevant evidence is admissible, except as otherwise provided by the Constitution of the United States, by Act of Congress, by these rules, or by other rules prescribed by the Supreme Court" (including Rule of Evidence 402). "'Relevant evidence' means evidence having any tendency to make the existence of any fact that is of consequence to the determination of the action more probable or less probable than it would be without the evidence" (Rule 401).

There can be no doubt that Federal Circuit judges do not "always possess the requisite knowledge of the meaning of terms of art or science used in letters patent." Trial courts may become aware "of the light furnished by experts relevant to the significance of such words and phrases," as Walker put it. It follows that Federal Circuit judges ought not to second-guess the testimony of experts presented to the trier of fact under oath and subject to cross-examination.

The safeguards of the Rules of Evidence–qualifications of witnesses, that "the testimony is based on sufficient facts or data" (Rule 702(1), "the testimony is the product of reliable principles and methods" (Rule 702(2)), that "the witness has applied the principles and methods reliably to the facts of the case"–are the governing law, not the preconceived notions of appellate judges substituted for facts determined at trial. The judicial perspective of federal courts is contrary to the Federal Circuit's "own law."

Rule 702 gives the judicial perspective on "testimony of experts." Contrary to the Federal Circuit's "own law" that disregards expert testimony as biased, the 2000 amendments specify five other factors to safeguard against unreliable expert testimony. Rule 703 adds the safeguard that all bases of the opinion testimony must be disclosed for cross-examination. Rule 704 expressly allows witnesses to testify on issues "to be decided by the trier of fact." Rule 705 adds the safeguard that all facts underlying the opinion of an expert must be disclosed.

The Federal Circuit violates all of these rules by disregarding both expert opinions and inventor testimony. The only explanation I can imagine is that none of the Federal Circuit judges (before the recent appointment of Judge O'Malley) has been a trial judge, as was Justice Souter (author of *Markman* opinion), or has sufficient patent trial experience to have a thorough grasp of the Federal Rules of Evidence.

Federal Circuit judges are not qualified on every fact issue "by knowledge, skill, experience, training, or education" to know the truth of every fact at issue in a patent claim. It is just wrong to assert that patent claims are "devoid of facts" when the patent claims define the invention. How can a patented invention not have any facts?

It is for the district court to determine the admissibility of evidence, subject to the Federal Rules of Evidence. Whether expert testimony is to be admitted is for the trial judge to determine, not the court of appeals years later. The Federal Circuit is not omniscient. The Federal Rules of Civil Procedure and of Evidence leave the facts for trial courts to determine under the judicial perspective.

It is astonishing that the injustice of substituting the view of the Federal Circuit for findings by a trier of fact based on expert testimony, inventor testimony of what the invention is, and the adoption of the findings by the trial judge, has endured for sixteen years without review by the Supreme Court. The Federal Circuit thumbs its nose at everything the Court's *Markman* decision stands for. There is a need for viewing patent law from the perspective of the judicial branch, not from patent specialists that are unfamiliar with judicial rules.

*Vitronics* cannot be squared with the Supreme Court *Markman* decision, yet the Federal Circuit very frequently cites it. A little boy or someone else should declare that the *Vitronics* emperor has no clothes.

Returning to Rule 50 JMOL, after the digression of *Vitronics*, the Supreme Court again reviewed a Federal Circuit JMOL decision in:

> *Unitherm Food Systems, Inc. v. Swift-Eckrich, Inc.,* 546 U.S. 394
> (2006)

Swift-Eckrich (called "ConAgra," its d.b.a, in the Supreme Court opinion) owned a patent on a process of making precooked meat products. Unitherm had a similar process and feared being sued by ConAgra for infringement of the patent.

Unitherm sued ConAgra seeking a declaratory judgment that the patent was invalid and violated section 2 of the Sherman Act because it was obtained by fraud. The basis for both counts was that the invention was made six years before ConAgra filed its patent application.

The patent infringement count was severed from the anti-trust claim and decided in favor of Unitherm. The anti-trust case went to trial before a jury. After the close of evidence, ConAgra moved for a directed verdict under Rule 50(a), claiming insufficiency of evidence. The district court denied the motion and the jury returned a verdict for Unitherm.

ConAgra did not renew its Rule 50(a) motion for JMOL, and did not move for a new trial under Rule 59 on the issue of anti-trust liability. It did, however, seek a new trial on the issue of anti-trust damages.

ConAgra appealed to the Federal Circuit. Ordinarily, anti-trust cases are appealed to the regional court of appeals, but because a patent count was joined with the anti-trust count, the Federal

Circuit arguably had jurisdiction. The Federal Circuit sought to follow Tenth Circuit (the regional circuit) law, which said that "a party that has failed to file a post-verdict motion challenging the sufficiency of the evidence may nonetheless raise such claim on appeal, so long as that party filed a Rule 50(a) motion prior to submission of the case to the jury" (399).

The Federal Circuit did not address the Rule 50 (b) provision for renewing the motion after trial. It held that Unitherm had failed to prove its fraud on the Patent Office claim, vacated the verdict, and remanded for a new trial.

Unitherm petitioned the Supreme Court and certiorari was granted. The Court reversed, citing numerous Supreme Court precedents holding that a court of appeals lacks the power to order JMOL. The majority, per Justice Thomas, said those precedents "underscore our holding today—a party is not entitled to pursue a new trial on appeal unless that party makes an appropriate postverdict motion in the district court" (404).

Justice Stevens, joined by Justice Kennedy, said, "This is not a case where an appellate court is limited by an explicit statute or controlling rule" (407). The controlling statute is 28 U.S.C. §2106, according to the dissent, which allows an appellate court to "affirm, modify, vacate, set aside or reverse any judgment, decree or order," and may remand to "require such further proceedings to be had as may be just under the circumstances."

The dissent noted that Rule 50(b) "precludes the *district court* from directing a verdict" (408; italics in the original). An appellate court is not so limited.

The Federal Circuit probably should not have heard ConAgra's appeal of the anti-trust damages; because the patent issue had been resolved by the district court in construing the patent claims and finding them invalid. Only the *Walker Process* anti-trust issue remained on appeal, and the Tenth Circuit should have resolved it.

While the "fraud on the Patent Office" issue is of interest to the patent court, it should not have sought to decide the antitrust issue on appeal. The patent court purported to follow Tenth Circuit law, but the wiser course would have been to refer the matter to the Tenth Circuit, avoiding a reversal on a non-patent issue.

The result was a reversal of the patent court decision.

*Merck KGaA v. Integra Lifescience 1 Ltd.*, 545 U.S. 193 (2005)

This case involved a Rule 50 JMOL. It is thoroughly discussed in chapter 10 and shall not be repeated here.

*Verdegaal Brothers, Inc. v. Union Oil Co. of California*, 814 F.2d 628

This case did not reach the Supreme Court, but it involved a Rule 50 JMOL. It is thoroughly discussed in chapter 2, and need not be further studied.

*Eastman Kodak Co. v. Goodyear Tire & Rubber Co.*,
114 F. 3d 1547 (Fed. Cir. 1997)

The last Rule 50 JMOL case discussed here did not reach the Supreme Court, but it covered so many tangents that it failed to apply common sense to the core issue.

Kodak had a patent on a process for making polyethylene terephthalate (PET) granulate, a material used to make two liter soft drink bottles. The process involved crystallization and polycondensation. We think of ice being crystallized at zero degrees Celsius (or thirty-two degrees Fahrenheit). The patented process crystallized at 220 to 260 degrees Celsius, which was vastly different. The PET was then polymerized "at a temperature equivalent to, or lower than, the crystallization temperature."

Goodyear used a similar process, except that the polycondensation step took place at a temperature higher than the crystallization temperature. Kodak sued Goodyear for patent infringement and Goodyear sued Kodak for an antitrust violation in monopolizing the PET market.

The two cases were consolidated and went to trial before a jury. After the close of evidence, Goodyear moved for JMOL. The district court granted the Goodyear motion as to most of the charged infringement, but denied the motion as to two of the PET lines.

The district judge construed the claims under *Markman* to mean that the crystallization temperature "between 220° C. to 260° C." related to the "temperature of the heating medium, not the granulate temperature" (1553).

The jury found that those two lines infringed and awarded twelve million dollars in damages to Kodak. The renewed JMOL motion was denied. Goodyear appealed to the Federal Circuit.

The Federal Circuit, as it often does, looked to the district court's claim construction for clues to resolve the dispute. It analyzed (1) "claim language and any syntactic signs of its meaning" and "precepts of English grammar" (1553); (2) what the prosecution history "suggests" by the use of the term "utilizing" either medium temperature or polymer temperature (1554); (3) what is "relevant evidence" on the issue of medium temperature or polymer temperature; (4) who is "best situated to gauge the relevance" as between the trial court and the appellate court (1555); and (5) which of the competing experts is to be believed (1555–56).

All five of these "tea leaves" are beyond the powers of the court of appeals. All are within the duties of the trial participants, especially the trier of fact who determines credibility of witnesses, weighs the evidence, and finds the facts. The trial judge, not appellate judges, determine the meaning of the claim language (and grammar rules). The trial judge decides relevance and admissibility issues.

Appellate courts must defer to district courts, unless the ruling "is manifestly erroneous" *Spring v. Edgar*, 99 U.S. 645 (1879). Credibility of witnesses is exclusively a matter for the trier of fact, not the court of appeals.

The case reveals an effort by the Federal Circuit to second-guess the trial judge in claim construction, relevance and admissibility of evidence, and the jury in fact-finding and witness credibility. Common sense dictates that when water reaches the crystallization temperature it becomes ice. It is the temperature of the water, not the temperature of the ice-box (the "medium") that controls.

The dissent cut through all of the nonsense about tangential matters, and correctly noted that Goodyear's process did not have the "critical feature" of the Kodak patent of "holding the subsequent temperatures below the first crystallization step" (1556), and "Goodyear's polycondensation occurred at a temperature greater than either crystallization step" (1563). Water will not crystallize at a temperature above freezing.

The dispositive fact was clear and undisputed, as the dissent noted. The majority lost focus on a just resolution of the dispute by trying to read tea leaves. The appellate court must affirm a decision by a trial court unless the appellate court finds clear error. Simply because the court of appeals disagrees with the facts found by the trier of fact, without finding clear error, is not a sufficient reason to reverse, as we explore in the next chapter.

What I find most interesting about this case is that it is the perfect example of why the Federal Circuit belief that "claim construction is devoid of facts" is wrong. The term "crystallization temperature" is a fact. It is not a matter of law. Water freezes at zero degrees Celsius, as a matter of fact. The polycondensate in the patent claims crystalized at a temperature of between 220 and 260 degrees Celsius, as a matter of fact.

If the jury or the district court had held that there was infringement by the Goodyear process, as a matter of fact, the finding could be set aside by the reviewing court as clearly erroneous under Rule 52(a)(6), because the accused process is above 260 degrees Celsius, as a matter of fact. This has nothing to do with "syntactic signs," "what the prosecution history suggests," "what is the relevant evidence," "who is best situated to gauge relevance," or what witness is to be believed, which are not matters for the reviewing court to determine, as a matter of fact. The trier of fact, not the reviewing court, weighs syntactic signs, grammar, meaning of terms, and relevance. The findings can be set aside only if they are clearly erroneous. They cannot be set aside simply because the reviewing court believes it is "best situated to gauge relevance."

This message is repeated throughout this book, not just here, and in chapter 2 and chapter 17, as the single most important failure of the Federal Circuit: we must distinguish between fact and law.

CHAPTER 17

# FED. R.CIV. P. 52(a)(6) SETTING ASIDE THE FINDINGS

The Seventh Amendment to the Constitution requires deference to facts found by a jury. But when a district court is sitting without a jury or with an advisory jury, Rule 52 requires deference to facts found by the district court.

Rule 52(a)(1) mandates that "the court must find the facts specially and state its conclusions of law separately." This seems straight-forward, and is rigorously enforced by regional courts of appeal. But when the jurisdiction over appeals of patent infringement cases was taken away from the regional courts of appeal and given to the new Federal Circuit in 1982, rigorous enforcement of the distinction between fact and law fell apart.

The reasons for the failure were two-fold. First, the regional courts of appeal have been committed to the separation of fact and law since the Federal Rules of Civil Procedure were adopted in 1937. Every case, not just patent infringement cases, had to have facts stated separately from conclusions of law.

Second, the CCPA and the Patent Office Boards of Appeal have never, since 1929 when the CCPA was created, been required to distinguish between the two. Patent examiners, charged with finding the facts and making conclusions of law, typically summarized the inventions described in the prior art and concluded that the claims of the patent application being examined were obvious, anticipated, or improperly described. Never were they required to specify in detail the facts contained in prior art, and separately state the conclusions of law.

Because the PTO did not separate facts from legal conclusions, the patent courts saw no reason to do so. Neither the CCPA nor the Federal Circuit followed Rule 56 requirements for making findings of fact separate from conclusions of law.

The second reason that Federal Circuit judges did not rigorously enforce the rule that fact-findings must be separately stated is that they were not trained to do so. Until Judge Kathleen O'Malley was appointed to the Federal Circuit on December 27, 2010, none of the Federal Circuit judges had ever served as a United States district judge, unlike some judges on regional courts of appeal. Many of the Federal Circuit judges were, before appointment to the Federal Circuit, primarily involved in PTO proceedings, to which Federal Rules of Civil Procedure do not apply. Very few, before their judicial appointments, were primarily practicing in district court litigation, where Rule 52 is most often applied.

The PTO, an administrative agency, is governed by the Administrative Procedure Act, which assumes expertise in the agency's affairs. It is not part of the judicial system, in which lay jurors determine facts based upon evidence adduced at trial. The differences between the two decision-making systems are enormous, and warrant some explanation.

### Grant of Federal Right versus Dispute Resolution

Although I have characterized the CCPA and the Federal Circuit as the two "patent courts," they were fundamentally different in how they made decisions. They had in common federal appellate jurisdiction, but the CCPA was limited to administrative agency appeals, and not to disputes between opposing parties.

The original jurisdiction of the Court of Customs Appeals in 1910 was appeals of the assessments of customs duties on imports of goods into the United States. The customs bureau had a rather arbitrary scheme of assessing customs duties on imports of goods from foreign countries. An importer dissatisfied with the assessment on imported goods could seek review of the assessment in the Customs Court, the court of first instance to hear customs cases.

In 1910, Congress created an intermediate appellate tribunal to review decisions of the Customs Court. A similar appellate procedure within the Patent Office existed, called the Board of Appeals, to hear appeals by inventors dissatisfied by the refusal to grant a patent to a patent applicant.

In 1929, Congress expanded the jurisdiction of the intermediate appellate court to include patent appeals, renaming the specialist court the "Court of Customs and Patent Appeals."

There are many differences between customs appeals and patent appeals. For example, a patent is a grant of a right to exclude others from using an invention for a limited time. This right, identified in the Constitution, has no counterpart in customs law. If a patent applicant prevails on appeal, a government grant is accorded to the successful appellant. If an importer prevails in an appeal of the customs duty imposed, the only consequence is that the importer pays less customs duty to the United States. There is no government right that may be asserted against competitors by prevailing in a customs appeal.

In law, this difference is described as being *ex parte*–the importer petitions the government for relief from the assessment of a high duty and the patent applicant seeks the relief of a grant of a patent.

The *ex parte* proceeding in the Patent Office is the examination of a patent application to determine whether a patent should be granted. There also is an *inter partes* proceeding in the Patent Office in which two or more different parties claim ownership of the same invention in patent applications.

When the owner of a patent seeks remedy from one using the patented invention without permission, the proceeding in a district court is *inter partes*, that is, between parties, rather from a single party seeking relief from the government in granting a patent.

Probably the most important difference between *ex parte* and *inter partes* proceedings is the kind of evidence used to prove facts. Documentary evidence is used in *ex parte* proceedings before an administrative agency because the agency deciding the case has expertise in assessing the facts involved. The agency is presumed to have knowledge of the state of the art in the subject matter of a patent application, to use the example of the Patent and Trademark Office.

Testimony under oath is not required in matters before the PTO, although it is allowed in the documentary form of an affidavit or a declaration. No live testimony is permitted in PTO proceedings, which means that the trier of fact cannot judge the credibility of a witness testifying about the facts. It also means that there cannot be any cross-examination of a witness in an *ex parte* PTO proceeding.

A judicial dispute between a claimant and a respondent is an *inter partes* proceeding before a US district court if it involves a federal matter. Facts may be proven by witnesses' testimony live in a courtroom with a robed judge elevated above everyone else. The formalities include not only the judge, but also the American flag; a clerk administering an oath to every witness asked to raise the right hand and swear to tell the truth; a jury of qualified citizens also under oath to do their duty; a court reporter making a permanent record of everything that transpires in the trial; and the witness box near the judge where the witness is observed by the jury during direct and cross-examination. All of these formalities make a scene in which the complete fabrication of lies is difficult to accomplish, though not impossible.

In contrast, a patent application is almost always drafted by a person licensed to practice before the PTO, but not always qualified to try patent infringement cases in federal courts. Because the cost of a jury trial in a patent infringement suit has escalated in recent decades to the point where numerous lawyers skilled in big case litigation (but not necessarily skilled in preparing patent applications) are required for the production of a judicial presentation in a district court.

On appeal, still other specialized skills are required to adequately present an appeal of the district court's decision. Perhaps the most important is the requirement for deference to the decision of the district court on findings of fact.

In a district court, the jury may find facts. For over two centuries, the Seventh Amendment has required deference to facts found by a jury unless contrary to "the common law."

Facts may also be found by a district court sitting without a jury if no jury has been demanded. The findings by the district court also require deference from an appellate court "unless clearly erroneous" (Rule 52(a)(6)).

The CCPA never had to abide by Rule 52(a)(6) because it never had jurisdiction over appeals from district courts. It was only after the Federal Circuit was created in 1982 that a patent court had to defer to findings of fact by lower tribunals. Before 1982, the CCPA would routinely substitute its view of the facts for that of the lower tribunals whose decisions were appealed. No deference was accorded to the facts found in lower courts because the CCPA believed it was the final authority on patent appeals.

No petition to the Supreme Court over a CCPA decision was ever granted from its beginning in 1929 until 1966, when the first Supreme Court review of a CCPA decision occurred.

Because none of the CCPA judges had ever tried a patent infringement case in a district court, when those same judges became Federal Circuit judges in 1982, they were not aware, given their prior judicial experiences, that deference is to be paid to findings of fact made by district courts.

The lack of experience in appeals from district court decisions was apparent in the very first Supreme Court review of a Federal Circuit decision in a patent infringement case:

*Dennison Mfg. Co. v. Panduit Corp.*, 475 U.S. 809 (1986).

This case marked the first time that the Supreme Court granted certiorari on a case decided by the Federal Circuit. It related to a Rule 52(a) decision in which the district court findings were reversed without an express holding that the lower court was clearly in error in finding facts.

The Supreme Court opinion was *per curiam,* or summarily decided by the court without a designated author of the opinion. The five paragraphs summarized the district court's opinion on why the patents at issue were invalid, and why the court of appeals disagreed with the district court's decision. The Supreme Court quoted its *Graham v. John Deere Co.* decision that the obviousness determination "lends itself to several basic factual inquiries," and held that those factual inquiries were subject to Rule 52(a) of the Federal Rules of Civil Procedure.

"The Federal Circuit, however, did not mention Rule 52(a), did not explicitly apply the clearly-erroneous standard to any of the District Court's findings on obviousness and did not explain why, if it was of that view, Rule 52(a) had no applicability to this issue. We therefore lack an adequate explanation of the basis for the Court of Appeals judgment: most importantly, we lack the benefit of the Federal Circuit's informed opinion on the complex issue of the degree to which the obviousness determination is one of fact."

The Court could not consider the petitioner's claim that the opinion could not be squared with Rule 52(a), and instead granted the petition, vacated the judgment, and remanded the case to the Federal Circuit "for further consideration in the light of Rule 52(a)."

This harsh treatment of the Federal Circuit's lengthy, detailed criticism of Judge Grady's holding that the Panduit patents were invalid because they were obvious appears simple and straight-forward. Every federal judge should know that findings of fact must not be set aside unless they are clearly erroneous. Unfortunately, the Federal Circuit judges in 1986 did not know this fundamental rule because they had never been bound by the Federal Rules of Civil Procedure before 1982, when they first had jurisdiction over appeals from district court decisions.

Summarily granting a petition, vacating the Federal Circuit decision, and remanding for an explanation, without even a hearing on the petition, is certainly harsh treatment. But the patent court had it coming because it routinely disregarded Rule 52(a) simply by ignorance.

A closer analysis of the labyrinthine history of Panduit's patent litigation reveals the patent courts' substitution of its omniscient view of the facts for that of the trier of fact. Rule 52 was adopted in 1937. That the patent courts ignored Rule 52(a) for almost half a century is shocking.

Although I have tried to be as objective as I can in discussing every case in this book, I deviate here because the legal proposition is straight-forward and the Court's decision is clear. The environment was unusual because of the people involved. This is the only time in this book that I give my personal speculation about developments in case law.

I deviate from not speculating about this case because of my involvement with the people involved. The facts discussed here formed no part of the Supreme Court decision in *Dennison v. Panduit.*

I was a patent examiner in Division 25 of the Patent Office from late 1959 to 1962, when I became a CCPA law clerk. A colleague in Division 25, Robert Conte, became a witness in the companion case of *Panduit v. All States Plastic Mfg.*, which was consolidated with the *Dennison* case in the district court. The cases against Dennison and All States were brought in the Northern District of Illinois and assigned to Judge Grady.

Panduit had many patents on plastic cable ties. Panduit had a series of patents in the United States and "approximately 170 Panduit applications" in foreign countries (223 USPQ, 466). Panduit also had a number of patent infringement cases in this and other countries.

Conte was a lawyer in a law firm that allegedly had a conflict of interest in *Panduit* litigation. My only contact with Conte was as a co-worker in the Patent Office, not as a litigation colleague.

As a law clerk at the CCPA, I came to know the first two patent lawyers to be appointed to the CCPA, Judge Giles Rich and Judge Arthur Smith. Not long after I left the court, I became acquainted with CCPA Chief Judge Markey through my work as Judge Almond's former law clerk. Judge Almond served under Chief

Judge Markey, and I kept in touch with Judge Almond until he retired. Judge Markey became chief judge of the Federal Circuit when it was created in 1982.

Markey had practiced law in Chicago and was a retired air force general. He was gregarious and politically connected. He was appointed chief judge straight from private practice, which is unusual. The chief is usually elevated by the promotion of a sitting judge on a court, not as an outsider. Chief Judge Markey was always congenial with former patent court law clerks, including me.

When the Federal Circuit was created, I argued the first case before one of the three-judge panels on its first day of hearings. I had pleasant relations with Federal Circuit judges in the early days.

In 1991, I joined the International Federation of Industrial Property Counsel (FICPI, the abbreviation of the French name of the federation). At the time, the president of the US national section of this international group was John Chrystal. Chrystal asked me to serve on the lowest rung of the ladder that eventually led to my becoming president of the US section.

Conte, Markey and Chrystal were all deeply involved in the various *Panduit* disputes. It had rigorously enforced its patents against competitors in various jurisdictions. An early series of disputes related to cable ties was between Panduit and companies that sell Bowthorpe cable ties in the US and in several other countries. The US disputes were resolved by Panduit obtaining a royalty-free license to foreign patents of Bowthorpe in return for Panduit discontinuing proceedings in foreign countries against the Bowthorpe companies.

In 1976, Panduit sued All States Plastic Mfg. Co., Inc. for infringement of the patents that Panduit had previously given the Bowthorpe Companies a royalty-free license to use. The case was assigned to Judge Grady of the Northern District of Illinois in Chicago.

Judge Markey, who had practiced in the rough-and-tumble forum of Chicago litigation before his appointment in 1972 to the first patent court, almost certainly knew District Judge Grady in Chicago, although I never heard Judge Markey speak of him. In any event, the relationship between Judge Markey and Judge Grady appeared to be unfriendly, as the several *Panduit* cases indicate.

In 1978, Panduit sued Dennison Manufacturing Company. The cases against All States and Dennison were both assigned to Judge Grady and were consolidated for trial of the patent validity issue.

In discovery in *Panduit v. All States*, All States learned about the prior deal between Panduit and Bowthorpe. All States moved for leave to file an antitrust and unfair competition counterclaim against Panduit. That motion was granted (*Panduit Corp. v. All States*, 205 USPQ 1063 (N.D. Ill. 1979)).

In 1981, Panduit dropped all claims of infringement by All States of one of its patents, and Judge Grady denied several of All States motions (213 USPQ 887).

In 1982, Judge Grady granted a motion to disqualify Laff, Whitesell, Conte and Saret from representing All States in the *Panduit v. All States* case because Robert Conte, who had worked at Ladas & Parry until 1976, had merged his practice with that of the Laff firm in 1981. Ladas & Parry was headed by John Chrystal, and had represented Panduit in foreign patent applications through correspondents in foreign countries. Ladas & Parry did not do patent infringement litigation in the United States.

Judge Grady held, as the third finding of fact, that "All States has proved clearly and effectively that Mr. Conte has not communicated to anyone at the Laff firm any confidential information concerning Panduit which he may have received while at the Ladas & Parry firm" (*Panduit Corp. v. All States Plastic Mfg. Co., Inc.*, 744 F. 2d 1564, 1569 (Fed. Cir. 1984)).

However, Judge Grady qualified that finding because he "cannot possibly find as a matter of fact that Mr. Conte has not already inadvertently passed on some confidence." He therefore disqualified the Laff firm from working on the All States case "until the disqualification was resolved on appeal," in case "the Court of Appeals will disagree with my findings and conclusions." Briefly disqualifying the Laff firm would do "the least harm to anyone."

The Federal Circuit reversed the district court's disqualification order because it put too high a standard for disqualification: "An absolute finding of no possible inadvertent sharing of confidences" was too high a bar for disqualification, so the appellate court relied upon the finding that Conte had not shared confidences in order to reverse the district court (at 744 F. 2d 1579).

In short, the Federal Circuit substituted its view of the facts for that of the district court without finding that disqualification pending appeal was clearly erroneous. Rule 52(a) was never cited in the Federal Circuit opinion in *All States*, just as it was not in the Federal Circuit opinion in *Dennison*.

In the *Dennison* appeal, the Federal Circuit opinion by Chief Judge Markey reversed Judge Grady's decision that the three Panduit patents were invalid. The appellate court began by asserting that the patent suit arose "out of the affairs of people, real people facing real problems," quoting Judge Markey's opinion in *Rosemount, Inc. v. Beckman Instruments, Inc.*, 727 F. 2d 1540, 1544 (Fed. Cir. 1984). The court in *Rosemount* went on to quote sixteen findings of the district court supporting its decision to affirm the district court's findings of fact.

In *Dennison*, Judge Markey's opinion reversed the district court decision finding that "Panduit gave 'insufficient attention to what is taught by general engineering principles and general principles physics and, indeed, the common experience of mankind'" (1089-90).

But the Federal Circuit quoted with approval at note 15 the district court's ambivalence about its decision: "All the documents are here, the testimony is there for [the appellate court] to read, and if they come to a different conclusion that I, then so be it." (1090).

Rule 52(a) does not allow setting aside findings it disagrees with; it must find clear error in the district court's findings. It is not enough to reverse because the district court "misevaluated the prior art," and "misconstrued its role" (1091); the finding must be "clearly erroneous."

On remand, the Federal Circuit adhered to its previous decision that Panduit prevailed and Dennison infringed the patent. Its opinion cited what it regarded as clear errors and reached the same result specifying findings that were clearly erroneous.

It treated the scolding it received from the Supreme Court as a cosmetic problem, correctible by using the words of Rule 52(a).

The Federal Circuit has continued to insist that its view of the facts is superior to the view of the district court. It is not a question of who is wiser or who is "right." Rather, Rule 52(a) is a recognition that a trier of fact, who observes the witnesses that give testimony and weighs the testimony to determine proof of facts, is in a better position to determine truth than is an appellate court years later, reading transcribed words without any signals from the courtroom drama.

The Federal Circuit must embrace the Federal Rules of Civil Procedure that govern the judicial process, and stop contesting them. Fact-finders, not appellate courts, should determine facts.

# CHAPTER 18

# RULE 56(c) SUMMARY JUDGMENT

The litigation load on the federal judicial system has increased dramatically over the years. It is no longer possible to try nearly every case that is filed in federal courts. Two alternatives to trying cases are used with increasing frequency. One is ADR (alternative dispute resolution), either under the supervision of the federal judicial system or outside the judicial system. Because no ADR case involving patents has ever reached the Supreme Court, that alternative is outside the scope of this book.

The other alternative is summary judgment, in which the trial judge receives affidavits setting forth the facts in favor of and in opposition to summary adjudication of whether there is a genuine issue of material fact requiring trial, or whether the matter of liability can be resolved as a matter of law.

Whereas Rule 52(a) is a summary determination of fact issues, Rule 56(c) is a summary determination of the entire case, both fact and law. It provides that the "judgment sought should be rendered if the pleadings, the discovery and disclosure materials on file, and any affidavits show that there is no genuine issue as to any material fact and that the movant is entitled to judgment as a matter of law."

These last six words are the same as the JMOL in Rule 50(a). All three of these rules: 50(a), 52(a), and 56(c), are intended to resolve cases short of a full trial on the merits. Rule 50(a) applies during a trial but before its conclusion. Rule 52(a) applies when there is no jury or an advisory jury and the court is able to make both findings of fact and conclusions of law. Generally speaking, Rule 56(c) motions are filed before trial and before Rule 50(a) and Rule 52(a) motions. Rule 50(a) motions are filed during jury trials. Rule 52(a) is after trial.

Rule 56(c) is a pretrial proceeding to be filed at least twenty days after the case is filed and at least 10 days before the date set for hearing. The pleadings must be filed along with discovery and disclosure materials. The moving party and the opposing party must have the opportunity to file affidavits. The case must be sufficiently developed to carry out the mission of summary judgment.

The 1963 advisory committee notes on Rule 56(c) explain that the "very mission of the summary judgment proceeding is to pierce the pleadings and assess the proof in order to see whether there is a genuine need for trial." Further, where "an issue as to a material fact cannot be resolved without observation of the demeanor of witnesses in order to evaluate their credibility, summary judgment is not appropriate."

Because it is impossible for an appellate court to observe the demeanor of witnesses in order to evaluate their credibility, it is imperative that appellate courts defer to trial courts in evaluating credibility.

Rule 56 has other safeguards to make the proceeding resemble a trial a closely as possible. Rule 56(e)(1) requires that supporting or opposing affidavits must be "made on personal knowledge, set out facts that would be admissible in evidence, and show that the affiant is competent to testify on the matters stated. If a paper or a part of a paper is referred to in an affidavit, a sworn or certified copy must be attached to or served with the affidavit. The court may permit an affidavit to be supplemented or opposed by depositions, answers to interrogatories, or additional affidavits."

The *Dennison v. Panduit* case discussed in the last chapter vacated the Federal Circuit decision for failure to address the Rule

52(a) requirement of deference to a decision of a district court unless the lower court clearly erred.

The Federal Circuit opinion in *Dennison* by Chief Judge Markey attempted to insert a quotation from his prior opinion in *Rosemount v. Beckman* (see chapter 17) that the patent suit arose "out of the affairs of people, real people facing real problems." That attempt was inappropriate, because the evidence of the "affairs of people" that the court of appeals sought to consider is inadmissible because: it is not in an affidavit; it is not the district judge's "personal knowledge;" the judge is not competent to testify about the matter in the quote; the paper is not in a sworn or certified copy; and the paper is not in the record.

The *Dennison* appellate opinion was related to Rule 52(a), not Rule 56(c), but it had several references to the "real world story" that was not addressed by Judge Grady in the district court.

If a witness in a trial or in a summary judgment proceeding attempted to testify about a "real world story," either live or in an affidavit or deposition, the witness would be challenged and probably not be allowed to testify about a matter beyond his personal knowledge.

In 1982, when the Federal Circuit was created, it was comprised of judges with varied backgrounds, but not experts in the Federal Rules and trials under civil procedure. Chief Judge Markey, in both *Rosemount* and *Dennison* did not rigorously apply the Federal Rules of Civil Procedure. Had he been more thoroughly familiar with Rule 56(e) regarding affidavits, he would not have said in *Dennison* that the case arose "out of the affairs of people, real people facing real problems."

*Dennison* was not a Rule 56(c) proceeding related to summary judgment in the trial court. It was a Rule 52(a) matter related to deference to the district court decision unless it was found to be erroneous. There has never been a Supreme Court review of a patent court decision involving Rule 56(c). There are, of course, many Rule 56(c) cases decided by the Supreme Court that provide guidance for the Federal Circuit in deciding summary judgment cases. Unfortunately, the Federal Circuit is selective in choosing which Supreme Court summary judgment cases it will follow.

For example, an early Supreme Court case involving Rule 56(c) is:

*Adickes v. S.H. Kress & Co.*, 398 U.S 144 (1970)

In the summer of 1964, a white schoolteacher from New York went to Hattiesburg, Mississippi, to volunteer in a Freedom School. While there, she went with several of her black students to a Kress lunch counter. The store refused to serve her and had her arrested. She sued Kress, alleging that the refusal of service and her arrest were the product of a conspiracy between Kress and the police.

Kress filed a Rule 56(c) motion for summary judgment on the ground that there was no conspiracy. The district court granted the motion because Adickes "failed to allege any facts from which a conspiracy might be inferred" (147). The court of appeals affirmed, and Adickes petitioned the Supreme Court.

The petition was granted, and a unanimous Court held that the conspiracy between Kress and the Hattiesburg police department was state action. Adickes was entitled to relief "if she can prove a Kress employee, in the course of employment, and a Hattiesburg policeman somehow reached an understanding to deny Miss Adickes service in the Kress store, or to cause her arrest because she was a white person in the company of Negroes" (152).

That statement of the issue suggests that *Adickes* must prove contact between a Kress employee and a Hattiesburg policeman. As it turned out, as the moving party seeking summary judgment, Kress had to prove the *absence* of a contact between Kress and the police. Rule 56(c) states that judgment sought by the moving party "should be rendered if the [evidence] show[s] that there is no genuine issue as to any material fact and that the movant is entitled to judgment as a matter of law."

Contact between Kress and the police was certainly a material fact needed to prove a conspiracy. The district court and the Second Circuit held that Adickes had failed to prove the conspiracy she alleged. The Supreme Court stated that its "scrutiny of the factual allegations of petitioner's complaint, as well as the material found in the affidavits and depositions presented by Kress to the District Court, however, convinces us that summary judgment was improper here, for we think respondent failed to carry its burden of showing the absence of any genuine issue of fact" (153).

Two of the students who accompanied Adickes to the lunch counter testified at trial that a policeman came into the store, looked at the group, went to the back of the store and left. In discovery, Kress had given an unsworn statement by a check-out girl in the store that Patrolman Hillman came into the store while the group was there, said hello to her, and went toward the back of the store, and a few minutes later left with "a group composed of several Negroes accompanied by a white woman." A police car came up and "Patrolman Hillman escorted the white woman away from the Negroes and into the police car" (note 14).

Kress did not provide affidavits from the waitress who actually refused service to Adickes or her supervisor. The affidavits of the two police officers only stated that neither the store manager nor anyone else had asked that the arrest be made (note 12).

The store manager testified that he had signaled the food counter supervisor not to serve Adickes because he feared a riot if she was served. He denied asking "any public official to have Miss Adickes arrested" (note 8).

The gaps in the Kress materials included as support for the motion led the Supreme Court to conclude that Kress "failed to fulfill its initial burden of demonstrating what is a critical element in this aspect of the case—that there was no policeman in the store. If a policeman were present, we think it would be open to a jury, in light of the sequence that followed, to infer from the circumstances that the policeman and a Kress employee had a 'meeting of the minds' and thus reached an understanding that petitioner should be refused service."

The Court cited *United States v. Diebold, Inc.*, 369 U.S. 654, 655 (1962) to support the proposition that inferences to be drawn from facts contained in Kress materials "must be viewed in the light most favorable to the party opposing the motion," and "failure to show there was no policeman in the store requires reversal" (158-59). If it was true, the police officers could have testified in their affidavits that they were not in the store. If the check-out girl had not seen and spoken to Patrolman Hill in the store when the group was there, and observed him "escort the white woman...into the police car," she could have corrected her unsworn statement that recited these facts. The inference that she told the truth favors the Adickes opposition to the motion. The Kress argument that "it was incumbent on [Adickes] to come forward with an affidavit properly asserting the presence of a policeman in the store" (159) was rejected.

The 1963 advisory committee note to Rule 56(e) is clear: "Where the evidentiary material in support of the motion does not establish the absence of a genuine issue, summary judgment must be denied, even if no opposing evidentiary material is presented." Adickes "was not required to come forward with suitable opposing affidavits" (160).

The Court added that an affidavit or deposition of one of the students, or the checkout girl, who saw the policeman in the store, "would have been the preferable course for petitioner's counsel to have followed." In other words, it is risky to rely solely upon the failure of the moving party to prove that no policeman was in the store because one of the two policemen who signed affidavits was not in the store. He could have sworn in an affidavit that he was not in the store, and the Court might have bought the Kress argument.

It would have been far safer, though expensive, to track down one or the other of the students who saw the policeman go to the back of the store, or depose the check-out girl who observed the whole sequence in order to have a sworn statement. The case was pending in New York, and the three potential witnesses were almost certainly far from New York. Adickes was lucky to have won without tracking down an eye witness years after the event took place.

To my knowledge, the Federal Circuit has never cited *Adickes*– or required the moving party to "show that there is no genuine issue as to any material fact and that the moving party is entitled to a judgment as a matter of law." Rather, the Federal Circuit substitutes its view of what the facts show, without regard to the moving party's burden.

*Celotex Corp. v. Catrett,* 477 U.S. 317 (1986)

Louis Catrett had worked with asbestos and allegedly died from asbestos exposure. His widow sued fifteen asbestos companies for wrongful death. One of the defendants, Celotex, moved for summary judgment under Rule 56(c) on the ground that plaintiff "failed to produce evidence that any [Celotex] product...was the proximate cause of the injuries within the jurisdictional limits of the district court" (319–20). The district court for the District of Columbia granted the Celotex motion. A divided panel of the D.C. Circuit reversed, relying upon Rule 56(e) and *Adickes* to support the holding that "the party opposing the motion for summary judgment bears the burden of responding *only after* the moving party has met its burden of coming forward with proof of the absence of any issues of material fact" (321, italics in the original). Judge Bork dissented, stating that the "majority errs in supposing that a party seeking summary judgment must always make an affirmative evidentiary showing, even where there is not a triable, factual dispute" (321), and the majority's decision "undermines the traditional authority of trial judges to grant summary judgment in meritless cases" (322).

The Supreme Court reversed, finding that Rule 56(c) does not expressly or impliedly require "that the moving party support its motion with affidavits or similar material *negating* the opponents claim. On the contrary, *Rule 56(c),* which refers to 'the affidavits, *if any,* suggests the absence of such a requirement. And if there were any doubt about the meaning of *Rule 56(c)* in this regard, such doubt is clearly removed by *Rules 56(a)* and *(b),* which provide that claimants and defendants, respectively, may move for summary judgment *with or without supporting affidavits"* (italics added). "The import of these subsections is that, regardless of whether the moving party accompanies its summary judgment motion with affidavits, the motion may, and should, be granted so long as whatever is before the district court demonstrates that the standard for the entry of summary judgment, as set forth in *Rule 56(c),* is satisfied" (323).

The use of the word "should" in the last quoted sentence in Justice Rehnquist's opinion for the majority in *Celotex* was prophetic. In 1986, when *Celotex* was decided, Rule 56(c) read in part "The judgment sought *shall* be rendered forthwith if the pleadings, depositions, answers to interrogatories, and admissions on file, together with the affidavits, if any, show that there is no genuine issue as to any material fact."

In 2007, that subdivision was altered to substitute "should" for "shall." The advisory committee notes for the 2007 amendments to Rule 56(c), (d), and (e) explain that the substitution of "should" was meant to indicate that "although there is no discretion to enter summary judgment when there is a genuine issue as to any material fact, there is discretion to deny summary judgment when it appears that there is no genuine issue as to any material fact...'Should' in amended Rule 56(c) recognizes that courts will seldom exercise the discretion to deny summary judgment when there is no genuine issue as to any material fact...Rule 56(d)(1), on the other hand, reflects the more open-ended discretion to decide whether it is practicable to determine what material facts are not genuinely in dispute."

The majority opinion in *Celotex* shows that a district court has discretion to grant summary judgment when the moving party— "points out to the district court...that there is an absence of evidence to support the nonmoving party's case" with respect to an issue on which the nonmoving party bears the burden of proof (325), such as proximate causation by Celotex products.

The majority was careful to point out that *Adickes* was properly decided and was not overruled: "We fully agree with the *Adickes* Court that the 1963 amendment to *Rule 56(c)* was not designed to modify the burden of making the showing generally required by *Rule 56*(c)" (325, italics in the original).

Justice White concurred with the judgment of the majority, but would have remanded for further proceedings because the court of appeals did not address whether Catrett could name witnesses to support her claim. He would have vacated rather than reverse the court of appeals decision.

Justices Brennan, Burger and Blackmun joined in a dissent, pointing out that Catrett had disclosed to Celotex that she had a witness, T.R. Hoff, a former supervisor of Mr. Catrett, who could testify about the asbestos products to which decedent had been exposed. "Celotex was required, as an initial matter, to attack the adequacy of this evidence. Celotex' failure to fulfill this simple requirement constitutes a failure to discharge its initial burden of production under *Rule 56*," which means that summary judgment was inappropriate. "This case is indistinguishable from *Adickes*." (336).

Because "Celotex has admitted that plaintiff had disclosed her intent to call Mr. Hoff as a witness at trial," Justice White's desire to remand for further proceedings (stated in his concurrence) would be "a waste of time," according to the Brennan dissent (337, note 7).

Justice Stevens dissented on the narrow ground that Catrett was not exposed to Celotex asbestos "within the jurisdictional limits" of the District of Columbia (337). Justice White was the fifth vote for overruling the court of appeals. If his vote was to remand so that Celotex could address the adequacy of the Hoff evidence, then the 5–4 Supreme Court split would have gone the other way, with the result obtained in *Adickes*.

Deference to the decision of the district court was paid in *Celotex*. Deference was not paid to the district court in *Adickes*, because it erred in finding that the moving party had shown that there was no conspiracy between the police and the store. The affidavits there did not establish the absence of a conspiracy. Although Adickes had the burden at trial to prove a conspiracy existed, Kress was unable to show that it was not a fact in dispute.

Reconciling *Adickes* and *Celotex* is difficult, but it is clear that *Celotex* did not overrule *Adickes*, since the Court in *Celotex* "fully agree[d] with the *Adickes* Court" (325).

*Nissan Fire & Marine Ins. v. Fritz Companies, Inc.*, 210 F. 3d 1099
(9th Cir. 2000)

The Ninth Circuit has addressed the question of reconciling *Adickes* and *Celotex* in *Nissan Fire*. Fritz, a freight forwarder, shipped a 530– kilogram disk drive from Miami to Buenos Aires by means of Tower Air, Inc. The disk drive arrived damaged and was a total loss. Nissan Fire, the insurer of the disk drive, sued Fritz and Tower.

The Warsaw Convention governs international shipment by air. Article 26 of the convention provides that no claim for damages against a carrier may be sustained unless the shipper dispatches a written complaint within seven days of the receipt of the damaged goods. Fritz and Tower moved for summary judgment, supported by affidavits indicating that notice was not received within seven days.

The shipper responded with affidavits "from a Nissan claims adjuster attaching an inspection certificate and letters purporting to constitute timely notice" (1102). The court explained the distinctions "among the initial burden of production and two kinds of ultimate burdens of persuasion: The initial burden of production refers to the burden of producing evidence, or showing the absence of evidence, on the motion for summary judgment; the ultimate burden of persuasion can refer either to the burden of persuasion on the motion or the burden of persuasion at trial" (*id.*).

"If a moving party seeking summary judgment fails to carry its initial burden of production, the nonmoving party has no obligation to produce anything, even if the nonmoving party would have the ultimate burden of persuasion at trial. *See Adickes v. S.H. Kress & Co.*" (1102–03).

If "a moving party carries its burden of production, the nonmoving party must produce evidence to support its claim or defense…If the nonmoving party fails to produce enough evidence to create a genuine issue of material fact, the moving party wins the motion for summary judgment. *See Celotex Corp. v. Catrett*…We recognize that the two cases [*Adickes* and *Celotex*] have caused some confusion in the lower courts, and that some academic commentators consider them inconsistent. However, we are constrained to treat the cases as consistent, for the Supreme Court in *Celotex* explicitly relied upon and distinguished *Adickes* rather than over-ruling it" (1103; footnote omitted).

There are two methods to meet the initial burden of production. "The moving party may produce evidence negating an essential element of the nonmoving party's case, or, after suitable discovery, the moving party may show that the nonmoving party does not have enough evidence of an essential element of its claim or defense to carry its ultimate burden of persuasion at trial" (1106). *Adickes* involved the first method; *Celotex* involved the second method. "The Supreme Court has clearly indicated that, in appropriate cases, a moving party may carry its initial burden of production by showing that the nonmoving party does not have enough evidence to carry its ultimate burden of persuasion at trial" (*id.*). In *Celotex*, interrogatory answers filed by Catrett had failed to identify "any witnesses who could testify about decedents exposure to [Celotex's] asbestos products" (1105).

### *Anderson v. Liberty Lobby, Inc.*, 477 U.S. 242 (1986)

On the same day that *Celotex* was decided, the Supreme Court decided another frequently cited summary judgment case, *Anderson*. The issue there was whether the requirement for "clear and convincing evidence" must be applied in the summary judgment stage, or whether it was limited to the review of trial holdings.

Reporters had published articles about public figures. The public figures sued the reporters for defamation. The reporters moved for summary judgment on the ground that the public figures had not proved "actual malice" on their part.

The district court granted the motion based on the *New York Times* precedent, which required a showing of actual malice (246). The court of appeals reversed, because "a jury could reasonably conclude that the...allegations were defamatory, false, and made with actual malice" (247).

The Supreme Court reversed, holding that Rule 56(c) requires the moving party to "show that there is no genuine issue as to any material fact." This does not mean that the fact has to be conclusively proved, just that there is no genuine issue for trial. What a jury might "reasonably conclude" is not the test; the test is whether or not there is a fact issue to be tried.

In *Anderson,* the Court relied extensively upon *Adickes* as it had in the concurrently decided *Celotex* case. It is clear that the Supreme Court did not overrule *Adickes.*

*Anderson* is an important case to keep in mind in patent infringement cases because the "clear—and–convincing standard" applies to overcoming the presumption of validity under 35 U.S.C. §282 (*North American Vaccine Co. v. American Cyanamid Co.* 7 F. 3d 1571, 1579 (Fed. Cir. 1993)). *Anderson* shows that the standard applies whether a district court is "ruling on a motion for summary judgment or for a motion for a directed verdict" under Rule 50 (*Anderson,* 255).

Unfortunately, the Federal Circuit does not review motions for summary judgment in the manner required by *Anderson:* to "view the evidence presented through the prism of the substantive evidentiary burden." Instead, it substitutes its view of whether it "thinks the evidence unmistakably favors one side or the other," a practice deplored by *Anderson.*

### *Dow Chemical Co. v. Sumitomo Chemical Co.,* 257 F. 3d 1364 (Fed. Cir. 2001)

This is a Federal Circuit decision that did *not* reach the Supreme Court. It is included in this chapter because a motion for summary judgment under Rule 56 was filed in the district court and granted, and the Federal Circuit vacated the judgment of the district court based upon its reading of the facts, which differed from the district court's reading.

Dow Chemical had a patent on a process of making high-purity epoxy resins suitable for encapsulating semiconductor chips for computers and other applications. In most countries of the world, claim drafting requires setting forth the environment in which the invention exists followed by "characterized in" (or words similar) followed by the specific improvement to be patented. In the United States, however, claims are drafted as a string of elements, some of which may be old and some new. This is because 35 U.S.C. §103(a) specifies that obviousness is determined on "the subject matter as a whole." There is no requirement that the specific improvement be separately evaluated for "inventive height" as in many countries. This is another of the many instances in which practice in the United States differs from that of most other countries.

In this case the claim at issue was "written in Jepson format" (1368), a relatively rare style named after *Ex Parte Jepson* (1917 Commissioner Decisions 62 (1917)), in which the known elements are first set forth and the improvement follows the words "the improvement comprising," not unlike the format used in other countries.

Claim 1 of the patent here "is directed to an improvement of this well-known method of preparing epoxy resins" (1367). Five steps are recited as the improvement: (1) conducting the reaction in the presence of an organic solvent that codistills with water and epihalohydrin at a boiling point below the boiling point of the lowest boiling compound among the components in the reaction mixture; (2) conducting the reaction under a reduced pressure sufficient to provide a distillate with a boiling point of between about forty-five and eighty degrees Celsius; (3) employing the alkali metal hydroxide as an aqueous solution and adding said aqueous alkali metal hydroxide in a continuous or intermittent manner over a period of about one-half to about ten hours; (4) continuously removing water by means of codistillation at a rate such that the water content in the reaction mixture is less than about 6 percent by weight; and (5) separating the water from the codistillate and returning the solvent and epihalohydrin to the reaction mixture (1368).

It should be apparent that these five steps are exceedingly fact intensive, and the task of showing that "there is no genuine issue as to any material fact" under Rule 56(c) would be daunting, to say the least. Several issues of material fact, very much in dispute, were decided by the district court in claim construction, and overruled by the Federal Circuit on appeal. Because disputed material facts may not be determined by summary judgment, it was an error for the district court to decide the disputed facts. It was also an error for the Federal Circuit to decide the same disputed facts the opposite way on appeal when no trier of fact has decided these issues.

First, the overriding issue of whether Sumitomo infringed the patent claim "is a question of fact, to be submitted to a jury" *Winans v. Denmead*, 15 How. 330, 338 (1854). It is not an issue to be decided on summary judgment if it is genuinely in dispute. Sumitomo, as the moving party on summary judgment, had the burden to show that there was no fact dispute regarding infringement. The eighteen page Federal Circuit decision is chock-a-block with disputed facts.

Second, a subsidiary disputed fact is the "boiling point of the reaction mixture." The district court construed step one of the claim as calling for codistillation "at a boiling point of the reaction mixture" (1370). This would seem to be a reasonable interpretation of the words of the claim: "a boiling point below the boiling point of the lowest boiling compound among the components in the reaction mixture" in step one (1368). However, Dow disputed this construction and the Federal Circuit agreed with Dow that codistillate vapor is the phase in which temperature is measured, not the temperature in the distilland (note 2, 1369, note 4, 1370). The disputed fact is for the trier of fact to determine, based upon suitable instructions and considering the credibility of the evidence. Neither the district court nor the court of appeals may decide disputed fact issues.

Third, the meaning of "continuous" in steps three and four was disputed, with the district court favoring Sumitomo's interpretation and the Federal Circuit adopting Dow's interpretation.

Fourth, is dioxane "interchangeable" with the solvents in Dow's patent (1371)? The district court held that Dow "failed to demonstrate interchangeability," while the Federal Circuit said (1368, note 1), that "dioxane is an organic solvent." Whether dioxane is a suitable organic solvent in step one was the subject of an experiment by Dow's expert. The district judge excluded that testimony and Dow argued that "the district court erred by excluding this testimony" (1371). The mere fact that the material fact is disputed means that summary judgment must be denied. Neither the district court nor the appellate court can usurp the function of the trier of fact.

The Federal Circuit failed to understand the mission of the summary judgment procedure "to pierce the pleading and to assess the proof in order to see whether there is a genuine issue for trial" (advisory committee note, 1963 amendment to Rule 52(e)). The same note explains: "Where the evidentiary matter in support of the motion does not establish the absence of a genuine issue, summary judgment must be denied even if no opposing evidentiary matter is presented."

It was the moving party Sumitomo that had to establish that there was no issue regarding "interchangeability," and Dow had no duty "to demonstrate interchangeability" (1371).

The Federal Circuit vacated the district court decision and remanded so the district court could "conduct additional fact-finding proceedings in accordance with the proper claim construction" (1371). It is not a claim-construction problem; it is a problem of the moving party failing to show that there is no need for trial. Summary judgment had to be denied because Sumitomo failed to carry its initial burden to show there was no genuine fact issue to be tried.

The *Dow* case is filled with instances in which the district court is shown no deference and is criticized only because the appellate court holds a different view. Six examples should suffice:

(1). The district court said "Clause 1 of claim 1 was developed on the model of a minimum boiling azeotrope" (1374). Instead of finding that statement to be clearly erroneous, the Federal Circuit said "The fact that the claim language was changed" in successive generations of the claims "suggests that the terms have different meanings" (1375).

A mere "suggestion," unsupported by any evidence, and counterintuitive when priority is claimed to the grandparent, is not a valid reason to substitute the reviewing court's interpretation of the perceived "suggestion" in a claim for the finding of fact by the district court. Whether the "codistillate disclosed in claim 1 of the '255 patent is not an azeotropic mixture" (1375) is a fact, and must not be set aside unless clearly erroneous. (The fact issue should never have been considered on summary judgment, because it is disputed, and thus for the trier of fact to decide).

(2). "Although the construction of the 'boiling point' limitation used in clause 1 requires a numerical comparison of boiling points, we conclude…that the district court was incorrect in ruling that the codistillate boiling point is determined by measuring the temperature of the reaction mixture" (1375). The appellate court found as a fact that "the boiling point of the codistillate is properly measured in the vapor phase," because "boiling point" must be given "its ordinary meaning as understood by one of ordinary skill in the art" (*id.*). Treatises are cited to show that "boiling point must be measured in the vapor phase" (*id.*).

In fact, clause 1 reads "Conducting the reaction in the presence of an organic solvent…at a boiling point…in the reaction mixture" (1368). To say that the district court's finding of fact was "incorrect" when the words "measured in the vapor phase" appear nowhere in the claim is not giving claim terms their ordinary meaning. Rather, it is substituting the Dow interpretation that has no basis in the claim language for the district court's interpretation, which uses the words in the claim.

Deference means that even if the Federal Circuit would have adopted the Dow interpretation instead of the Sumitomo interpretation had it been the trier of fact, substitution of its view for that of the trier of fact is improper. The district court chose to rely upon the Hala treatise and stated that measuring in the vapor phase is of "dubious value" (1376). It did not rely upon the treatises that the appellate court found more probative. That is not deference, and it is not proof that the district court's finding of fact was clearly erroneous under Rule 52.

(Again, the disputed fact cannot be determined on summary judgment by either the district court or the Federal Circuit, because it is a task for the finder of fact. Had a jury chosen to believe Hala instead of the Dow treatises, setting aside the jury finding of fact would have violated the Seventh Amendment. Summary judgment cannot avoid a jury determination of a disputed fact.)

(3). "Claim 1 of the '255 patent specifically calls for measuring the boiling point of the *distillate,* not the *distilland*" (1376). The

Federal Circuit quoted a dictionary as stating that distillation is "a separation process in which a liquid is converted into a vapor and the vapor then condensed to a liquid" (id.). As with brandy or vodka, the liquid at the end is purer than the starting liquid that has components that do not vaporize at the boiling point. From this, the Federal Circuit concluded that this proves that the ordinary meaning of boiling point "entails the measurement of the codistillate in the vapor phase" (*id.*).

The Oxford English Dictionary defines "boiling point" as the "temperature at which a liquid, (esp. water) boils." *Webster's Third New International Dictionary* defines it as the "temperature at which a liquid boils." Neither of these standard sources of ordinary meaning of terms links "boiling point" with "vapor phase." The distilland is a liquid below the boiling point, not above. *Markman* teaches that claim construction should be by the district court "following receipt of evidence." It should not be done by an appellate court that prefers other evidence than that relied upon by the district court.

(4). "The ordinary meaning of the reaction temperature is different than the ordinary meaning of the boiling point of the codistillate" (1377). This appears to be a *non sequitur*. If the liquid enters the vapor phase at a given temperature, why would the distilland enter the liquid phase at about the same temperature? If it is disputed whether the temperature at evaporation differs from the temperature at condensation, as the Federal Circuit states, then summary judgment is not proper and the motion must be denied. A trial to determine the fact issue is appropriate.

(5). "The claim language calls for the measurement of the boiling point of the codistillate" (1378). If the distillate is the liquid output of the distillation step, as the dictionary relied upon by the Federal Circuit states, then the condensation temperature is not measured. Rather, the boiling point of that condensed liquid entering the vapor stage of the next distillation step must be measured. This seems counterintuitive, given the claim language. The boiling point of a distillate, the condensed liquid, would seem to be the boiling point of the distilland, unless pressure differences between boiling and condensation steps alter the two temperatures.

These issues should be resolved at trial, not by speculation by an appellate court on appeal of a summary judgment motion.

(6). Whereas the Sumitomo accused process maintains the temperature of the reaction mixture at a level recited in the claim, is there infringement? Dow conceded that the first stage of the Sumitomo process does not infringe, but it argued that the second stage infringes if the boiling point is measured in the vapor phase of the starting liquid. Whether the Sumitomo process infringes is an issue of fact. It is disputed, so summary judgment is inappropriate.

The net result of the *Dow* case is that these six issues show that there is a need for trial. The advisory committee note to the 1963 amendment to Rule 56(e) states: "The very mission of the summary judgment procedure is to pierce the pleadings and to assess the proof in order to see whether there is a genuine need for trial." It is abundantly clear that there was a genuine need for trial and that both the district court and the Federal Circuit wasted a huge amount of effort trying to *decide* the facts when they lack the power to do so on a summary judgment motion.

### *Phonometrics Inc. v. Northern Telecom Ltd.*, 133 F. 3d 1459 (Fed Cir. 1998)

This is another case that did not reach the Supreme Court. It is an example of the failure of the Federal Circuit to defer to the nonmoving party, as required by Rule 56(c).

The title of the patent in the suit showed that the invention was a "computer and recorder" for long distance call costs. The specification showed that the invention was "a computing and recording apparatus" useful for "facilitating expense allocating procedures." The drawings showed how the system calculated telephone call costs for the first three minutes, and for each minute thereafter. Claim 1 recited a "long-distance telephone call cost computer apparatus for computing and recording the cost of each long-distance telephone call."

Northern Telephone moved for summary judgment on the ground that its system did not display the call cost as it accrued during the call, but rather only after the call was concluded. The district court held that the apparatus had to display the call cost to the caller during the call, rather than provide a record of the cost of each long distance call made by the user of the system, such as a hotel guest.

The Federal Circuit affirmed, not based upon the evidence that the district court relied upon (a passage from the preferred embodiment in the specification that was not present in any claim), but upon three other passages in claim 1 that used the phrase "substantially instantaneously." The district court did not rely upon any of these three passages; they appeared for the first time in the appellate decision. If the three passages about "substantially instantaneously" were dispositive of the case, the Federal Circuit should have remanded the case to the district court to reconsider the summary judgment motion as to facts genuinely in dispute.

Neither the district court nor the Federal Circuit deferred to the nonmoving party, as *Adickes* and Rule 56(c) require. No claim of the patent used the words "as charges accrue during the call"; "cumulated costs as they accrue, in real time"; or "the register is current throughout the duration of the call." All three of these statements are *inferences* drawn in favor of the *moving* party, not the non-moving party.

If these conclusions were interpreted according to the ordinary meaning of the claim's language, the call-cost register means is merely a means to tote up the cost of each long distance call. It is not a means for "recording the cost of each long distance telephone call," which is the purpose of the invention and what claim 1 specifies.

A register showing "charges as they accrue during the call" is worthless information when the claimed goal is to know "the cost of each long-distance telephone call" for "facilitating expense allocation procedures."

The district court and the court of appeals substituted words found in the specification, but not in the claims, for the words in the claims in order to limit the claims to features that the accused devices did not have. It was a question of fact whether the claims specified calculating the cost "during the call." Summary judgment under Rule 56(c) was not appropriate because the issue was material and genuinely in dispute.

The error was repeated by the Federal Circuit in many later Phonometrics cases because the fact was said to be *res judicata*, or already decided, even though no trier of fact had decided the disputed issue. There never was a trial in any of the dozens of *Phonometrics* cases. The Federal Rules of Civil Procedure were ignored, and result-oriented decisions were made on summary judgment on genuinely disputed issues of fact.

These are just a few of the Federal Circuit decisions that decide facts arising in motions for summary judgment, without deference to the trier of fact. The Federal Circuit has not followed Rule 56(c). In many cases, including in the *Phonometrics* cases, Rule 56(c) has been trashed.

CHAPTER 19

# DOCTRINE OF
# EQUIVALENTS

In *Graver Tank & Mfg. Co., Inc. v. Linde Air Products, Inc.*, 339 U.S. 605 (1950), Justice Jackson, for the majority, noted that "courts have also recognized that to permit imitation of a patented invention which does not copy every literal detail would be to convert the protection of patent grant into a hollow and useless thing. Such a limitation would leave room for–indeed encourage- -the unscrupulous copyist to make unimportant and insubstantial changes and substitutions in the patent which, though adding nothing, would be enough to take the copied matter outside the claim, and hence outside the reach of the law. One who seeks to pirate an invention, like one who seeks to pirate a copyrighted book or play, may be expected to introduce minor variations to conceal and shelter the piracy. Outright and forthright duplication is a dull and very rare type of infringement. To prohibit no other would place the inventor at the mercy of verbalism and would be subordinating substance to form. It would deprive him of his invention and would foster concealment rather than disclosure of inventions, which is one of the primary purposes of the patent system.

"The doctrine of equivalents evolved in response to this experience. The essence of the doctrine is that one may not practice a fraud on a patent. Originating almost a century ago in the case of

*Winans v. Denmead*, 15 How. 330 (1854), it has been consistently applied by this Court and the lower federal courts, and continues today ready and available for utilization when the proper circumstances for its application arise" (607-08).

These pro-patent words of the Supreme Court came in the same term as the decision in *Great A. & P. Tea Co.*, the last case decided before the long drought of Supreme Court decisions in patent cases that extended from 1950 to 1966, when the Court once again granted review of a patent case in *Graham v. John Deere Co.*

*Winans v. Denmead*, cited in *Graver Tank*, was also cited in the *Markman* case, in which the Federal Circuit said that *Winans* supported the proposition that claim construction was a matter of law. In contrast, the Court in *Graver Tank* held that *Winans* was the source of the doctrine of equivalents, a fact issue.

As to the difference between fact and law, *Graver Tank* held that a "finding of equivalents is a determination of fact. Proof can be made in any form: through the testimony of experts or others versed in the technology; by documents, including texts and treatises; and, of course, by the disclosures of the prior art. Like any other issue of fact, final determination requires a balancing of credibility, persuasiveness, and weight of evidence. It is to be decided by the trial court and that court's decision, under general principles of appellate review, should not be disturbed unless clearly erroneous. Particularly is this so in a field where so much depends upon familiarity with specific scientific problems and principles not usually contained in the general storehouse of knowledge and experience" (609-10)

This teaching of *Graver Tank* (which is remarkably similar to Rule 52(a)), is completely at odds with the Federal Circuit rule in *Vitronics* that "In those cases where the public record [specification, claims, and prosecution history] unambiguously describes the scope of the patented invention, reliance on any extrinsic evidence is improper" (90 F. 3d at 1583, see chapter 11). Testimony of experts or others versed in the technology, documents, including texts and treatises, and disclosure of the prior art, held to be proper in *Graver Tank*, are improper under the peculiar Federal Circuit's "own law," as expressed in *Vitronics*.

Congress has never said that reliance by a district court on evidence in the form of expert testimony, documents, and prior art not included in the file wrapper is "improper," as the Federal Circuit has repeatedly said. The Federal Circuit's "own law" on this evidentiary point has no statutory support.

On the contrary, the Federal Rules of Evidence allow courts to rely on such expert and extrinsic evidence. The Federal Circuit does not follow Supreme Court precedents, including *Graver Tank*, or Rules requiring deference to the district court's reliance upon proper evidence.

Justices Black and Douglas, who were in the majority in *A. & P.*, dissented in *Graver Tank*. They said that the majority "invoked the judicial 'doctrine of equivalents' to broaden the claim for 'alkaline earth metals' so as to embrace 'manganese'" (613). Such a finding "relies upon what the specifications revealed" (*id.*), which violates the statute requiring claims to particularly point out and distinctly claim the subject matter that the applicant regards as his invention. The statute in 1950 was slightly different from the language adopted by Congress in 1952, but the meaning was the same. According to the dissent, "The claim is a statutory requirement, prescribed for the very purpose of making the patentee define precisely what his invention is; and it is unjust to the public, as well as an evasion of the law, to construe it in a manner different from the plain import of its terms" (614, quoting *White v. Dunbar*, 119 U.S. 47, 51 (1886)).

The first case involving the doctrine of equivalents decided by a patent court was *Warner-Jenkinson Co., Inc. v. Hilton Davis Chemical Co.*, 520 U.S. 17 (1997). The doctrine allows protection for an invention even when the accused product falls outside the four corners of the patent claim. Because the CCPA had no jurisdiction over patent infringement disputes, it was not possible for the Supreme Court to review a CCPA decision on the doctrine. It was fifteen years after the Federal Circuit began hearing appeals from district court decisions related to the doctrine of equivalents in 1982 that the Supreme Court considered the first doctrine-of-equivalents case from the Federal Circuit.

The Federal Circuit decision that was reviewed by the Supreme Court was titled *Hilton Davis Chemical Co. v. Warner-Jenkinson Co., Inc.*, 62 F. 3d 1512 (Fed. Cir. 1995). Five opinions were prepared by the twelve patent court judges. The unsigned *per curiam* opinion represented the view of six judges. One judge filed a concurring opinion, and five judges dissented in three different opinions.

There were eight *amicus curiae* briefs, indicating concern over the scope of the doctrine of equivalents after forty-five years of silence by the Supreme Court. One of the considerations in granting certiorari by the Supreme Court is when one "United States court of appeals has entered a decision in conflict with the decision of another United States court of appeals on the same important matter" (Supreme Court Rule 10(a)). Because there is only one court of appeals for patent matters, having two opinions supporting the decision by seven judges of the Federal Circuit and three opinions by five of those judges opposed is tantamount to a conflict between courts of appeals, indicating that certiorari might be appropriate. The conflict was not between decisions of two courts of appeal. Rather, it was between majority and minority of the Federal Circuit.

The opinion of the majority of the Federal Circuit traced the history of the doctrine from Circuit Justice Story's decision in *Odiorne v. Winkley*, 18 F. Cas. 581 (C.C.D. Mass. 1814) through *Graver Tank* and Federal Circuit cases from 1982, comparing the "insubstantial differences" and "function-way-result" tests for applying the doctrine.

When the Federal Circuit decided to consider the case en banc, it asked the parties to brief three questions:

1. Does a finding of infringement under the doctrine of equivalents require anything in addition to proof of the facts that there are the same or substantially the same (a) function, (b) way, and (c) result, the so-called triple identity test of Graver Tank v. Linde Air Products Co., 339 U.S. 605 (1950), and cases relied on therein? If yes, what?
2. Is the issue of infringement under the doctrine of equivalents an equitable remedy to be decided by the court, or is it, like literal infringement, an issue of fact to be submitted to the jury in a jury case?

3. Is application of the doctrine of equivalents by the trial court to find infringement of the patentee's right to exclude, when there is no literal infringement of the claim, discretionary in accordance with the circumstances of the case?

After the Federal Circuit received briefing on these questions, it answered the three questions this way:

In answer to the first question posed by this court en banc, a finding of infringement under the doctrine of equivalents requires proof of insubstantial differences between the claimed and accused products or processes. Often the function-way-result test will suffice to show the extent of the differences. In such cases, the parties will understandably focus on the evidence of function, way, and result, and the fact-finder will apply the doctrine based on that evidence. Other factors, however, such as evidence of copying or designing around, may also inform the test for infringement under the doctrine of equivalents. No judge can anticipate whether such other factors will arise in a given case. Instead, the presence of such factors will depend on the way the parties frame their arguments. Neither the Supreme Court nor this court limits the types of evidence that either party may proffer in support of a factor it considers probative of infringement under the doctrine. The trial judge, however, has a duty to decide whether the proffered evidence is relevant. This duty to assess relevance is no different in a doctrine of equivalents case than in any other type of case. Relevance will be self-evident to the judge in a case tried to the bench. In a jury trial, however, the judge must admit only relevant evidence, and instruct the jury to consider only the admitted evidence in reaching its decision.

In answer to the second question posed by this court en banc, infringement under the doctrine of equivalents is an issue of fact to be submitted to the jury in a jury trial with proper instructions, and to be decided by the judge in a bench trial. The answer to the third question posed by this court en banc necessarily flows from the answer to the second question. The trial judge does not have discretion to choose whether to apply the doctrine of equivalents when the record shows no literal infringement.

The Federal Circuit thus held that function, way and result were not the only factors to consider, and that other factors may be weighed in determining whether the differences were "insubstantial."

This holding by the Federal Circuit resembles its holding in the *Pfaff* case involving the on-sale bar under 35 U.S.C. §102(b) (see chapter 5). The Federal Circuit in *Pfaff* applied what it called the "totality of the circumstances" test to determine the trigger for the on-sale bar (525 U.S., 66). The Supreme Court rejected that test and applied a much simpler two-part test of (1) commercial offer for sale, and (2) ready for patenting (67). In *Warner-Jenkinson*, the Federal Circuit held that other factors– besides function, way and result, were to be considered, and the trial judge had to determine the relevance of evidence of these other factors before allowing the jury to be presented with evidence on the issue of "insubstantial differences." Again, the Supreme Court rejected the *Graver Tank* multiple-factor test.

The dissents in the Federal Circuit pointed out that the claims define the invention, not the specification, much as the dissent by Black and Douglas in *Graver Tank* did, among other arguments.

Justice Thomas, for a unanimous Court in *Warner-Jenkinson*, addressed the petitioner's arguments that the doctrine runs afoul of the statutory requirement that the claims define the invention. The same arguments were made by the dissent in *Graver Tank*, and were insufficient to "command a majority" (520 U.S., 26). Indeed, the dissent argument in *Graver Tank* resembled the dissent argument in *Winans v. Denmead* that the Patent Act of 1836 required an applicant to "particularly 'specify and point'" out what he claims as his invention" (id.). The 1952 act and the 1870 act were substantially the same and "have no bearing on the result reached in *Graver Tank*, and thus provide no basis for overruling it" (id.).

The fact that the word "equivalent" appears in 35 U.S.C. §112, paragraph 6 does not mean that Congress was overruling *Graver Tank*. The "lengthy history of the doctrine of equivalents strongly supports adherence to our refusal in *Graver Tank* to find the Patent Act conflicts with that doctrine. Congress can legislate the doctrine of equivalents out of existence any time it chooses. The various policy arguments now made by both sides are best addressed to Congress, not this Court" (28).

The Court created a new presumption in *Warner-Jenkinson*: that any amendment to a claim may be presumed to be for reasons related to patentability, in which case prosecution history estoppel may apply. The presumption is rebuttable, and if a patentee can show that an amendment was not made to distinguish over the prior art, the doctrine of equivalents may still apply. Because the new presumption was not before the Federal Circuit, the case was remanded to determine whether the "theory of equivalence would entirely vitiate a particular claim element" (39), in which case judgment as a matter of law would be rendered to the accused infringer under the doctrine of prosecution history estoppel by motion under Rule 56 or Rule 50.

The Supreme Court reversed the decision of the Federal Circuit which sought to substitute "insubstantial differences" as a less helpful analytical approach than function-way-result. The doctrine of equivalents was upheld, as was the doctrine of prosecution history estoppel. Because a new presumption was created to reconcile those two doctrines, the case was remanded.

Five years after *Warner-Jenkinson*, the Court again revisited the doctrine of equivalents on certiorari to the Federal Circuit. *Festo Corp. v. Shoketsu Kinzoku Kabushiki Co., Ltd.*, 535 U.S. 722 (2002) was part of the continuing effort of the Federal Circuit to limit, if not abolish, the doctrine of equivalents. The Federal Circuit succeeded in *Warner-Jenkinson* in making the doctrine of equivalents subservient to the doctrine of prosecution history estoppel unless it could be established that a claim limitation was not added in an amendment for reasons of patentability. That is, if an amendment is in response to a rejection of a claim and is intended to limit the invention in order to render the claim patentable, the patentee is estopped from arguing that the amended claim is infringed under the doctrine of equivalents. This is a severe limitation on the doctrine of equivalents.

The Federal Circuit in *Festo* considered the case *en banc*, just as it had considered *Warner-Jenkinson*. Like the earlier case, it asked the parties to brief a series of questions. The first question was whether "a substantial reason related to patentability," as the Supreme Court said in *Warner-Jenkinson*, was limited to amendments made to overcome prior art, or whether "patentability" included any reason affecting the issuance of the patent.

The question was relevant to the *Festo* case because the examiners' rejection of the Festo patent applications was not only based upon prior art, but also on form. The claims were rejected as unclear (that is, not in the "full, clear, concise and exact terms" that 35 U.S.C. §112, paragraph 1, requires), and not in proper form (that is, failing to point out and distinctly claim the subject matter as required by 35 U.S.C. §112, paragraph 2).

Festo amended the claims by adding limitations that were not present in the original claims. SMC, a competitor of Festo, came out with a competing product that failed to fall within the scope of the patented claims, but did fall within the scope of the original, rejected claims that had been canceled in order to overcome the rejections.

The Federal Circuit asked the first question in order to determine whether prosecution history estoppel applied to all grounds of rejection that were later overcome by an amendment. The Federal Circuit answered the question by holding that any ground of rejection (i.e. the denial of patentability by the examiner) can be a basis for prosecution history estoppel.

Justice Kennedy, for a unanimous Supreme Court, wrote "We agree with the Court of Appeals that a narrowing amendment made to satisfy a requirement of the Patent Act may give rise to an estoppel" (736). The Court did so after a careful explanation of the two doctrines of equivalents and prosecution history estoppel.

As to the doctrine of equivalents, the Court said "the nature of language makes it impossible to capture the essence of a thing in a patent application," and quoted *Autogiro Co. v. United States*, 384 F. 2d 391, 397 (Ct. Cl. 1967): "An invention exists most importantly as a tangible structure or a series of drawings. A verbal portrayal usually is an afterthought written to satisfy the requirements of patent law. This conversion of machine to words allows for unintended idea gaps which cannot be satisfactorily filled…Things are not made for the sake of words, but words for things…" (731).

"If patents were always interpreted by their literal terms, their value would be greatly diminished. Unimportant and insubstantial substitutes for certain elements could defeat the patent, and its value to inventors could be destroyed by simple acts of copying. For this reason, the clearest rule of patent interpretation, literalism, may conserve judicial resources but is not the most efficient rule. The scope of a patent is not limited to its literal terms but instead embraces all equivalents to the claims described" (731–32).

This explanation of the doctrine of equivalents emphasizes the difference between patent prosecution and patent infringement. The scope of a patent is determined in patent prosecution literally, because there is no allegedly infringing product in patent prosecution. The words in the application are all that there is–there is nothing to compare the literal words to. The scope of a patent claim in infringement litigation, on the other hand, is a comparison of the literal words to the accused product. The comparison must be measured by the invention *in pais* (to use the words of *Bischoff v. Wethered*, 76 U.S. 812 (1870)), rather than the literal words resulting from patent prosecution.

The CCPA considered patent prosecution, not patent infringement. While the Federal Circuit has jurisdiction over both patent prosecution in the PTO and patent infringement in the district courts, the expertise of the judges in the second patent court is much stronger in patent prosecution than it is in patent infringement cases. As a result, the Federal Circuit favors reliance upon the doctrine of patent prosecution estoppel rather than the doctrine of equivalents.

That is why the Federal Circuit in *Festo* held that the doctrine of prosecution history estoppel trumps the doctrine of equivalents. The Federal Circuit before its *Festo* decision applied a flexible rule for prosecution history estoppel. As the Supreme Court noted in reviewing *Festo*, the "Court of Appeals held that prosecution history estoppel is a complete bar, and so the narrowed element must be limited to its strict literal terms. Based upon its experience the Court of Appeals decided that the flexible-bar rule is unworkable because it leads to excessive uncertainty and burdens legitimate innovation" (737). In other words, the Federal Circuit abolished the doctrine of equivalents for amended claims.

The Supreme Court rejected this *per se* rule, and followed its precedents that acknowledge "this uncertainty [in determining equivalents] as the price of ensuring the appropriate incentives for innovation and... affirmed the doctrine [of equivalents] over the dissents that wanted a more certain rule..." (732). "Most recently, in *Warner-Jenkinson*, the Court reaffirmed that equivalents remain a firmly entrenched part of the settled rights protected by the patent" (732-33).

The Court continued: "Prosecution history estoppel ensures that the doctrine of equivalents remains tied to its underlying purpose. Where the original application once embraced the purported equivalent but the patentee narrowed his claims to obtain the patent or protect its validity, the patentee cannot assert that he lacked words to describe the subject matter in question. The doctrine of equivalents is premised on language's inability to capture the essence of innovation, but a prior application describing the precise element at issue undercuts that premise. In that instance the prosecution history has established that the inventor turned his attention to the subject matter in question, knew the words for both the broader and narrower claim, and affirmatively chose the latter" (at 734-35).

The Court found "no reason why a narrowing amendment should be deemed to relinquish equivalents unforeseeable at the time of the amendment and beyond a fair interpretation of what was surrendered" (738). Rather that abolish the doctrine of equivalents for amended claims, as the Federal Circuit attempted to do, the Supreme Court adhered to the "appropriate balance [between the two doctrines] by placing the burden on the patentee to show that an amendment was not for purposes of patentability" that it struck in *Warner-Jenkinson* (739). Because the Federal Circuit failed to explore the reasons for the amendments with the rebuttable presumption in mind, its judgment was vacated and the case remanded.

The Court said in *Warner-Jenkinson*, that "Congress can legislate the doctrine of equivalents out of existence any time it chooses" (526 U.S., 28), but the Federal Circuit lacks that power. The Federal Circuit must defer to the Supreme Court, as it was reminded in both of the doctrine-of-equivalents cases decided by the patent court that were reviewed by the Supreme Court.

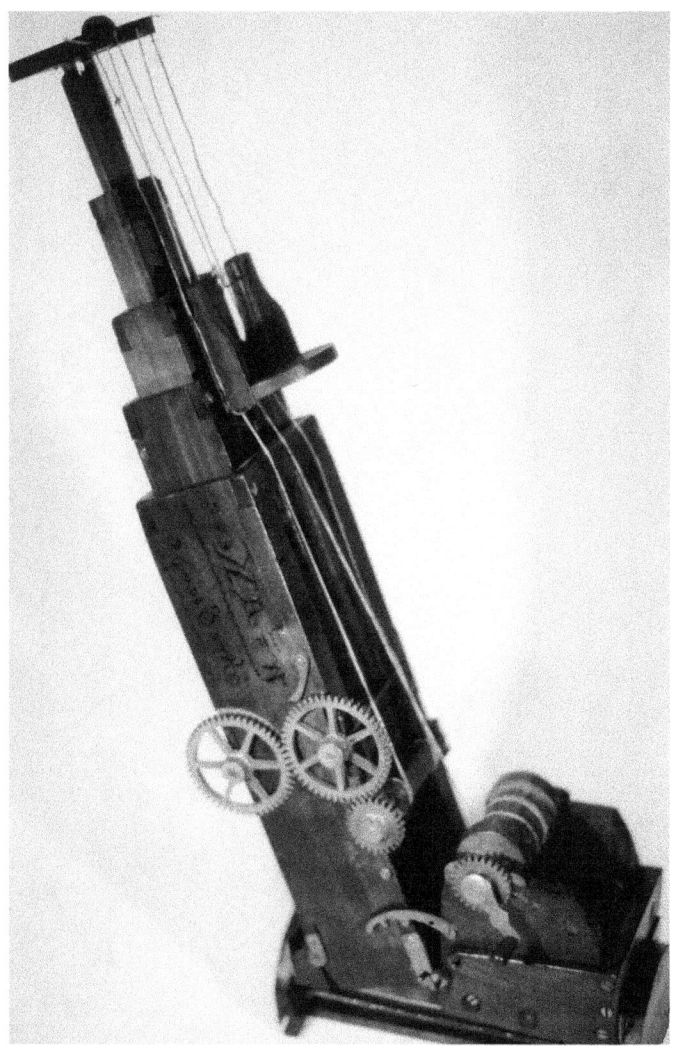

# CHAPTER 20

# WELL-PLEADED COMPLAINT

Although the Federal Circuit sometimes seeks to expand its jurisdiction for policy reasons (e.g. *Cardinal Chemical Co. v. Morton International, Inc.*, 508 U.S. 83 (1993), at other times it resists expanding its jurisdiction over matters that are not within the congressional mandate of patent law. The case of *Christianson v. Colt Industries Operating Corp.*, 486 U.S. 800 (1988) is in the latter category. In *Christianson*, both the Seventh Circuit and the Federal Circuit believed that jurisdiction rested with the other circuit and transferred the case back and forth like a Ping-Pong ball. Each insisted that it did not have jurisdiction.

In 1959, Colt Industries acquired a license to sixteen patents related to making rifles that became the M16, the army's standard rifle for many years. Although Colt obtained other patents for making the rifles, it also owned trade secrets about manufacturing specifications and the like. Employees and contractors who had access to the proprietary information were required contractually to agree to preserve the secrets.

Christianson was a former Colt employee who had signed such a contract; he later left Colt and set up his own business selling M16 parts. Colt sued Christianson and others involved in a sale of 16's to El Salvador for patent infringement. The case was voluntarily dismissed by Colt when its motion for an injunction against the defendants was denied, but Colt told Christianson's customers that they were illegally using Colt trade secrets. Colt also told certain customers that they should refrain from doing business with the perpetrators.

Christianson and his affiliates then sued Colt for antitrust violations and damages for driving them out of business. The Christianson et al complaint had a provision alleging that the Colt patents were "invalid through the wrongful retention of proprietary information in contravention of United States Patent Law (35 U.S.C. §112)" (805). In any event, they alleged, the patents had expired and Christianson, his company and its affiliates had "the right to manufacture, contract for the manufacture, supply, market and sell the M-16 and M-16 parts and accessories" (805).

The plaintiffs later amended the complaint to plead a state law claim for tortuous interference with their business relationships. Colt defended against this claim by asserting trade secrets and counterclaimed for misappropriation of Colt M16 specifications.

The plaintiffs moved for summary judgment, arguing that the Colt patents were invalid and the trade secrets claims could not protect the same inventions contained in the invalid patents. They sought a ruling that "Colt's trade secrets are invalid and that its claim of invalidity shall be taken as established with respect to all claims and counterclaims to which said issue is material" (806).

The district court granted the motion as to liability on both the antitrust and the tortuous-interference claims. Nine Colt patents were held to be invalid, all trade secrets relating to the M16 were unenforceable and Colt was enjoined from enforcing "any form of trade secret right in any technical information relating to the M16" (id.).

Colt appealed to the Federal Circuit, which held that it lacked jurisdiction because the case did not arise "under any Act of Congress relating to patents" under 28 U.S.C. §1338(a). The Federal Circuit transferred the case to the Seventh Circuit, the regional circuit in which the district court was located. The Seventh Circuit held that the Federal Circuit was "clearly wrong" and transferred the case back to the Federal Circuit. The Federal Circuit held that the Seventh Circuit was "clearly wrong" in its interpretation. Instead of bouncing the ball back to the Seventh Circuit, the Federal Circuit decided the case on the merits. Having a clear conflict between the decisions of two United States courts of appeal, the Supreme Court granted certiorari (806-07).

The Court cited its nineteenth century precedent *Pratt v. Paris Gas Light & Coke Co.*, 168 U.S. 255, 259 (1897), stating that "in order to demonstrate that a case is one 'arising under' federal patent law, 'the plaintiff must set up some right, title or interest under the patent laws, or at least make it appear that some right or privilege will be defeated by one construction, or sustained by the opposite construction of these laws'" (807-08). It also cited other cases, including *Franchise Tax Board of California v. Construction Laborers Vacation Trust*, 463 U.S. 1, 13 (1983), stating "Federal law is a necessary element of one of the well-pleaded...claims" (808). Section 1338(a) jurisdiction is limited "only to those cases in which a well-pleaded complaint establishes that either that federal patent law creates a cause of action or that the plaintiff's right to relief necessarily depends on resolution of a substantial question of federal patent law, in that patent law is a necessary element of one of the well-pleaded claims" (809).

The Christianson complaint is clear "that patent law did not in any sense create petitioners' antitrust or intentional interference claims...Under the well-pleaded complaint rule, as appropriately adapted to §1338(a), whether a claim 'arises under' patent law 'must be determined from what necessarily appears in the plaintiff's statement of his own claim in the bill or declaration, unaided by anything alleged in anticipation or avoidance of defenses which it is thought the defendant may interpose.' Thus, a case raising a patent law defense does not, for that reason alone, 'arise under' patent law, 'even if the defense is anticipated in plaintiff's complaint, and even if both parties admit that the defense is the only question truly at issue on the case'" (id. citations omitted).

The complaint continued:

Both the Seventh Circuit and Colt focus entirely on what they perceive to be 'the only basis Christianson asserted in the complaint for the alleged antitrust violation... namely, that Colt made false assertions in its letters and pleadings that petitioners were violating its trade secrets, when those trade secrets were not protected under state law because Colt's patents were invalid under §112. Thus, Colt concludes, the validity of the patents is an essential element of petitioners' prima facie monopolization theory and the case 'arises under' patent law...The well-pleaded complaint rule, however, focuses on claims, not theories...and just because an element that is essential to a particular theory might be governed by federal patent law does not mean that the entire monopolization claim 'arises under' patent law." (811).

"Our agreement with the Federal Circuit's conclusion that it lacked jurisdiction, compels us to disapprove its decision to reach the merits anyway 'in the interests of justice.' Courts created by statute have no jurisdiction but such as the statute confers. The statute confers on the Federal Circuit authority to make a single decision upon concluding that it lacks jurisdiction-whether to dismiss the case or, "in the interest of justice," to transfer it to a court of appeals that has jurisdiction...That does not mean, however, that every borderline case must inevitably culminate in a perpetual game of jurisdictional Ping-Pong until this Court intervenes to resolve the underlying jurisdictional dispute, or (more likely) until one of the parties surrenders to futility...Under law-of-the-case principles, if the transferee court can find the transfer decision plausible, its jurisdiction inquiry is at an end...We vacate the judgment of the Court of Appeals for the Federal Circuit and remand with instructions to transfer the case to the Court of Appeals for the Seventh Circuit" (818-19, citations omitted).

Accordingly, although the Federal Circuit's judgment on the merits was vacated, and the case was transferred to the Seventh Circuit to decide the merits, the Supreme Court agreed with the Federal Circuit's decision that it lacked jurisdiction to consider Colt's appeal. The Court ruled that the Federal Circuit decision on jurisdiction was the law of the case, and binding on the Seventh Circuit.

The Federal Circuit's decision quoted both the *Pratt* case and the *Franchise Tax Board* case regarding the well-pleaded complaint rule, just as the Supreme Court did. This is remarkable because in 1987, when the Federal Circuit decided *Christianson v. Colt*, 822 F, 2d 1544, 1553-1554 (1987), it had only been in the business of reviewing district court patent cases for five years. Before 1982, the CCPA had never considered the well-pleaded complaint rule because it never reviewed a district court decision in which there was a federal complaint. Whether a complaint was well-pleaded or not was never an issue before the CCPA.

Chief Judge Markey, author of the *Christianson* opinion in the Federal Circuit, had been Chief Judge of the CCPA. He could not have been familiar with the well-pleaded complaint rule while at the CCPA because judicial complaints were not within the jurisdiction of the CCPA. However, Chief Judge Markey was diligent in sitting on occasion with regional courts of appeals in order to be sure all circuit courts were following the same rules in deciding cases within their jurisdictions. It may well be that Judge Markey became familiar with the well-pleaded complaint rule when sitting with other courts of appeal. Whenever he learned the rule, his opinion for the Federal Circuit was thorough, cited the appropriate Supreme Court precedents, and was followed by the Supreme Court in *Christianson* in every way except in deciding the merits of the case over which the Federal Circuit had no jurisdiction.

Unlike so many of the Federal Circuit decisions that were overturned by the Supreme Court in the first twenty-five years, the legal doctrine in question (here the well-pleaded complaint rule) was correctly and convincingly set forth by the Federal Circuit and adopted by the Supreme Court. Overstepping its jurisdictional authority in deciding the merits of the controversy is merely a manifestation of the Federal Circuit's relative inexperience with judicial disputes.

The other well-pleaded complaint case in the Supreme Court on certiorari to the Federal Circuit was *The Holmes Group, Inc. v. Vornado Air Circulation Systems, Inc.*, 535 U.S. 826 (2002). After *Christianson* was decided, the Federal Circuit decided several cases extending its jurisdiction over disputes similar to, but not exactly like patent disputes. For example, in *Aerojet General Corp. v. Machinery Tool Works*, 895 F. 2d 736 (Fed. Cir. 1990), held that a well-pleaded, non-frivolous, compulsory counterclaim is different from the mere argument regarding a defense, as was the case in *Christianson*, and was within Federal Circuit jurisdiction.

The Supreme Court called a halt to the creeping expansion of Federal Circuit jurisdiction in *Holmes*. The well-pleaded complaint rule means that the *complaint* is the controlling document for determining jurisdiction. "It follows that a counterclaim-which appears as part of the defendant's answer, not as part of the plaintiff's complaint-cannot serve as the basis for 'arising under' jurisdiction" (831). "Since the plaintiff is 'the master of the complaint,' the well-pleaded complaint rule enables him, 'by eschewing claims based on federal law...to have the cause heard in state court.' (id, citation omitted.). In *Christianson*, the Court held "that the Federal Circuit's jurisdiction, like that of the district court, 'is determined by reference to the well-pleaded complaint, not the well-tried case'" (832). If, after hearing all of the policy arguments that allowing regional circuits to consider patent law issues simply because they are raised in a counterclaim returns patent law to where it was before the Federal Circuit was created, Congress could codify the rule with additional words like "except where a counterclaim is pleaded." This would amend the rule in the manner that the Federal Circuit wished. However, it is not for the Federal Circuit to amend a long standing Supreme Court rule in cases involving federal jurisdiction "arising under" §1331. The term "arising under" is the same in §1338 as it is in §1331.

The Court in *Holmes* essentially said that the well-pleaded complaint rule means what it says, and inferior courts may not narrow or amend it. Tinkering with jurisdictional rules does not advance the policy objective of patent law uniformity of patent law that guided Congress to create the Federal Circuit. "Our task here is not to determine what would further Congress's goal of ensuring patent-law uniformity, but to determine what the words of the statute must fairly be understood to mean" (833). Policy matters are for the legislative branch to resolve, not the judiciary.

Vornado started the fight by suing a third party, Duracraft, for theft of its trade dress in a fan grill design that was not patented. Vornado lost that battle in the Tenth Circuit, which ruled that it had no trade dress rights. Later, Vornado sued Holmes for patent infringement based on the same fan grill design, which was no longer a trade dress but by then a patented design-a federal claim. Next, Holmes sued Vornado for a declaratory judgment that the fan grill design was not infringed, and sought an injunction against Vornado asserting the same trade dress claim that the Tenth Circuit had held Vornado was not entitled to protect in the *Duracraft* case. Vornado answered and asserted the compulsory counterclaim of patent infringement. The district court granted the Holmes motion for an injunction, based on collateral estoppel by the *Duracraft* case. The patent counterclaim was stayed pending appeal.

Vornado appealed to the Federal Circuit, and Holmes challenged its jurisdiction. The Federal Circuit vacated the district court's decision and remanded for consideration of a recent Federal Circuit decision on the trade dress conflict among circuits. The Supreme Court granted Holmes's petition for certiorari.

Because the Holmes complaint related to the trade dress claim and Vornado's patent claim was asserted as a counterclaim, the Supreme Court vacated the Federal Circuit's judgment and remanded with instructions to transfer the case to the Tenth Circuit, which had already decided the trade dress issue. "Because [Holmes's] complaint did not include any claim based on patent law, we vacate the judgment" (834).

Accordingly, in the two well-pleaded complaint cases decided by the Federal Circuit and reviewed by the Supreme Court, the Federal Circuit was overturned both times. The first time, in *Christianson*, the Supreme Court agreed with the Federal Circuit's jurisdictional ruling entirely. The problem was that instead of simply dismissing the appeal for lack of jurisdiction after transferring the case to the Seventh Circuit and having it transferred back, the Federal Circuit decided the case on the merits. It assumed jurisdiction when it should have declined jurisdiction and suggested that a party dissatisfied with the result should seek review.

In the *Holmes* case, the Federal Circuit made its own decision on what policy would promote uniformity and extended its jurisdiction to include counterclaims as well as well-pleaded complaints asserting patent claims. Had the Federal Circuit simply followed its own decision in *Christianson* in applying the well-pleaded complaint rule in *Holmes*, it would not have strayed into a power grab for broader jurisdiction.

# CHAPTER 21

# SUMMATION

The thirty-three patent court decisions that have been reviewed by the Supreme Court between 1966 and 2012 have all been explored, as well as many other decisions that have not reached the Supreme Court, but may have raised issues that might be considered by the Court.

A summation of some of the lessons learned and lessons not yet learned is appropriate. I will not address here every issue raised in this book, only some of the more important ones. A report card on the lessons, either "pass" or "fail," will be used to assess whether the patent courts have learned some of the lessons taught by the Supreme Court in reviewing patent court decisions.

## 1. The Patent Courts' "Own Law."

Perhaps the greatest failure of the Federal Circuit is the belief that Congress empowered it to create its "own law." The belief in that power is evident throughout this book. In the prologue, we explored the conventional wisdom that Congress created the Federal Circuit to provide uniformity in patent law by having a single court of specialists instead of twelve circuit courts of generalists reviewing district court decisions in patent cases. But "uniformity" in the resolution of patent law disputes is a task for the judicial branch of government, not the legislative branch.

The legislative branch lacks the ability to determine how judicial disputes should be resolved, and it lacks the power to grant the Federal Circuit the power to make uniform rules to resolve judicial disputes. The judicial branch is headed by the Supreme Court, which promulgates the rules.

One set of rules is the Rules of the Supreme Court of the United States. Rule 10(a) deals with the issue of uniformity. One thing the Court may consider in deciding to grant certiorari is whether "a United States court of appeals has entered a decision in conflict with another United States court of appeals on the same important matter."

Congress lacks the power to overrule Supreme Court Rule 10(a) or to make the Federal Circuit the resolver of conflicts among courts. The conventional wisdom fails to consider Rule 10(a).

Another set of rules promulgated by the judicial branch is the Federal Rules of Civil Procedure. When there is a conflict between two commentators on the interpretation of the rules, the advisory committee can amend the rules to clarify the interpretation. An example is the 1985 amendment to Rule 52(a) to make it clear that trial courts determine facts, not appellate courts. The Federal Circuit has not learned that lesson, and continues to substitute its view of the facts for the district court's view of the facts. If the Federal Circuit can create its "own law," it must encompass only the law, and cannot extend to findings of fact, which is the duty of the fact-finder.

But the Federal Circuit cannot write its own rules for conducting its judicial business. Like all courts, it must abide by the Federal Rules of Civil Procedure and the Federal Rules of Appellate Procedure on procedural matters. It must follow the Federal Rules of Evidence, and, of course, the advisory committee notes accompanying all of the federal rules. It also must abide by the substantive acts of Congress on patents, trademarks, and other matters within its jurisdiction. All of these constraints leave precious little room for the Federal Circuit to promulgate its "own law."

For example, the advisory committee notes to the 2000 amendments to Evidence Rule 702 require that expert testimony (1) be by a "qualified" expert, (2) must "address a subject matter on which the fact-finder can be assisted by an expert;" (3) be reliable; and (4) must "'fit' the facts of the case."

Instead of following these safeguards in Rule 702, the Federal Circuit's "own law" simply disregards inventor and expert testimony and substitutes its own omniscient interpretation of facts. *Vitronics Corp. v. Conceptronic, Inc.*, 90 F. 3d 1576 (Fed Cir. 1996), held that reliance on "extrinsic evidence, such as expert testimony" is improper if the public record is unambiguous. "Allowing the public record to be altered or changed by extrinsic evidence introduced at trial, such as expert testimony, would make this right [to rely on the public record] meaningless."

*Vitronics* is contrary to Evidence Rule 702, but the Federal Circuit repeatedly relies upon its own precedents instead of the governing federal rules.

A trier of fact may rely upon expert testimony at trial. There is nothing to support the belief that a public record, which is not prepared for deciding facts in future disputes, is inherently superior to the sworn testimony of a qualified expert regarding the facts of the case.

The Supreme Court has repeatedly corrected the misconceptions of the Federal Circuit's "own law." These two examples of Supreme Court approved rules (Rule 52(a) and Rule 702) are just two that the Court has not yet finally corrected. It is clear that the Federal Circuit must reassess its "own law" to be sure it fits the judiciary standards. To that end, it would be wise to have impartial "advisory committees," as the Federal Rules do, instead of biased law organizations like the New York Patent Law Association which sponsored Giles Rich to help write the 1952 patent act. I suggest that the patent court's "own law" has no foundation and must give way to the mainstream judicial branch of government.

To hold that an appellate court may ignore expert testimony weighed by the fact-finder in the district court is not mainstream law.

## 2. Facts v. Law

A related problem is distinguishing between facts and law. The CCPA never reviewed decisions of district courts. That jurisdiction only came to the Federal Circuit when it was created in 1982. Federal Rule 52(a), which requires an appellate court to defer to facts found by the trier of fact unless "clearly erroneous," did not apply to the CCPA review of facts found by the PTO. The PTO has never instructed patent examiners to separately set forth findings of fact apart from conclusions of law. Instead, patent examiners are trained to cite the statutory basis for a rejection (e.g. section 102 or 103), followed by a summary of what the references teach that makes the claims unpatentable. This puts the cart of conclusions of law before the horse of findings of fact- -the opposite of district court findings of fact and conclusions of law.

On appeal, the CCPA did not hesitate to substitute its interpretation of the facts in the prior art for that of the patent examiner. This is easily accomplished by picking and choosing among the terms used in a patent application for a reading that fits the conclusion the court of appeals chooses to follow. No deference was paid to the determination of facts by the tribunal of first instance, because there is no live testimony in patent prosecution, and thus no opportunity to judge the credibility of the inventor as would be the case if the inventor were cross-examined about the facts surrounding the invention.

Worse, even the written word of the patent application is seldom prepared by the inventor. It reflects the view of the facts relevant to both the invention and the prior art through the eyes of the patent application. Sometimes, more than one drafter stands between the inventor's view of the facts and the patent examiner- -none of whom has sworn to tell the truth, the whole truth, and nothing but the truth. For example, the inventor may not be trained in factual presentations of what happens when the invention is used. Also, in a corporation or in a large law firm, there may be a junior patent agent or patent attorney that prepares a first draft of a patent application, subject to review and revision by a senior drafter. The more application drafters, the less the facts known to the inventor are likely to be presented.

Likewise, a junior patent examiner may draft a version of the facts that is subject to review and revision by a senior patent examiner. Although patent examiners are assumed to have expertise in the technology involved in the patent application, applications are *never* prepared with a numbered list of facts about the invention claimed in the patent as well as the facts shown in the prior art that the inventor attests are true or believed to be true, followed by separate conclusions of law. Rather, an agent for the inventor writes a narrative of what he or she believes is true with no numbered facts regarding what the invention is, as a matter of fact, and what the prior art teaches, as a matter of fact.

The ultimate test of the truth of facts, cross-examination of a live witness before a judge or jury, is nowhere to be found in patent prosecution. I do not advocate cross-examination of live witnesses in patent prosecution. I only assert that the safeguards of a trial in a United States district court are much more likely to establish the truth of facts than is the present patent prosecution system.

On the other hand, should the lack of safeguards in the PTO permit the CCPA to ignore the facts found by the patent examiner and the Board of Patent Appeals and Interferences and substitute wholesale its views of the facts? I think not, because our judicial branch is geared to defer to the trier of fact. The patent examiner is trained to judge the facts (although the procedure has law set forth first and facts thereafter).

It would help if patent examiners were taught to be finders of fact, not adversaries to patent agents and attorneys. Also, examiners should learn that facts need to be proved by credible evidence, not speculation by an inventor's agent. Instead of drawing inferences from narratives, whether written in patent applications or in briefs by the agents, it is important to focus on the truth of facts, rather than the conclusions to be drawn from those facts.

A great many improvements should be made in the quasi-judicial patent examination process, but the focus of this book is on the judicial process, which needs equally important safeguards.

To be sure, the patent examination process is not like the adversarial process of determining which of two rival claimants is the first and true inventor (an interference proceeding).

An interference proceeding involves taking testimony from rival claimants to an invention in order to decide which one was first. It resembles the findings of fact made by a trial court after receiving evidence. An appellate court must presume that findings of fact by a trial court are correct and worthy of deference unless clearly erroneous. That should include interference proceedings.

A "mere appeal from a decision of the Patent Office" is not entitled to a presumption as strong as that afforded to a district court's findings of fact, as noted by the Supreme Court in *Morgan v. Daniels*, 153 U.S. 120, 124 (1894). The presumption of administrative correctness is grounded on the expertise of patent examiners in doing their job. But that presumption is not as strong as the presumption of Rule 52(a). It would be helpful if the judicial branch of government defined precisely the deference warranted by a patent examiner's findings of fact. Before that, we need to train examiners to carefully distinguish facts from law in order to base rejections on factual findings.

The deference paid to *ex parte* determinations to grant a patent must not exceed the deference owed to *inter partes* determinations such as interferences and judicial proceedings.

The Manual of Patent Examining Procedure (MPEP) needs revision from top to bottom to perform the quasi-judicial process in sync with the judicial branch of government, rather than making decisions according to the conclusions sought, as the political branches (executive and legislative) of government do.

## 3. Facts In Patent Claims

Probably the worst Federal Circuit decision that has not yet been corrected by the Supreme Court is *Cybor Corp. v. FAS Technologies*, 138 F. 3d 1448 (Fed. Cir. 1998).

It not only failed to distinguish between findings of fact and conclusions of law, but it also held that patent claims are devoid of facts and may be interpreted as a matter of law. If it is true that claims define the invention in a patent (and no one seems to doubt that), then how can a claim not have any facts?

The Federal Circuit decided *en banc* in *Cybor* that claim construction was purely a question of law that had no factual component, and it was not bound to defer to the district court findings of fact under Rule 52(a) and could decide *de novo* the meaning of claim terms without deference to the trial court's findings.

A superb criticism of *Cybor* and related cases that was published not long after the decision was handed down is Don Dunner's "*Cybor Corp v. FAS Technologies*: The Final Say on Appellate Review of Claim Construction?" in the Journal of the Patent and Trademark Society, (1998). Dunner, a former CCPA law clerk, has reportedly argued more cases before the Federal Circuit than any other lawyer. Rather than summarize the article here, I conclude that *Cybor* may be the worst Federal Circuit decision that has not yet been corrected by the Supreme Court.

Former District Court Judge O'Malley recently joined the Federal Circuit, a first for the patent courts since 1929. Perhaps deference by the patent court to district court fact-finding may follow. One can only hope so.

My own experience as a law clerk at the CCPA in 1962-64 established that patent claims contain facts. Nobel Prize-winner Glenn Seaborg was the inventor of two patent applications before the court on appeal from the rejections by the PTO while I was there. The CCPA reversed the rejections in each case.

My all-time favorite patent claims were in these two cases. The first, reported in 328 F. 2d 993 (CCPA 1964), claimed "Element 96." The other, reported at 328 F. 2d 996, claimed "Element 95." If patent claims before the patent court are "devoid of facts," as *Cybor* holds, these two claims recite inventions that cannot exist. If elements 95 and 96 are not facts, then these claims are meaningless.

## 4. Precedential Value of Decisions by Sister Courts

My last summation relates to the first decision by the Federal Circuit. In 1982, the former Chief Judge of the CCPA became Chief Judge Markey of the Federal Circuit. The very first decision of the new patent court, *South Corp. v. United States*, 690 F. 2d 1368

(Fed. Cir.1982), held that the decisions of the generalist regional courts of appeals in patent cases since 1890 would not be binding precedents on the specialist patent court.

The Federal Circuit did not say that decisions by non-specialist judges (for example Judge Learned Hand, who wrote important patent decisions as judge in the Southern District of New York and in the Second Circuit Court of Appeals) would not be considered as binding precedents. Rather, the patent court said in *South* that only "the holdings of our predecessor courts, the United States Court of Claims and the United States Court of Customs and Patent Appeals...shall be binding as precedent in this court."

This appears to be a response to the comments in Congress that the new patent court was intended to avoid "intercircuit inconsistency" in patent decisions, in which some circuit courts seemed to be "pro-patent" and other circuit courts seemed to be "anti-patent."

The problem was that the statute creating the Federal Circuit was silent on the value of decisions of sister circuit courts of equal rank in the federal judiciary. Congress had never said that precedents of one circuit would be binding on another circuit. Although a decision in one circuit may not be binding on a decision of another circuit, it should be taken seriously by a sister court. It was for the Supreme Court to determine the outcome of intercircuit differences.

The *South* opinion, stating that only Claims Court and CCPA decisions would be binding precedents, was a declaration that the specialist patent court was *not* bound to take seriously important precedents in sister courts, particularly unanimous decisions authored by giants in patent law, such as Learned Hand.

The assertion by the new specialist court in its first decision that it was unique, capable of writing its "own law" without paying heed to precedents of sister courts of appeal was, in a word, arrogant.

The implication was that the new specialist patent court would be omniscient as the sole source of patent law. It was ready to ignore precedents by courts of appeal having equal rank and be bound to follow only precedents from two administrative courts that had never reviewed decisions by district courts in patent disputes or any other federal disputes.

It was unfortunate for an inferior court to rule, in its very first opinion, that only Court of Claims and CCPA decisions would be binding precedents. The Supreme Court has, in the decisions reviewed here, followed precedents of other circuit courts in patent matters decided before the Federal Circuit was created as sounder precedents that those of the Federal Circuit. The fact that two out of every three Federal Circuit decisions are reversed or vacated by the Supreme Court confirms that the precedential value of Federal Circuit decisions is no greater than that of patent decisions of regional courts of appeal.

The assumption that Congress made the Federal Circuit the omniscient, supreme law of the land in patent matters is not supported by any congressional act or any Supreme Court decision. It is important to note that there are two paths for review of decisions of the PTO.

First, 35 U.S.C. §144 provides for Federal Circuit review of the decision "on the record before the" PTO. Alternatively, 35 U.S.C. §145 provides that if the inventor does not appeal to the Federal Circuit, the inventor may "have remedy by civil action against the Director in the United States District Court for the District of Columbia." It is clear that Congress did not make the Federal Circuit the single, omniscient, specialist court for deciding all appeals from decisions by the PTO.

If the inventor dissatisfied with the decision of the PTO chooses to do so, he may seek remedy before non-specialist district court judges, with the right to appeal to non-specialist judges of the District of Columbia Court of Appeals, followed by the possible review by the non-specialist Supreme Court justices on certiorari.

The District of Columbia Court of Appeals is of the same rank as the Federal Circuit. It is neither superior nor inferior to the Federal Circuit. Both are inferior to the Supreme Court.

The Federal Circuit is not the only court of appeals for reviewing district court decisions in patent matters.

### 5. Article 1, Section 8, Clause 8 of the Constitution

Next year, it will be 225 years (2 and a quarter centuries) that Congress has ignored the mandate of the Founding Fathers "To promote the progress of science and he useful arts, by securing for limited times to authors and inventors the exclusive right to their respective writings and discoveries."

Instead of securing exclusive rights to the writings of authors and to the discoveries of inventors, Congress has secured rights to investors, employers, masters of all types that have deprived the servants, employees, and creators of all types, the fruits of their labors. Contracts of adhesion, by which inventors promise to give their inventions to their employers in order to be employed, are the norm in United States, and their rights to their inventions are not secured, they are appropriated.

Congress follows the money from investors, employers, and masters to achieve or retain their positions, and disregards the Constitutional goal of securing rights to creators. While those of us in the patent bar feed at the same trough as inventors and authors and are funded by employers and investors as well as inventors, I suggest that the Constitutional goal of securing to inventors the rights in their inventions is more important than securing fees for legal work. If nothing more, securing exclusive rights to creators rather than to their employers serves the purpose of "establishing justice," another goal in the Preamble of the Constitution. It is just to secure rights to inventors.

Master-servant law came to this country with colonists that gave us slavery redemptionism, and indentured servitude. The Founding Fathers did away with those unjust doctrines, but Congress has passed laws favoring the government, the investors, and the employers, as explained in the book.

It is time, after two centuries, to embrace the effort to secure rights to authors and inventors rather than allocate those rights to the wealthy, the owners, and the employers. A good starting point is to abolish contracts of adhesion, as other countries have done.

Although it is not a "Summation," I want to end by drawing attention to the failure of Congress, the Patent and Trademark Office, the CCPA, the Federal Circuit, and the Supreme Court, commentators, and the general public to honor the Constitutional goal of securing exclusive rights to inventors, as argued in Chapter's 4 and 8, rather than securing rights to the government, masters, employers, owners, and industry. 220 years of failing to do what the Founding Fathers intended is too long. Congress and the courts must be prodded to promote progress of the useful arts by securing to inventors the exclusive rights to their discoveries. The facts that members of the legislative, executive and judiciary departments of government are dependent upon the wealth of masters, employers, owners and industry is not a reason to fail to support the Constitutional goal. Slavery has ended: it is time to end master-servant law.

# APPENDIX

# ABOUT THE PHOTOS

**"L**etters patent" is a government grant by a nation conferring upon the patentee a grant of right, title, and interest that could not otherwise be enjoyed in a form readily open for inspection by all seeking confirmation of the grant conferred. The purpose is to disclose as completely as possible the invention covered by the patent. Drawings, descriptions, designs deposits, and illustrations have been submitted to disclose the limits of protection.

One form of illustration, that as far as I know, was required by the Patent Office only of United States inventors, and only from 1836 to 1880 (with a handful later), was a model showing how the invention worked. The invention can have complicated features that exist outside the patent document itself.

The Supreme Court explained the difference between the invention and the document in *Bischoff v. Wethered*, 76 U.S. 812 (1870). The patent documents describe "mechanisms and complicated machinery, chemical compositions and other manufactured products, which have their existence *in pais*, outside the documents themselves; and which are commonly described by terms of art or mystery to which they respectively belong; and these descriptions and terms of art often require peculiar knowledge and education to understand them aright." The working patent models were intended to dynamically illustrate an invention *in pais* better than static words and drawings. Because the patents cover the entire range of technology (including a lot more than the *Bischoff* court mentioned), even working models are not adequate for everything *in pais* as opposed to in court.

During the forty-four years that each inventor had to have a working model when seeking a U.S. patent, a modest industry of model-makers came into being. Later, the law was changed to limit the requirement of a working model to patent applications in which the patent examiner expressly required a model. Apparently, storage of patent models had been a problem. Also, several fires over the years had destroyed many of the earlier models.

After the law was changed, the Patent Office tried to dispose of the models. That proved to be difficult. After several failed efforts, the entire collection of models was sold at a bankruptcy auction in 1940 in Foley Square in New York City. There were two bidders at the auction; one was a Japanese scrap metal dealer who presumably wanted the metal values in the models (a year before Pearl Harbor). The other bidder was O. Rundle Gilbert, an antique dealer and auctioneer in Garrison, New York, who assumed that the models filed before 1880 would qualify as antiques in 1940. Gilbert was successful in obtaining more than 100,000 models, sight unseen, for $5,000, or an average of fifty cents each.

He tried auctioning the models off, but value at an auction is relative to what a competing bidder thinks the item is worth. That is, the successful bidder thinks the item being sold is worth more than the unsuccessful bidder thinks it is worth. Each patent model is, by definition, unique, so one cannot compare, for example, a pristine chair to a scratched chair in deciding what to bid. One patented chair is patentably different from another patented chair, and no one can accurately evaluate the patented feature.

Gilbert tried for thirty years, until 1970, to get rid of the patent models. He then held a series of nationally advertised auctions over many years to dispose of his collection of models. I had, since 1956, been a patent examiner, law clerk at the patent court, and a practicing patent lawyer in San Francisco. I had seen patent models at the Smithsonian Institution and was fascinated by the history, beauty, and detail of the models in virtually every area of inventions. I had a big house in San Francisco and decided to collect patent models. One of my daughters, who majored in photography in college, took all of the photos that appear at the end of each chapter out of my collection of about a hundred and fifty models.

The cover photo pays homage to Ralph Waldo Emerson, who wrote: "Build a better mousetrap and the world will beat a path to your door." That, in patent law jargon, is called "commercial success." When I sold my big house in San Francisco and moved into our tiny Victorian cottage in the Sierra Nevada foothills, I faced the problem Gilbert had faced in 1940: what to do with the models. I gave nearly all of them to the Oakland Museum in California. I share the photos here because they are at once works of art and scientific illustrations of inventions in a short period of the American patent system.

John P. Sutton

www.ingramcontent.com/pod-product-compliance
Lightning Source LLC
Chambersburg PA
CBHW051446170526
45166CB00001B/140

* 9 7 8 1 4 6 7 9 4 6 2 6 1 *